QUESTIONS OF CONSPIRACY

THE TRUE FACTS BEHIND
THE ASSASSINATION OF
PRESIDENT KENNEDY

By
Mel Ayton

HORSESHOE PUBLICATIONS . WARRINGTON . CHESHIRE

ISBN 1.899310.32.0
British Library Cataloguing in Publication Data
A catalogue record for this book is available from
The British Library

First published 1999 by
HORSESHOE PUBLICATIONS
BOX 37, Kingsley, Frodsham, Cheshire WA6 8DR

Cover designed and illustrated by DAVID NOLAN

Printed and bound in Great Britain by
REDWOOD BOOKS LTD
Trowbridge, Wiltshire

This book is dedicated to
Arlen Specter and David Belin,
Warren Commission Attorneys
and honourable public servants whose reputations
have been maligned for the past 35 years.

PREFACE

In 1964 the Warren Commission, which had been instituted by President Kennedy's successor Lyndon Johnson, to bring an end to speculation about the assassination, concluded that Kennedy had been killed by a lone assassin, Lee Harvey Oswald. The findings were greeted with instant skepticism. A public opinion poll immediately afterwards revealed that 56% of the American public accepted the Commission's conclusions. By the 1990's and especially following the release of Oliver Stone's movie "JFK" skepticism had turned to incredulity. Opinion polls were now showing around 10 or 11% of Americans believed that Lee Harvey Oswald acted alone in killing President Kennedy.

As of this writing, the skepticism continues unabated with the release of book after book and dozens of feature films, documentaries and newspaper articles claiming various assassination theories and elaborate conspiracies.

No event has provoked as much speculation, enquiry, rumor or initiated an industry so prolific and lucrative. There have been some 600 books published on the assassination. There have been 2 major government enquiries - The Warren Commission and the U.S. House of Representatives Assassinations Investigation.

So it may well be asked - Why another book on the Kennedy Assassination? The answer is simple. I believe that the history of the assassination has been gravely distorted by the Conspiracy Theorists who have acted, in most cases, in an irresponsible way and I wanted to clarify many issues surrounding the assassination and correct the record. I believe that Conspiracy Theorists have chipped away at the very foundations of Democracy which ultimately resulted in a major part of the American people not trusting their government. Needless to say the consequences of this distorted history has implications for future generations. Can we allow cynicism and hysteria to govern our affairs?

I also recognised that no British author, since the 1960's, has written anything other than highly speculative conspiracy theories. From the late 1980's I began to assemble evidence that the Conspiracy Theorists were presenting a distorted view of what occurred that tragic November weekend. Accordingly, I have selected a number of best-selling books which posit conspiracies of one sort or another and examined them.

In 1993, as I was writing this book, Gerald Posner published his excellent research on the Kennedy assassination, in his best-selling book, "Case Closed". In no way would I pretend my study surpasses Posner's but, I believe, complements it.

I continued with my book for a number of reasons. Firstly, I believe I have provided a different perspective on the assassination from Posner; my work extends the considerations of why Oswald killed Kennedy and, as Posner completed his book in 1993, I have been able to assess new evidence which has arisen this past 5 years. Furthermore, as there are approximately 60 different assassination theories, ranging from the "Manchurian Candidate Theory" to the "Horrible Accident Theory" (Kennedy was killed accidentally by a Secret Service Agent) it is evident that Posner could not examine every issue and theory. There was room for another work which could take speculation and supposition out of the equation.

Most conspiracy books seem to be written for assassination buffs. However it has been my experience that there are many people who wish to read a comprehensive study of the assassination and find answers to intriguing questions without having to search through dozens of finely detailed narratives for the answers. This type of reader simply does not have the time to enter the complex and sometimes impenetrable world of conspiracy theories and has no desire to read assassination books which are infused with paranoia.

I state at the outset that my book supports the lone assassin theory and my research has lead me to strongly criticise conspiracy authors who, I believe, have misunderstood or misinterpreted the evidence. Paranoia must be replaced with common sense.

Since the 1960s I have collected some 50 books about the assassination of President Kennedy as well as numerous newspaper and magazine articles, audio tapes, video tapes of documentaries and T.V. news programmes, recordings of Oval office conversations by Presidents Kennedy and Johnson and recordings of the New Orleans radio programme in which Oswald appeared when he lived in New Orleans. My main sources are the Warren Commission Report and the Report of the House of Representatives Select Committee on Assassinations. I have also used some records acquired by other authors who obtained them through the U. S. Freedom of Information Act and the JFK Records Act of 1992. All of these sources can be readily examined by any interested parties.

This book was initiated by a conversation with Warren Commission lawyer and now United States Senator, Arlen Specter. But it was also a result of conversations with friends and colleagues who invariably asked the same questions about the assassination. I hope I have succeeded in answering most of them.

Mel Ayton

Durham, England.
October 1998

QUESTIONS OF CONSPIRACY
- The True Facts Behind the Assassination of President Kennedy.

By Mel Ayton

PREFACE

INTRODUCTION

Discovering how Conspiracy Theorists have misled the American Public. How conspiracy theories reflect major shifts in the American national psyche.
The Kennedy Assassination as popular myth.
Why questions are still asked.

CHAPTER 1: CAMELOT BEGINS

Why his death moved a nation.
Why his presidency is still the most abiding of our time.
Why the Kennedy myth still prevails.

CHAPTER 2: DEALEY PLAZA

Who planned the motorcade route?
Did Oswald have knowledge of the route?
How did Oswald come to work in the Dealey Plaza area?
Was the route changed for sinister reasons?
Why weren't Secret Service Agents and Police Officers stationed on rooftops throughout the motorcade route?
Did anyone see Oswald shoot President Kennedy.

CHAPTER 3: INVESTIGATING THE ASSASSINATION
THE WARREN REPORT

Who were the members of the Warren Commission and why were they chosen?
What were the Warren Commission findings?
Did the Warren Commission do a thorough job?
Why was the Warren Commission criticised in the years after it's release?
What mistakes did the Warren Commission make?
Why did the American Congress investigate the assassination?
Did the House Select Committee on Assassinations differ to the Warren Report in it's conclusions?

THE RIFLE

Did Oswald bring the rifle to the Texas Book Depository?

Did Oswald own the rifle?

Did the bullets from the rifle kill President Kennedy and wound Governor Connally?

Why was the Mannlicher- Carcano rifle initially described as a German Mauser?

Was the rifle reliable?

Was the telescopic sight defective and unreliable?

Could Oswald have fired in the time-span available?

Were the photographs of Oswald holding the rifle fakes?

Did Oswald have marksmanship capabilities?

THE SINGLE BULLET THEORY (THE MAGIC BULLET)

Did one bullet cause the neck wounds to President Kennedy and the wounds to Governor Connally?

Were the wounds consistent with shots fired from the Book Depository?

Why was the bullet which caused wounds to Kennedy and Connally pristine?

Why do some eyewitnesses say there were from 2 to 8 shots fired?

THE HEAD WOUND

Why does the Zapruder film show Kennedy's head being thrown backwards and to the left, which, if true, would indicate shots fired from in front and to the right of the Presidential limousine?

Are the wounds consistent with shots fired from behind?

Were President Kennedy's wounds altered?

THE GRASSY KNOLL

Is there photographic evidence of gunmen on the Grassy Knoll or behind the picket fence?

Did witnesses see any gunmen?

Why did some witnesses see men fleeing from the scene of the assassination?

Why did some witnesses see bogus Secret Service Agents behind the picket fence?

What were the "puffs of smoke" behind the picket fence?

Why did spectators and police officers run towards the Grassy Knoll after the shots were fired?

Was Oswald in the doorway of the Book Depository when the shots were fired?

Does acoustical evidence, in the form of a Dallas police tape recording, indicate shots were fired from the grassy knoll?

CHAPTER 4: **CONSCIOUSNESS OF GUILT**

OSWALD'S FLIGHT AND ARREST
Did Oswald have time to flee from the 6th floor to the second floor before being confronted by a Dallas police officer?
Why did Oswald flee the scene of the crime?
Did witnesses see Oswald during his journey to his rooming house across the Trinity river?
Why was Oswald's description broadcast so soon after the assassination?
Why did a Deputy Sheriff testify he saw Oswald being taken from the scene of the crime in a car?

THE MURDER OF OFFICER TIPPIT
Why were eyewitness testimonies of the Tippet shooting so different?
Is the ballistics evidence consistent with the shots being fired from Oswald's gun?
Why did Officer Tippet stop Oswald?
Is there any evidence to suggest someone else shot Officer Tippit?

OSWALD'S ARREST
Why did numerous police cars descend on the Texas Theatre to arrest Oswald?
Who was the 'Mystery Man' who 'fingered' Oswald in the Texas Theatre?
Did Oswald try to shoot a police officer when he was arrested?

OSWALD'S INTERROGATION
Did Oswald lie to his interrogators?
Who were Oswald's interrogators?
Why did Oswald maintain his innocence?

CHAPTER 5: **JACK RUBY & THE MURDER OF LEE HARVEY OSWALD**

Was Jack Ruby a member of the U.S. Mafia?
Was Ruby ordered or paid to shoot Oswald?
Was Oswald's murder a "typical gangland killing"?
How did Ruby gain access to the Dallas Police Department basement?
Did Oswald know Ruby?
Did Ruby "stalk" Oswald?
Did Dallas police officers allow Ruby to shoot Oswald?
Was Ruby involved with mobsters in gun running activities to Cuba?
Was Ruby connected to anti-Castro Cubans?

Did Ruby confess he was part of a Conspiracy to kill President Kennedy?
Did Government officials ignore Ruby's pleas to "get him out of Dallas so he could tell the truth"?
What did Ruby say in his "deathbed statement"?
Did Jack Ruby make numerous telephone calls to "mobsters" in the weeks prior to the assassination?
Did Ruby know Officer Tippet?
Did Oswald show recognition of Ruby just before he was shot?
Were Oswald and Ruby seen together at the Carousel Club?

CHAPTER 6: DID OSWALD WORK FOR MILITARY INTELLIGENCE, THE K.G.B., THE C.I.A., CASTRO'S INTELLIGENCE SERVICES, ANTI-CASTRO CUBANS, OR ANY COMBINATION OF THESE?

MILITARY INTELLIGENCE

Was Oswald recruited by military intelligence whist serving as a Marine?
Is there any evidence to conclude that Oswald had special intelligence training as a marine?
Why was Oswald able to return so quickly to the United States after his defection to the Soviet Union?
Did the military send Oswald to a Russian language school?
How did Oswald come to work at top secret military bases?
Was Oswald sent to the Soviet Union by Intelligence agencies?
Was Oswald a "double agent"?

K.G.B.

Did Oswald reveal intelligence secrets to the K.G.B.?
Did Yuri Nosenko defect to the United States for the sole purpose of leading investigating authorities astray in their examination of Oswald's potential links to the K.G.B.?
Have former K.G.B. agents spoken about Oswald's activities in the Soviet Union?

C.I.A.

Did Oswald work for the C.I.A.?
Did the C.I.A. cover up Oswald's links to that Agency and keep important information from the Warren Commission?

F.B.I.
Was Oswald an F.B.I. informant?
Did the F.B.I. know of Oswald's intentions to shoot the president?

CASTRO AGENT
Did Castro hire Oswald to kill Kennedy?

ANTI-CASTRO ASSASSIN.
Was Oswald in the employ of anti-Castro Cubans?

CHAPTER 7: MAFIA ASSASSIN

Was Oswald hired by the Mafia?
Did Oswald's uncle work for New Orleans mob boss Carlos Marcello and did he have anything to do with the assassination?
Did New Orleans mob boss Carlos Marcello, Chicago mob boss Sam Giancana or Florida mob boss Santos Trafficante hire Oswald and / or other conspirators?
Did Teamster's boss Jimmy Hoffa have anything to do with the assassination?
Why did the House Assassinations Select Committee blame the Mafia for Kennedy's assassination?

CHAPTER 8: NEW ORLEANS

Did New Orleans District Attorney Jim Garrison have a case for conspiracy?
Why did Oswald move to New Orleans in the spring of 1963?
Did Oswald know David Ferrie?
Was Oswald's library card in the possession of David Ferrie?
Were David Ferrie, Guy Bannister and Lee Harvey Oswald seen together?
Did Clay Shaw lead a conspiracy to kill President Kennedy?
Did New Orleans District Attorney Jim Garrison find out the truth about the assassination?
Were Garrison's witnesses credible?
What evidence is there to support Garrison's claims that the military, C.I.A., anti-Castro Cubans conspired together to kill Kennedy?
Are Oliver Stones claims, made in the movie 'JFK', credible?

QUESTIONS OF CONSPIRACY

- The True Facts Behind the Assassination of President Kennedy.

By Mel Ayton

Introduction

I have been interested in the assassination of President Kennedy for some 35 years now since the publication of the Warren Report and works criticising it's findings in the 1960's. To me the assassination was the 'Great Whodunit' of the 20th. Century. As the years went by new books and new revelations by Conspiracy Theorists placed the tragic story evermore into a morass of intrigue and wonder. Would we ever make sense of the events of November 22nd.1963?

My book is the culmination of research into how JFK Conspiracy Theorists have investigated and reported the Assassination of President Kennedy. I have sought to explain how the Kennedy Assassination has become an American myth and how the American public eventually, throughout the 1970's, 80's, and 90's, became susceptible to conspiracy theories as a result of national disillusion with government institutions and governmental abuse of power during the Kennedy, Johnson, Nixon and Reagan Administrations.

The Kennedy assassination investigation became a national obsession since the publication of The Warren Commission Report and works criticising it's findings in the mid 1960's. Like most people during that period I believed the report's major premise-that Lee Harvey Oswald alone killed President Kennedy.

However, during the 1970's, U.S. Senate Committee revelations of assassination attempts against Fidel Castro and government files indicating that New Orleans and Florida Mafia bosses had discussed the "elimination" of the President, persuaded me that various investigatory agencies as well as individual researchers were now beginning to unravel some of the conundrums of the case. A conspiracy to kill President Kennedy seemed likely.

During this period (1976-1979) the American Congress (House of Representatives Select Committee on Assassinations) initiated an investigation and concluded, primarily on the basis of acoustical evidence from a Dallas Police Department Dictabelt, that:

"the President was probably assassinated as a result of conspiracy".

The House Assassinations Committee also expressed suspicion that elements of the Mafia, or anti-Castro activists, or both, may have taken part in the plot. It said pointedly that two living Mafia bosses, Carlos Marcello and Santos Trafficante, "had the motive, means, and opportunity to kill President Kennedy". It appeared that the Conspiracy Theorists had been right all along and American history books would have to be amended. The truth had finally come out.

It was not until a conversation in 1988, whilst living and teaching in the United States as a Fulbright Exchange teacher, that I began to question what had become accepted "historical fact" by the American People. This "historical fact" was -

* Lee Harvey Oswald was innocent, a "patsy";

* a second gunman fired the fatal shot from the "Grassy Knoll";

* anti-Castro Cubans, rogue elements of the C. I. A. or the Mafia conspired to kill the President;

* Oswald had been a spy for American intelligence;

* a vast network of State and Federal Government officials, including the Warren Commission members, had conspired to "cover- up" the facts to prevent the American public from knowing the truth.

The conversation was with Warren Commission attorney and now United States Senator Arlen Specter, the author of "The Single Bullet Theory". The key to understanding the assassination, Senator Specter said, was to re-read the conspiracy theorists' books. He said he did not believe their claims and their theories, especially the 'Mafia-Did-It' theory had no foundation in truth. Most authors, I eventually found out, had relied heavily on evidence contained in the Warren Commission's 26 volumes of sworn testimony and exhibits and they had taken some of this testimony out of context and were highly selective because they wanted to prove conspiracy. Others had engaged in speculation and presented it as fact. Yet others had used fractured logic and imagination to construct a false theory.

I was surprised that someone with Specter's knowledge of the case did not now accept the findings of the House Assassinations committee's report and I began to reconsider my acceptance of the Conspiracy authors' claims. I selected a number of conspiracy books which I had acquired over the years, and looked at the way they had used the Warren Commission's published testimony. It was immediately apparent that Senator Specter had been right. Amongst the many mistakes I found was one dealing with a particular area of the Warren Report Investigation - the testimony given by Jack Ruby, Oswald's killer. Many authors had pointed to Ruby's request to Chief Justice Earl Warren to transfer him to Washington so he could reveal a "Conspiracy".

The actual testimony is less dramatic. Ruby, in his mentally unstable frame of mind, had been talking about a 'conspiracy', by elements unknown, to kill "the Jews". Medical records show that Ruby suffered from organic brain damage and was mentally and emotionally ill and his condition had severely deteriorated whilst in jail. The Conspiracy writers failed to mention this fact thus taking Ruby's statements out of the proper context. During my research of the methodology of conspiracy authors and their abuse of the Warren Report's findings, I bought Jean Davison's excellent book 'Oswald's Game' and she confirmed my worst suspicions - a false history of the assassination was being promulgated by authors who were mismanaging and manipulating the facts of the case. Her own reading of the Warren Report also showed how Conspiracy Theorists had taken many of Ruby's statements out of context to suggest conspiracy. This was the first major work on the assassination, since the release of the HSCA Report in 1979, which approached the subject from an unbiased perspective and I acknowledge her research as an invaluable tool in finding the true facts of the case. Unfortunately, her book was not met with the same favourable publicity as Anthony Summers' 'Conspiracy'.

I also found that Conspiracy authors were continually presenting "evidence of guilt by association" when making their case for conspiracy. For example, when discussing Ruby's links with Mob figures they ignored the simple logical fact that anyone who ran a night club in cities like Dallas, New Orleans and Chicago during that period would inevitably associate in some way with disreputable people connected with the entertainment industry and related labour unions. There is certainly truth in the allegations that Ruby had "mob connections" but there is no evidence whatsoever that he received "instructions" to eliminate Oswald or was part of any conspiracy. Association does not prove conspiracy.

The assassination has become an industry in the United States and the "plot" to kill Kennedy has, I suspect, become one of the outstanding myths of the 20th. Century mainly as a result of these efforts to prove conspiracy. New revelations came yearly and this trend has continued into the late 1990's. It began as soon as the Warren Report was issued and since then there has been a flood of articles, books, T.V. programmes and films alleging various kinds of plots to kill the President. All of these plots are labyrinthine in their complexity. The Mafia, the C.I.A., the military-industrial complex, Texas oilmen, pro-Castro Cubans, anti-Castro cubans, the K.G.B., J. Edgar Hoover and the F.B.I., Lyndon Johnson, southern racists, the joint chiefs of staff or any combination of these.

This wealth of books and theories have created problems of evaluation and verification of facts. Government investigations alone have amassed volumes upon volumes of information which has only intensified the problem of knowing exactly who killed Kennedy. Each increment of data requires a proportionate increment of time spent evaluating evidence and linking facts together, which is why many commentators have averred that the truth of the matter will never be disclosed. Evaluation of the assassination data requires reasoned judgement and where books about the Kennedy assassination fail is precisely because they do not communicate the true facts of the case in a communicable, intelligible and succinct manner. Conspiracy Theorists are thus at an advantage in that their use of facts and evidence which supposedly support their theories are not easily verifiable. How many amongst us are willing to wade through volume upon volume of Government reports written in language which is only suitable for civil servants? I hope my work overcomes these problems.

The most notable of the "Who Killed Kennedy?" books have all indicated a conspiracy to murder the President but the authors have used flawed methodology and they often let their imaginations run wild. Yet their ruminations have come to be accepted as legitimate historical "truths"— In my book I have attempted to expose their fraudulent claims, a sample of which follows:

* Mark Lane's "Rush to Judgement" exonerated Oswald completely and pointed to the C.I.A. with little or no credible evidence to support this.

* Anthony Summers "The Kennedy Conspiracy" argued for conspiracy, basing some of his evidence on unreliable witnesses who can only testify to a tenuous connection between Oswald and a number of characters who were linked to Carlos Marcello, the New Orleans head of the Mafia. His book is fascinating and lucid but he fails to prove his case.

* David E. Scheim points the finger at Mafia leaders yet no credible witness (i.e. a mafia member) has come forward who has had direct knowledge of the "conspiracy". If the Mafia had indeed been involved certainly some sane, if criminal, member of that organisation would have talked. There is nothing more untrue than the Mafia law of "Omerta". Any criminal in his 30's or 40's who is facing a life sentence will most certainly "plea bargain" to gain a lighter sentence or his freedom with a new identity.

*Sam and Chuck Giancana, the brother and nephew of Chicago Mafia boss Sam Giancana wrote a book telling of the mob boss' involvement in the assassination but again they offer no credible evidence, only hearsay evidence of Giancana's "confession". The writers named a Jack Lawrence as a co-conspirator in the assassination. Lawrence's reputation was greatly damaged by such irresponsible reporting.

*David S. Lifton in his well researched but speculative "Best Evidence", maintained that Kennedy's body had been altered to eliminate traces of shots from his front, thus pointing to a conspiracy at the highest level. The doctors who performed the autopsy say that nothing of the kind occurred.

*Henry Hurt names the second assassin as Robert Easterling—an ex-convict, raging alcoholic, and a diagnosed psychotic and schizophrenic.

*Michael Eddowes in his book "November 22nd - How They Killed Kennedy" claimed that the Oswald who was captured, killed and buried was not the real Oswald who returned from the Soviet Union-ipso facto he must have been a Russian spy. The exhumation of the body in the early 1980's proved otherwise.

*British author Matthew Smith's "J.F.K. The Second Plot" paints Oswald, preposterously, as a "good guy, good marine and loyal American"- and intelligence agent. Like most conspiracy theorists he promises to reveal all. Unfortunately he posits his theories without credible or substantiated evidence and he uses witnesses who cannot substantiate any of their claims. Like other theorists he selects some facts and omits others. His book is fraught with speculation. Smith gives the House Assassination Committee's acoustical findings as 'definite evidence of conspiracy' but glosses over the fact they were found to be in error by the Ramsey Panel (a team of scientists who were appointed by the prestigious National Academy of Sciences).

* Channel 4 relied on Smith to help research their 1988 documentary "The Men Who Killed the President". It named the killers as French Mafia members. The conspirators were either in the army or completing prison sentences at the time of the assassination. Unfortunately this fact has not been as well publicised as the original claims. It is small wonder the general public believe conspiracy is a "proven fact".

* Robert Groden, a supposed photography expert published two books in the period 1993-1995-"The Search for Lee Harvey Oswald" and "The Killing of a President". Groden purports to find 'conspirators' all over Dealey Plaza in his examination of photographs taken of the assassination. In 1997 he was discredited as a photographic expert during the O.J. Simpson civil trial.

Most conspiracy theorists continue to refer to the findings of the House of Representatives Assassinations Committee Report and it's conclusion that

Kennedy was killed as a result of a conspiracy. Conspiracy Theorists do not, however, inform their readers that the committee, two weeks before it's findings were due to be published, arrived at virtually the same conclusions as the Warren Commission and quickly amended it's conclusions only on the basis of acoustical evidence which was dramatically presented at the last minute. In 1982 this evidence, as noted earlier, was challenged by prestigious scientists chosen by the National Academy of Sciences and they reported that it's analysis of the House Committee's experts' report and the acoustical evidence it relied on did not persuade them that there was adequate evidence of a second shot coming from the infamous 'Grassy Knoll'.

I have come to believe that there is a mountain of evidence, ignored by the general media outlets and reputable publishers, which indicates the conspiracy theories are baseless. But this willingness to accept dramatic works of far-fetched conspiracies for publication has changed the killing of Kennedy from a national calamity and tragedy into a bottomless pit of rumor, assertion and innuendo. In some cases outright fakery has been peddled to gullible American and British publics.

The apex of conspiracy paranoia occurred in the early 1990's with the release of Oliver Stone's movie "J.F.K." The otherwise excellently written and directed movie was a litany of supposition, half-truths and lies yet the American public and leading figures in academia, according to polls taken by C.B.S. and A.B.C. news, believe Stone's theory that Kennedy was assassinated by "Dark Forces", the members of which are never named. We are then required by Stone and others to make a "logical" conclusion—it was a successful conspiracy therefore no-one has been caught or can be named.

Oliver Stone's conspirators remain faceless Government agents who somehow manage to manipulate thousands of people connected with the assassination; not one of whom has come forward after all these years to give some insight into this incredible feat. Consequently a new generation of Americans are growing up believing an alternative and false part of their history. It has been said that it is virtually impossible to prove a negative but I have attempted to build on the works of a nearly silent minority of intelligent and rational authors like Gerald Posner and prove that their is indeed a preponderance of evidence to assume the likelihood that Lee Harvey Oswald killed President Kennedy -- if not "beyond a reasonable doubt" at least to the satisfaction of historical truth.

My work includes an examination of authoritative scientific evidence which has reinforced many conclusions of the Warren Report. Computer analysis of Dealey Plaza, for example, has shown that the single-bullet theory first posited by Arlen Specter, remains intact. Spectrographic analysis of photographs purporting to show gunmen on the "Grassy Knoll" reveal only light and shadows. Neutron- activation analyses of bullet fragments support the single bullet theory which postulates a single shot caused wounds to both Kennedy and Governor Connally thus confirming that Oswald could have fired the shots in the time sequence required by the Zapruder film of the assassination. Ballistics tests showing that the sharp movement of Kennedy's head backwards is consistent with a shot fired from the rear was examined by a Nobel Prize-winning physicist, Luis Alvarez, who agreed with this finding. Other tests prove that the shots were fired from behind from Oswald's rifle to the exclusion of all other weapons and the tests prove that the shots could have been fired in the necessary time.

Part of my work includes an examination of why there was so much conflicting evidence from audio and visual witnesses at the assassination scene. It is true that there were many witnesses who said there were more than 3 shots or who saw suspicious activity in a number of areas other than the Book Depository. But it is common in shootings for there to be different recollections on matters such as the number of shots and their origin. The witnesses in Dealey Plaza were focusing their attention on the President of the United States, a mesmerising event for most of them. In the chaos, hysteria and confusion which engulfed the assassination scene it is remarkable that there was any similarities at all to accounts of what they saw and heard. Human observation, notoriously unreliable in even the most optimum of situations has to give way to hard scientific evidence and logical explanations of anomalous events.

If these scientific techniques had been available at the time of the Warren Commission investigation much of the speculation and suspicions would never have arisen or accepted as legitimate areas of enquiry.

The historian A.J.P. Taylor has written that it was a popular fallacy to believe that a great event must necessarily have a great cause. He said this about the origins of the first World War, but I believe it can offer a clue in explaining why Conspiracy Theorists have had such an impact on the American public. There was a huge reaction to the shocking events and the knowledge that the perpetrator was a pathetic figure like Lee Harvey Oswald took away meaning to the life and leadership of President Kennedy. If he had died for one of the causes he fought for the assassination myth may never have been advanced. The american psyche could not deal with this stark fact. It was difficult to accept this premise which is one reason why the majority of Americans give credence to incredible theories. They give a meaning to Kennedy's life and death. Furthermore, conspiracy theories are a form of denial, a way of avoiding unpleasant truths about the basic competence of their agencies of government to protect and defend the President of the United States and all American citizens.

Irresponsible Conspiracy Theorists can take some of the blame for the historical distortions which exist in the Kennedy case- but not all. If the Dallas Police and the F.B.I. had not "botched" the case there would have been little room for the Conspiracy Theorists to manoeuvre. The Dallas police were certainly careless with their prisoner, if not conspiratorial. Yet not perhaps as careless as the F.B.I. For Director J. Edgar Hoover the assassination was a disaster. The F.B.I. had a file on Oswald stretching back to his time in the Soviet Union. Two weeks before the assassination Oswald marched into the local F.B.I. office in Dallas and created a scene complaining about the harassment his wife was receiving from its agents. The F.B.I. failed to keep Oswald under observation during the Presidential visit. Furthermore the C.I.A. were not forthcoming in the handing over of files to the House Assassinations Committee which may have shed light on Oswald's alleged 'subversive' activities. Allen Dulles, a Warren Commission member and ex-Director of the C.I.A. failed to tell the Warren Commission about the assassination attempts against Castro. In this sense the "cover-up" is an historical truth.

The media can also take some responsibility. After the assassination every witness, no matter how remote from first-hand knowledge became a 'news - maker'. The spotlight confused many of them - seldom did any respond with a 'don't know' answer to media questions. The result was a flood of distortion and misinformation. Nor were the motives of various 'conspiracy witnesses' questioned. For example, Beverly Oliver gave an interview to the makers of the documentary 'The Men who Killed Kennedy'. Oliver is not mentioned in the Warren Report but she claimed to have seen Oswald and Ruby together at Ruby's night-club. At the beginning of the second episode of the 4 part documentary she is filmed in a recording studio. She states that she is developing her career. Whilst this does not necessarily make her conspiratorial statements incorrect it should have been treated by the documentary researchers as 'suspect'.

The Warren Commission must also take some blame for the way in which loose ends were not tied up and left the way open for innuendo and speculation.

Again, in this limited sense, there was a cover-up. Lyndon Johnson must also be held "historically culpable". He was fearful that there had indeed been a conspiracy to kill Kennedy and this would have dire consequences for Soviet-American relations. He may have had some hand in wanting the Warren Commission to disprove allegations of conspiracy at any cost to historical truth. If there was a conspiracy he did not want it laid at the door of the Kremlin.

The House of Representatives Select Committee on Assassinations, which issued its report in 1979, must also be held accountable. It worked under financial constraints and political considerations and, accordingly, failed to pursue many leads which could have annulled much speculation.

The actions of various American administrations can also explain why the American public have been open to persuasion by Conspiracy Theorists. The American people faced a litany of lies, distortions and half-truths by Government agencies and the White House during the administrations of Kennedy (attempted assassinations of foreign leaders), Johnson (Vietnam war), Nixon (Watergate) and Reagan (Iran-Contra), therefore allegations of a cover-up did not appear unusual or outrageous.

From my reading and research it can be said that in this case, which is now in it's 35th year, the truth cannot be established with absolute precision. However, it does not always follow that an untruth should prevail in it's place. I have found that many mistakes have been made in trying to establish the truth surrounding the circumstances of the assassination, some by investigating agencies and others by Conspiracy Theorists. However it can be argued that the biggest mistake of all was in not releasing Dallas Police, F.B.I. and C.I.A. files-a mistake which resulted in incredible theories masquerading as objective truth.

During my research into the way Conspiracy Theorists have investigated the assassination I was inevitably drawn into researching the assassination itself and I have attempted to explain not only why this event has gripped the imagination of the American people but what is valid historical truth and untruth in the case. I believe I have demonstrated the preponderance of evidence proves Lee Harvey Oswald killed President Kennedy and he acted alone. I have also examined Lee Oswald's character as a means to answering the question which the Warren Report and the House Assassinations Committee Report failed to answer to the satisfaction of the American Public - What was it in Oswald's make-up that led him to kill the President of the United States?

CHAPTER 1

CAMELOT BEGINS

"Lifting us beyond our capacities, he gave his country back to it's best self, wiping away the world's impression of an old nation of old men, weary, played out, fearful of the future; he taught mankind that the process of rediscovering America was not over. He transformed the American spirit."
Arthur Schlesinger, Jr.

"People will remember not only what he did but what he stood for. He had confidence in man and gave men confidence in the future. Just as no chart on the history of weapons could accurately reflect the advent of the atom, so it is my belief that no scale of good and bad presidents can rate John Fitzgerald Kennedy."
Theodore Sorenson.

John Kennedy's brilliant life and career abruptly ended 35 years ago and his life still has a large impact even now. Three million visitors still come to his grave at Arlington National Cemetery in Washington D.C. every year. Although fewer photographs of Kennedy are now displayed in households in western nations than they once were, they can still be found in homes all over the Third World next to those of the late Mother Teresa and Pope John Paul. His image stands forever with other sixties icons - a 'Che Guevara' of American idealism.

The moment 35 years ago when one learned the news is forever fixed in the memory and many have been trying to come to terms with the tragedy ever since. It was the most traumatic news event since the end of the Second World War. We remember the day Kennedy died, November 22nd 1963, not his birthday. History suddenly changed and we were left with an endless list of possibilities of what he might have done. Would Civil Rights have continued? Would the deepening gaps between rich and poor have narrowed? Would the war in Vietnam have reached a settlement? The myth making about John Kennedy, as a politician and as a person, began. Who would have guessed then that Kennedy's assassination would also enter the pantheon of myths?

For the 60's generation the Kennedy administration was a new beginning to the post-war world. At the start, under the glaring sun in the biting January cold of Washington D.C. everything seemed about to change. Americans and Europeans together were captured by this seemingly American pop culture figure. We were as one with the leader of the western world. In Britain the old fashioned MacMillan was not for us. We saw the figure of John Kennedy as the representative of our generation. Watching the Inauguration on television we had only to look at the two men sharing the platform-benign and ageing 'Ike' Eisenhower and the youthful and vigorous 'Jack' Kennedy - to sense this incredible change.

When Kennedy spoke our generation listened. And 35 years later we still remember. He occupies a special place in the roll call of post-war presidents, partly because his assassination cut him down in his prime and the myth of John Kennedy has warped our judgement of his 1000 day presidency ever since. He was probably not president long enough to be judged by conventional standards of solid achievement in office. It was the promise not the performance that we responded to. And historians have always maintained that a president cannot be judged until a generation has passed. But we can say today, paradoxically, that Kennedy's status and prestige as a president, if not a man, has increased rather than diminished with the passing years. Could we say the same of Eisenhower or Truman, let alone Johnson or Ford?

Some have argued that the myth has not interfered with their judgements of his presidency and he did indeed achieve much during his short time in office. Merely by getting elected president Kennedy opened the way for other Catholic presidential candidates. He had destroyed forever the religious issue in American politics. Kennedy presided over a change of political generations in America much as Bill Clinton did in the 1992 elections. And he did it with brilliant style. He brought youth and idealism to Washington and he refreshed the country with a vision of idealistic change throughout the world. But his presidency contained a dark side. His reckless involvement with Judith Campbell Exner, the mistress of mob boss Sam Giancana, and his affair with Marilyn Monroe, if revealed at the time, could have led to his impeachment by Congress. Kennedy's frustration with a communist dictator only 90 miles from American shores led to murder plots which could have been laid at the door of the Oval Office.

But Kennedy, when he died, was moving towards a new American world view. He was so shocked by the implications of the Cuban Missile crisis that his position vis a vis Russia helped steer the world away from the Cold War. He made an eloquent and one of the most memorable speeches by any statesman, at the American University in June 1963, in which he asked us all to consider our national antagonisms :

"If we cannot end our differences, at least we can make the world safe for diversity. For, in the final analyses, our most basic common link is that we all inhabit this small planet. We all breath the same air. We all cherish our children's futures. And we are all mortal."

Kennedy also accomplished a limited test ban treaty on nuclear weapons and he had plans for Medicare for the aged and Civil Rights for African-Americans. He began the race to put a man on the moon before the end of the 60's and without Kennedy's leadership it is unlikely this would have been accomplished. The 'Mercury' astronauts, especially John Glenn, the first American to orbit the earth, are forever linked to the Kennedy years.

He also had an impact on us in other ways. Not since the New Deal had Washington seen such an influx of idealistic young people. Never before had the White house been such a haven for the nation's cultural life. Intellectuals suddenly found themselves popular in Washington. The sense and the semblance of culture was everywhere and a feeling of optimism prevailed. The President's young family fascinated the nation and were 'celebritised'.

Kennedy captured the imagination of the world through the medium of television. In the presidential news conference Kennedy was eloquent and inspired. He enthralled the nation with his sardonic wit and confident style. No president had ever allowed the press so much access. He was anxious to be recorded for history in the making and even let cameras into the Oval Office during times of national crisis. Kennedy was criticised, however, for soliciting the friendships of newsmen thereby 'managing' the news. It probably did affect the autonomy of the press but in those days the president and the press were not engaged in an adversarial relationship. Kennedy was a keen student of history and he felt an obligation to the historical record. Kennedy's favourite reading matter was biography and he swiftly learned the lessons of past statesmen using their lives as a compass in avoiding the pitfalls of arrogance and pride. Like Harry Truman he made every effort to use history to inform his decisions.

In contrast to the Eisenhower years everything the Kennedy's did was news. The Kennedys were called America's 'Royal Family'. JFK's brother-in law, Peter Lawford was a movie star and Kennedy had close links to Frank Sinatra, at least until his brother Robert warned him off because of Sinatra's ties to the Chicago 'mob'. And White House dinners were attended by celebrities from the arts, sciences and the world of entertainment.

But beneath the glamour lay international tensions and a growing risk of nuclear confrontation with the Soviet Union over Berlin and Cuba. And at home Afro-Americans were no longer willing to wait for the American Dream.

It has to be accepted that Kennedy's style exceeded his performance. He confessed to interviewer Walter Cronkite, near the end of his life, that it was much easier to make speeches than to finally make the judgements. But he was successful in confronting the Soviet threat of missiles in Cuba, securing a strong NATO alliance, responding in a positive way to Civil Rights and inspiring the American people to confront the issues of caring for the poor and the aged, not just in the United States but in countries around the world. His 'Peace Corps' and 'Alliance for Progress', which were designed to aid Third World countries, stands as a monument, like the post-war Marshall plan, to American ideals.

The crises, especially in the unceasing struggle with Soviet power around the globe, came with startling frequency. The new Administration had been in office just three months when the disastrous 'Bay of Pigs' invasion unnerved the nation. Although Kennedy had inherited the Cuban invasion plans from the Eisenhower Administration he took the blame for the debacle. The botched invasion revealed Kennedy's personal qualities for a new emerging presidential style of governing: an openness and candour, and an honesty and forthrightness which was missing in more than one president who came after him. Kennedy made no effort to escape blame for the recklessness, to cover it up or excuse it. It taught Kennedy several important lessons. One was that self-confident 'experts', such as generals and C.I.A. officials, can be disastrously wrong. After the 'Bay of Pigs' Kennedy came to mistrust military solutions and more than one government 'insider' has testified to the fact that these personal qualities in the president would have prevented the 'Vietnam Quagmire'. They are convinced he would have chosen a political, as opposed to a military solution, to the problem of Vietnam. Kennedy was too worried that the war would damage his domestic programme which he needed to concentrate on fully in his second term.

He told more than one advisor that the time to get out of Vietnam would be after his re-election in 1964.

Just two months after the Bay of Pigs fiasco, in June 1961, Kennedy had his first face to face meeting with the Soviet leader Nikita Kruschev - the portentous Vienna summit - probing for any areas of agreement on Berlin. The young and inexperienced president had returned to the United States depressed and despondent. He felt he had not shown 'steel ' to the Soviet leader. His bad back had been a factor causing him many moments of searing pain. Accordingly he was not up to negotiating with an aggressive Kruschev and he believed that the Soviets would risk nuclear war over the divided city of Berlin. In August the defiant Soviets put up the Berlin Wall. The optimism of those January days had taken a downturn.

Despite the problems of the first months in office Cuba was eventually to provide Kennedy with his most satisfying triumph and set the stage for an era of detente with the Soviet Union. From the start, Kruschev had dangerously misread the president's resolution. The Cuban leader, Fidel Castro, had persuaded the Soviets that the new president would not go to war over the positioning of Soviet nuclear missiles in Cuba. The crisis was sparked by the C.I.A.'s discovery of the partially hidden missiles through its U2 regular overflights of the island. The discovery brought the superpowers dangerously close to nuclear war. This was even more profound when, years later, it was revealed after the end of the Cold War that Soviet Commanders in Cuba were given strategic autonomy over the launching of the missiles.

Kruschev had expected a repetition of the tactical fumbling of the 'Bay of Pigs' adventure but he was wrong. The American show of strength forced the Soviet leader to back down not from a threat of nuclear war but from the 'quarantine' Kennedy had imposed around the island. If nuclear war was to start it was the Russians who had to make the first move and forever to be seen as the 'aggressors'. But Kennedy, with the mature advice of his brother Robert, would not allow Kruschev to be humiliated and gave the Soviet leader an 'out'. Kennedy rejected the idea of a 'first strike' against the offensive missiles and instead imposed a Naval quarantine on Cuba and allowed Kruschev to reconsider. Kennedy replied to Kruschev's less belligerent first letter to the president instead of the second letter which was obviously written on the advice of 'hawks' in the Kremlin. This allowed Kruschev to make an accommodation without losing face. It was history's first nuclear confrontation and President Kennedy's finest hour.

The Missile Crisis, more than any other single event of his presidency, demonstrated the way in which Kennedy matured in office, the way in which he could master complexities and to wait and question. Great Presidents are remembered by simple sentences "He freed the slaves." - "He lifted us out of the Depression and carried us through a war." Kennedy will be remembered in history by "He saved us from nuclear war."

More respectful now of the young president Kruschev adopted a new approach and he was ready to deal. President Kennedy, for his part, was willing to assure the Russians that his goal was peaceful coexistence. It laid the groundwork for the limited nuclear test ban treaty which was to be one of Kennedy's lasting legacies.

At home the major problem was the growing confrontation between black and white Americans. The grave domestic issue brought Kennedy to grips with a national crisis as no president had been since Abraham Lincoln. The 'Freedom Riders', young black and white students who challenged segregated public places in the South, began during Kennedy's first months in office and as the Civil Rights movement gained momentum racial violence became a commonplace of American life. Kennedy federalised troops in Mississippi and Alabama and he spoke out on the issue firmly and forthrightly, more than any other president had done. He was not a leader on the subject. He was no Martin Luther King, but he did respond in a moral and courageous manner to what was, essentially, a human rights movement.

In the spring of 1963 there were 2000 civil rights demonstrations in more than 300 cities. Kennedy now faced the civil rights call directly. He responded by an eloquent and emotional speech:

"We are confronted primarily with a moral issue ... It is as old as the scriptures and is as clear as the American constitution ... The heart of the question is whether all Americans are to be afforded equal rights and opportunities, whether we are going to treat our fellow Americans as we want to be treated. If an American, because his skin is dark, cannot eat lunch in a restaurant open to the public, if he cannot send his children to the best public (state) school available, if he cannot vote for the public officials who represent him, if, in short, he cannot enjoy the full and free life which all of us want, then who among us would be content to have the colour of his skin changed and stand in his place? Who among us would then be content with the counsels of patience and delay?" This speech, more than any other, was to endear JFK in the hearts and minds of African-Americans.

In November 1963, then, John F. Kennedy was set to become a two term president with notable successes behind him. But hatred for President Kennedy matched his popularity. Anti-Castro Cubans detested Kennedy for not allowing air strikes to aid the invading guerrilla brigades during the 'Bay of Pigs' fiasco. Their C.I.A. controllers believed Kennedy to be weak, indecisive and ineffectual. In 1961 John Kennedy's brother, Attorney-General Robert F. Kennedy, targeted the Mafia and their corrupt associates in major workers' unions across America. Castro warned Kennedy, who he believed may have initiated murder plots against him, that he would possibly retaliate 'in kind'. Racial supremacists loathed Kennedy, believing he pandered to Civil Rights leaders. Right-wing organisations like the John Birch Society taunted Kennedy, claiming he was communist inspired. It was in this climate of hatred that President Kennedy and his wife Jacqueline left the White House embarking on their journey to Texas to shore up the Democratic Party base in that state.

CHAPTER 2

DEALEY PLAZA

"The world is a comedy to those who think, a tragedy to those who feel."
Walpole.

"We participate in a tragedy; at a comedy we only look."
Aldous Huxley.

The beginning of 1964 was election time in the United States and the Democratic Party were confident that Kennedy would be re-elected to a second term in Office. He was riding high in the opinion polls and his expected Republican Party opponent was the right-wing Senator Barry Goldwater, who was to go down in disastrous defeat against the new president, Lyndon Johnson, one year later. But America was about to witness the most notorious murder in modern American history as Kennedy embarked upon his visit to Texas.

The President was in Texas primarily for political reasons - to heal a rift in the Democratic Party and to raise money for the coming Presidential election. On Monday, November 18, he spoke to audiences in Tampa and Miami Beach. That night he flew back to Washington for a two day interlude of official business. At a White House reception for the Justices of the Supreme Court, Jacqueline Kennedy returned to her work after a two month hiatus after the death of her infant son in August. On Thursday the President and his wife flew to Texas.

There were warnings that the President's reception might be hostile. Lately Texas had been in an unfriendly mood toward the Kennedy Administration. Partly, this arose from the Civil Rights Movement which Kennedy had supported; partly it was aroused by right - wing militant groups like the John Birch Society. Vice- President Lyndon Johnson himself a Texan was frequently vilified. Ambassador to the United Nations Adlai Stevenson had recently been spat upon and hit with a picket sign in Dallas. Placards were being distributed bearing the President's picture and the legend "Wanted for Treason". Even Governor John Connally was worried and argued against a motorcade through Dallas but withdrew his objection. Some of JFK's aides were uneasy about the trip.

Yet Thursday's reception in San Antonio, Houston, and Fort Worth were warm and enthusiastic. Everything was obviously going well. In Fort Worth Kennedy and his wife discussed the risks that a President inevitably faces when he makes public appearances. What Kennedy said was remembered by his special assistant Kenneth O'Donnell and told to the Warren Commission:

"If anybody really wanted to shoot the President of the United States it was not a very difficult job-all one had to do was get a high building some day with a telescopic rifle and there was nothing anybody could do to defend against such an attempt."

This was not the first time that Kennedy had worried about his own mortality. After his election in November 1960 he retired to his father's estate in Palm Beach. On Sunday morning, December 11th 1960 a car slowed down and came to a halt across the street from the Kennedy residence. Inside the house were members of the Kennedy family including John and Jackie Kennedy and their children. According to Secret Service files, the driver of the car was a retired 73 year old postal clerk from Belmont, New Hampshire named Richard P. Pavlick, who had previously made threats against the life of President-elect Kennedy. Pavlick's car contained seven sticks of dynamite that could be detonated by the simple closing of a switch. Pavlick's intention was to wait until Kennedy entered his car then drive his own forward into Kennedy's blowing himself and the President-elect up. Pavlick watched the house and knew Kennedy would be going to Sunday mass at 10.00am Kennedy opened the door of the house surrounded by agents and accompanied by his wife and children. In an instant, according to Pavlick, he changed his mind about killing Kennedy because he did not wish to harm Jackie or the children. Pavlick drove off in the opposite direction. On Thursday December 15th he was arrested for reckless driving and admitted the dynamite found in the car was to assassinate Kennedy. He was eventually handed over to Secret Service agents who charged him with attempted murder and unlawful possession of explosives. He subsequently spent six years in various federal prisons and mental institutions. Pavlick was not alone in his desire to kill Kennedy. The threats and Secret Service investigations would grow to incredible proportions over the following 3 years.

The next stop on the presidential itinerary was Dallas, where Kennedy was to be driven through the city in a motorcade. The motorcade route has been endlessly speculated upon by Conspiracy Theorists. It was agreed by all parties concerned, including Kennedy's advisors, that the President should be seen by as many people as possible and a motorcade was proposed by Kenneth O'Donnell. The actual route was selected by Secret Service Agents Forrest V. Sorrels and Winston G. Lawson to traverse the distance between the Dallas airport and the site of the luncheon where the President was to speak to business and political leaders.

There were three potential sites for the luncheon. One building, known as Market Hall, was unavailable for November 22. The second building, located at the state fair grounds and known as the Women's Building, had the practical advantage that it was a one- storey building with few entrances and it was easy to make secure. However, it lacked food facilities. This left a third possibility-the Trade Mart. The Secret Service was very concerned about security at this venue as there were several entrances and a balcony. The President's advisors overruled them and the Trade Mart was selected.

Once the Trade Mart was selected the motorcade route was easy to determine. Most people would congregate in Downtown Dallas. From Downtown Dallas the motorcade would then have to head north on to Stemmons Freeway to get to the Trade Mart. But there was a problem. Main Street did not have a direct access on to Stemmons Freeway. To get around this problem the motorcade would have to make a 90 degree turn onto Houston Street and then another sharp turn onto Elm Street which would lead to Stemmons Freeway. This would take the motorcade past the Texas School Book Depository. Contrary to some speculation it was not normal practice to have Secret Service Agents in every tall building along motorcade routes. Agents scanned crowds in buildings to anticipate trouble. City police assisted by lining the route and keeping crowds away from the limousine. Kenneth O'Donnell made the decision to remove the "Bubble top" protective covering from the car, hardly a conspiratorial move by an official who was both a friend and an advisor to the President. O'Donnell was later to absolve the Secret Service of any responsibility. Moreover it was President Kennedy who ordered that no Secret Service Agents were to ride on the running boards at the rear of the car. If this normal procedure had been carried out President Kennedy would have had some protection although the 'bubble-top' was not bullet-proof.

On the drive into Dallas from Love Field Kennedy twice called the car to a halt, once to respond to a sign asking him to shake hands, the second time to talk to a Catholic nun and a small group of children. There was a large crowd of people at the triangular Dealey Plaza. There the motorcade slowed to 11.2 mph and moved past the Book Depository building. Inside the Lincoln limousine Mrs. Connally, who was sitting directly in front of Jackie Kennedy turned to the President and smiled: "Mr. President, you can't say that Dallas doesn't love you." Kennedy replied, "That is very obvious."

At 12.30pm Jackie Kennedy heard a sound similar to a motor cycle noise and a cry from Governor Connally, which caused her to look to her right. On turning she saw a quizzical look on President Kennedy's face. As Jacqueline Kennedy told author Theodore H. White:

"They were gunning the motorcycles. There were these little backfires. There was one noise like that. I thought it was a backfire. Then next I saw Connally grabbing his arms and saying no, no, no, no with his fist beating. Then Jack turned and I turned. All I remember was a blue-gray building up ahead. Then Jack turned back so neatly, his last expression was so neat... you know that wonderful expression he had when they'd ask him a question about one of the ten million pieces they have in a rocket, just before he'd answer. He looked puzzled, then he slumped forward. He was holding out his hand... I could see a piece of his skull coming off. It was flesh-coloured, not white-he was holding out his hand... I can see this perfectly clean piece detaching itself from his head. Then he slumped in my lap, his blood and his brains were in my lap... Then (Secret Service Agent) Clint Hill, he loved us, he made my life so easy, he was the first man in the car... We all lay down in the car... And I kept saying, Jack, Jack, Jack, and someone yelling he's dead, he's dead. All the ride to the hospital I kept bending over him, saying Jack, Jack, can you hear me? I love you, Jack. I kept holding the top of his head down, trying to keep the brains in."

Governor Connally testified that he recognised the first noise as a rifle shot and the thought crossed his mind that it was an assassination attempt. From his position in the right jump seat immediately in front of the President, he instinctively turned to his right because the shot appeared to come from over his right shoulder. Unable to see the President as he turned, the Governor started to look back over his left shoulder, but he never completed the turn because he felt something strike him in the back. The Governor was lying with his head on his wife's lap when he heard a shot hit the President. At that point both Governor Connally and his wife observed brain tissue splattered over the interior of the car.

Two cars to the rear, in the Lincoln carrying the Johnsons and Texas Senator Ralph Yarborough, Secret Service Agent Rufus Youngblood heard an "explosive noise". In the second car behind Johnson Mrs. Earl Cabell, wife of the Mayor of Dallas, saw a "projection" sticking out of a window of the Book Depository. From a press car at the rear of the motorcade, Robert Jackson, a Dallas Times Herald photographer, saw a rifle being slowly drawn back through an open window. Directly across from the building, Amos Euins, a 15 year old schoolboy, saw a man shoot twice from a window. Euins then hid behind a bench.

Arnold Rowland had seen a figure silhouetted in a window, holding what appeared to be a high-powered rifle, like a Marine on a rifle range. He assumed that the figure must be a Secret Service agent protecting the president and said to his wife, "Do you want to see a Secret Service agent?" "Where?", she asked. "In that building there", he said, pointing. Shortly afterwards Robert Edwards and Ronald Fischer, who were watching the motorcade from a high building overlooking Dealey Plaza also noticed Oswald but his weapon was below their line of sight. They were struck by something peculiar in his stance and expression. He never moved, he didn't even blink his eyes. He was just gazing like a man mesmerised.

The most important witness to the shooting, however, was Howard L. Brennan. Standing across from the Book Depository building, he had noticed a man at the 6th floor corner window. While waiting for the motorcade to arrive he had watched him leave the window "a couple of times". After Brennan had heard a shot, he looked up again:

"And this man that I saw previous was aiming for his last shot. Well, as it appeared to me, he was standing up and resting against the left window sill, taking positive aim, and fired his last shot. As I calculate, a couple of seconds. He drew the gun back from the window as though he was drawing it back to assure hisself (sic) that he hit his mark, and then he disappeared."

Brennan stopped a policeman, gave a description of the man: slender, about 5ft 10ins, in his early 30's. The description was radioed to all Dallas patrol cars. Brennan later picked Lee Harvey Oswald out of a line-up. After the assassination Brennan would not positively identify Oswald as the gunman and Conspiracy Theorists have made much of this fact. However Brennan reacted this way because he feared for his own safety, believing initial reports of a communist conspiracy, a natural assumption in right-wing Texas.

Another witness, Ronald Fischer, sitting near Brennan, saw a man in the window for 10 or 15 seconds. He said that the man held his attention until the motorcade came because the man:

"... appeared uncomfortable for one, and secondly, he wasn't watching. ... he didn't look like he was watching for the parade. He looked like he was looking down towards the Trinity river and the Triple Underpass down at the end-toward the end of Elm Street. And... all the time I watched him, he never moved his head, he never-he never, moved anything. Just there transfixed."

According to the Warren Report Fischer could see the 'man':

" from the middle of his chest to the top of his head", and that as he was facing the window the man was in the lower right-hand portion of the window and "seemed to be sitting a little forward." The man was dressed in a light-coloured, open-necked shirt which could have been either a sports shirt or a T-shirt, and he had brown hair, a slender face and neck with light complexion, and looked to be 22 or 24 years old. The person in the window was a white man and 'looked to me like he was looking straight at the Triple underpass' down Elm Street. Boxes and cases were stacked behind him."

The only place where witnesses conclusively saw a gunman and a rifle at the time of the assassination was in the southeast corner of the 6th floor window of the Book Depository. Furthermore Harold Norman heard the action of the rifle bolt and the sounds of the cartridges as they hit the floor. Norman was sitting in the south-east corner of the 5th floor. He heard 3 shots. He told the Warren Commission:

"... and I can't remember what the exact time was but I know I heard a shot, and then after I heard the shot, well, it seems as though the president, you know, slumped or something, and then another shot and I believe Jarman or someone told me, he said, 'I believe someone is shooting at the President,' and I think I made a statement 'It is someone shooting at the President, and I believe it came from up above us.' Well, I couldn't see at all during the time but I know I heard a third shot fired, and I could also hear something sounded like the shell hulls hitting the floor and the ejecting of the rifle."

Many Conspiracy Theorists maintain that Oswald had assistance within the Book Depository and they point to movie footage named the 'Hughes film' which, they say, indicates figures moving around the 6th floor minutes before the assassination. The movie was examined by Frances Corbett, an image processing analyst, and the claims were found to be erroneous. Furthermore, consider the scenario. The Texas Book Depository was occupied by dozens of employees who had free run of the building. From the Warren Commission's testimonies of many of those employees it is clear some of them only decided on their motorcade viewing position only minutes before the assassination. How would conspirators depend upon employees staying clear of their snipers' positions? Obviously they could not. Oswald did not appear suspicious in his movements around the building. Other conspirators would have.

After the shots there was a mass of confusion, in part because Dealey Plaza is surrounded on all three sides by tall buildings which acted as an echo chamber leading many witnesses to look to the Grassy Knoll and other places for the origin of the shots. Experienced police officers, however, have always recognised the fact that when you get two or more witnesses to a sudden event you generally get two or more stories as to what exactly happened and the stories are often conflicting. In the case of Dealey Plaza there were hundreds of witnesses milling around in a state of excitement.

Five minutes after the shooting the presidential limousine swept into the driveway of the Parkland Memorial Hospital. Vice-President Johnson's car and two cars loaded with Secret Service Agents arrived almost simultaneously. Agent Clint Hill removed his suit jacket and covered the President's head wound to prevent photographs.

The braking of the car jolted Governor Connally back to consciousness. Despite his grave wounds, he tried to stand up and get out so that doctors could reach the President. But he collapsed again. Mrs. Kennedy held the President in her lap, and for a moment refused to release him. She only relented when Agent Clint Hill covered the President's head with his jacket. Then three Secret Service Agents lifted him onto a stretcher and pushed it into trauma room one.

Twelve doctors had rushed into the emergency room. Surgeon Charles Carrico was the first to examine Kennedy and found him to be still alive. His condition, however, was hopeless. One bullet had hit near the base of the neck slightly to the right of the spine, ripped his windpipe and shot out the front of his neck, nicking the knot on his tie. This wound was not necessarily lethal. The second bullet that hit President Kennedy bored into the right rear of his skull causing a massive and fatal wound. So extensive was the damage that doctors were unsure whether the bullets had entered from the front or the rear. They did not discover the wound in the back (lower neck/right shoulder) because they did not roll him over to examine him concentrating instead on the right side of his head where the damage was most extensive. Dr. Malcolm Perry performed a tracheotomy, making an incision that cut away the wound in the front of the throat. It was a futile effort and President Kennedy died at 1pm

CHAPTER 3

INVESTIGATING THE ASSASSINATION

"There is little doubt that the Government needlessly and wastefully classified and then withheld from public access countless important records that did not require such treatment ... Such secrecy had led the American public to believe that the Government had something to hide."

Assassination Records Review Board, September 1998

THE WARREN REPORT

The Warren Commission was appointed by President Johnson to investigate the circumstances surrounding the assassination and was headed by the Chief Justice of the Supreme Court, Earl Warren. The other members of the Commission were distinguished Americans but the actual investigative work was carried out by lower ranking staff members like Arlen Specter and David Belin, experienced lawyers who were noted for their integrity. However, they had little contact with the Commission members and they had to rely largely on F.B.I. reports since the Warren Commission had no investigating staff of it's own.

President Johnson urged the Commission on to get the Report out to stop rumours of conspiracy and members did not fully investigate many aspects of the case. It was later disclosed that President Johnson had intimated to one insider that Kennedy had indeed been assassinated as a result of a conspiracy. He stated that the United States had been running a 'damn Murder Incorporated' in the Caribbean (C.I.A. murder plots against Castro) and Castro had taken revenge. Recently released LBJ Library tape recordings (October 1997) also revealed that Johnson told Senator Richard Russell, a Commission member, that he did not believe in the 'Single-Bullet Theory'. However, according to his wife Lady Bird, Johnson accepted the findings of the Warren Commission.

Notwithstanding these facts, the Warren Report was impressive - 27 volumes of witness testimony, exhibits and reports. The Warren Commission heard 552 witnesses and received more than 3000 reports from law enforcement agencies which had conducted 26, 000 interviews. It is this fact that many Conspiracy Theorists miss-the inevitability of imperfection given the volume of evidence.

The Commission's first conclusion was that the shots that killed President Kennedy came from the Texas School Book Depository. This conclusion was based on medical evidence which showed that at least two of the shots came from the general direction of the depository; on the testimony of eyewitnesses who saw a rifle in the 6th floor window of the depository; and on the fact that the murder weapon and 3 cartridges were found on the 6th floor of the depository.

The second conclusion concerned the sequence of events. The film of the assassination taken by Abraham Zapruder, showed that the President and Governor Connally were hit less than two seconds apart, and that the rifle tests showed it was physically impossible for the murder weapon to be accurately fired twice within this period of time. Thus, either both men were hit by the same bullet or there had to be two assassins. The Report decided on the "Single-Bullet Theory" which had first been proposed by Arlen Specter.

Thirdly, the Commission concluded that the assassin was Lee Harvey Oswald. This conclusion was based on 7 sub-conclusions:

1. The murder weapon was Oswald's.
2. Oswald carried the weapon into the Depository.
3. At the time of the assassination Oswald was at the window from which the shots were fired.
4. The murder weapon was found in the Depository after the assassination.
5. Oswald possessed enough proficiency with a rifle to have committed the assassination.
6. Oswald lied to the police.
7. Oswald had attempted to kill General Walker, a right-wing public figure living in Dallas.

The Commission's fourth conclusion concerned Oswald's motive. Although the Commission could not make any definite determination of Oswald's motives it listed 5 factors which might have influenced Oswald's decision to assassinate President Kennedy.

1. Oswald's resentment of all authority.
2. His inability to enter into meaningful relationships with people.
3. His urge to find a place in history.
4. His capacity for violence.
5. His commitment to Marxism and Communism.

Finally there was the conclusions concerning whether or not Oswald acted alone.

"Because of the difficulty of proving a negative to a certainty the possibility of others being involved with either Oswald or Ruby cannot be rejected categorically, but if there is any such evidence it has been beyond the reach of all investigative agencies and resources of the United States and has not come to the attention of this Commission."

However it soon became evident that the Warren Report was flawed and inadequate in many ways. Critics seized on a number of issues and their criticisms turned mainly on technical points:

* Witnesses differed on identifying Lee Harvey Oswald, a 24 year old ex-Marine and former defector to the Soviet Union, as the man firing a rifle from the Texas School Book Depository building. The only one who claimed to have seen him positively did not identify Oswald later in a police line-up.

* Many witnesses thought the first shot came from the railway overpass, or the Grassy Knoll, ahead of the presidential car, instead of from "above and behind", as the Commission found.

* There was a wide difference among eye and ear witnesses as to how many shots were actually fired: some thought they heard only 2 shots, others up to 5 or 6.

* The murder weapon originally was identified by a Deputy Sheriff as a 7.6 Mauser, rather than a 6.5 Mannlicher-Carcano, indicating that there might have been more than one weapon, or a switch of weapons.

* Oswald was said to be a poor shot, using a second hand rifle with a defective gunsight, who couldn't possibly have fired 3 shots with such accuracy.

* A paper bag the Commission concluded Oswald used to bring a rifle into the building showed no chemical or physical evidence of ever having contained a rifle, and was of a different size than witnesses remembered.

* The single bullet - Commission exhibit No.399 - which the Commission said hit both President Kennedy and Governor Connally was so clean and undamaged it seemed impossible that it could have gone through two bodies.

* This same bullet, found on the floor at Parkland Hospital in Dallas, originally was thought to have come from the President's body during heart massage, but later was identified as having fallen from Governor Connally's stretcher.

* The weight of fragments found in Governor Connally's wrist, added to the weight of the bullet found at the hospital, was alleged to add up to

more than the weight of a complete bullet-indicating that more shots were fired than the Commission report indicated.

* The bullet found on the hospital floor could have been 'planted' there, and certain other evidence 'faked', to implicate Oswald, while the real killer escaped.

* The Commission was accused of shutting off testimony from some witnesses and failing to call others who claimed to have pertinent information.

* The Dallas police failed to keep a record of their interrogations of Oswald while he was alive and in their custody.

* The Commission failed to reckon with testimony of witnesses who claimed to have seen Oswald, or persons resembling Oswald or giving his name, at times when the Commission found he was elsewhere.

* The Commission failed to get the X-rays and photographs taken at the time of the autopsy at Bethesda Naval Hospital, which might have cleared up any doubt about the number and position of the wounds in the President's body.

* Many critics said Oswald's guilt was not established by due process of law under legal rules of evidence. Had he lived, they believed, and if there had been a trial, a good lawyer could have established such a case of 'reasonable doubt' as to enable Oswald to go free.

There is a consensus amongst historians that the Warren Commission was inadequate in the manner in which it investigated the assassination:

* The Commission did not demand to see all the C.I.A. files on Oswald who had been 'tracked' by the C.I.A. and F.B.I. from the time he defected to the Soviet Union to the time he made his trip to the Soviet and Cuban embassies in Mexico City in September of 1963.

* The Commission did not do a thorough job in investigating Oswald's killer, Jack Ruby and his alleged links to the Mafia.

* The Commission did not investigate Kennedy's natural 'enemies'- Teamster boss, James R. Hoffa, New Orleans Mafia boss Carlos Marcello, Chicago mob boss Sam Giancana, Florida mob boss Santos Trafficante and the various Anti-Castro organisations.

* The Commission did not investigate fully the possibility that Cuban leader, Fidel Castro, hired Oswald to kill Kennedy as a reprisal for C.I.A. attempts to kill him. The Warren Commission was not told about C.I.A. attempts to kill Castro even though ex-C.I.A. Director Allen Dulles was a Commission member and knew about the plots.

These were definite major failings of the Warren Commission and were rightly criticised by legitimate and sober assassination researchers. But then the nit-picking and fantasising began and the greatest 'Whodunit' of the 20th Century captured the imagination of the American public. After the Watergate scandal and the revelations that the C.I.A. had attempted to eliminate heads of various foreign governments growing public distrust of governmental agencies forced the United States Congress to investigate the assassination of President Kennedy and the House of Representatives instituted the House Select Committee on Assassinations which investigated the affair over a period of 3 years in the 1970's. Their report was issued in 1979 and supported many of the conclusions of the Warren Commission but eventually decided, on the basis of acoustical evidence, that a conspiracy was likely. Since that investigation many of the anomalies and supposed discrepancies in the evidence have been re-investigated by numerous government bodies and independent investigators. I believe further new evidence and interpretation of events surrounding the assassination can satisfactorily negate the claims of Conspiracy Theorists that there was a conspiracy to kill President Kennedy.

THE RIFLE

Shortly after the assassination Dallas Police started a floor by floor search of the Book Depositories. When police came to the south-east corner 6th floor window, they found stacked boxes that had been used as a rifle perch. Officer Luke Mooney found 3 cartridge shells. Minutes later a Mannlicher-Carcano 6. 5 mm rifle was found by Deputy Sheriff Boone. It had been placed between boxes of books. Boone did not touch the rifle but called Captain Will Fritz of the Dallas Police Homicide Bureau who arrived with Lieutenant J.C. Day of the Crime Scene Search Section Identification Bureau. Day noticed its serial number - C 2766 -, photographed it and scratched his initials on the stock. Boone commented that it looked like a 7.65 Mauser because 'Mauser' was a generic term used at that time for a bolt-action rifle.

This mis-identification of the weapon used to shoot President Kennedy has been seized upon by Conspiracy Theorists who have continually claimed for 35 years that another rifle was involved in the assassination. Deputy Sheriff Boone has repeated his testimony concerning the rifle as late as 1991 in the television programme "The Trial of Lee Harvey Oswald" and reiterated that he thought the rifle was a Mauser because it had a bolt action and there were a lot of Mausers around at the time. He said he was not an expert on firearms. This simple mistake has frequently been seen by Conspiracy Theorists as evidence of a cover-up. As late as 1996 Ray and Mary La Fontaine were using this honest mistake to imply that a Mauser and a Mannlicher Carcano were found in the Book Depository.

When Lt. J.C. Day took the rifle apart he found and lifted a palm-print which he sent to the F.B.I. laboratories in Washington. It was later identified as the palm -print of Lee Harvey Oswald. Palm-prints are just as unique as fingerprints. In Oliver Stone's movie "J.F.K." conspirators can be seen to imprint the rifle with the dead Oswald's palmprint. There is absolutely no credible evidence to suggest this ever happened. However, the fingerprints which were found on the rifle were too blurred to make any conclusive opinion as to who had handled the weapon.

The question of fingerprints, or supposed lack of them, was finally resolved in 1993 by one of America's leading fingerprint experts, Vincent Scalese, during the making of a BBC 'Timewatch' documentary. In 1963 the latent fingerprints on the trigger guard were initially ignored by investigating agencies because they were less defined than the palm print.

"The F.B.I. examined these latent prints," Scalese said, "and determined that they were worthless for identification purposes. I re-examined the photo of these latent prints again in 1978 for the Select Committee on Assassinations and came to the same conclusion due to the faintness of the prints. I determined that they were of no value for identification purposes."

However, Rusty Livingstone, who worked in the Dallas Crime Lab 35 years ago found a second set of photographs of the prints which he took for himself and stored. This long neglected evidence was re-examined by Vincent Scalese in 1993. On examination, the prints on the trigger guard were found to have 3 positive and 3 possible points of identity though not enough for an 'absolute' identity. Using a new technique Scalese was prepared to go much further:

"I took the photographs, there were a total of 4 photographs in all. Then I began to examine them and as I did I saw 2 faint prints which had been taken at different exposures and it was necessary for me to utilise all of the photographs to compare against the ink prints. As I examined them I found that by manoeuvring the photographs in different positions I was able to pick up some details on one photograph and some details on another photograph. Using all of the photos at different contrasts I was able to find in the neighbourhood of about 18 points of identity between the 2 prints. I feel that this is a major breakthrough in this investigation because we're able, for the first time to actually say that these are definitely the fingerprints of Lee Harvey Oswald."

The F.B.I. later learned that this same rifle that was found in the Book Depository had been posted in March 1963 from a Chicago mail order house to "A. Hidell P.O. Box 2915" in Dallas. Handwriting experts told the Warren Commission that the coupon ordering the rifle, the signature on a money order to pay for it and the address on the envelope were all written by Oswald's hand. Oswald's wallet contained fake identification cards for "Alek James Hidell"; one such card carried Oswald's photograph. "Alek" had been Oswald's nickname in Russia because his Russian friends thought that 'Lee' sounded too 'Chinese'.

"Hidell", however, most probably came from several sources. In Atsugi, Japan, Oswald had known a fellow marine who came from New Orleans and whose name was John Rene Heindell, nicknamed "Hidell". If the name is pronounced "Heedell", the connection with Oswald's hero "Fidel" becomes evident. It was Marina Oswald who spotted the similarity. The name "James" may have been taken from "James Bond". Oswald was an avid reader of Ian Fleming's novels and he frequently commented that he would have liked to have been a spy.

The F.B.I. also found a tuft of cotton fibres-blue, grey-black and orange-yellow-clinging to the rifle butt. Under microscopic examination, the fibres matched those in a shirt worn by Oswald the day of the assassination. And the rifle was linked to Oswald by a fingerprint and palm-print found on the paper sack which held the rifle.

There has been much speculation as to Oswald's skill with a rifle. Nelson Delgado's name appears in many conspiracy books, mainly because he testified that Oswald was a poor rifle shot when he was in the Marines. He has testified that Oswald's shooting was a "big joke" because he got a lot of "Maggie's drawers"-a red flag indicating the shots had missed their target-and that he had barely qualified. He had scored just one point above the score necessary to qualify.

As a young recruit, however, Oswald had done better. His rifle score book showed him making 48 and 49 points out of a possible 50 in rapid fire at 200 yards from a sitting position, without a scope.

Sergeant Zahn, one of Oswald's trainers, has confirmed Oswald's ability with a rifle and described him as an excellent shot. In December 1956, at the end of his training, Oswald was tested and scored 212-2 points above the minimum for 'sharpshooter' on a scale of expertise ranging in ascending order from 'Marksman' to 'sharpshooter' to 'expert'. By civilian standards he was an excellent shot. Moreover Oswald now had a 4 power scope.

However, many Conspiracy Theorists maintain the shootings have never been duplicated. Of the 3 professional marksmen used by the Warren Commission to try to duplicate Oswald's performance-only one was able to fire 3 shots in the time stipulated by the Commission (they were later found to be mistaken about the timing-the time Oswald had to shoot the rifle was 8 seconds and not 6 as the Commission thought because the original timing was taken from the Zapruder film which was found to have a faulty time frame and the Commission also assumed Oswald did not fire his first shot until the limousine reappeared from behind a tree.)

Yet the feat was duplicated by Howard Donahue, an expert on firearms and ballistics. In his book 'Mortal Error', Bonar Menninger stated:

"Remarkably, Donahue's shots had all hit within a 3 inch circle on the (moving) target's head. More importantly, the elapsed time from first shot to last was only 4.8 seconds, well under the 5.6 maximum."

Oswald's wife Marina identified the rifle, in testimony to the Warren Commission during its 1964 hearings, as "the fateful rifle of Lee Oswald". She said she had taken some photographs of Oswald with the rifle in the backyard of their Neely Street, Dallas, apartment. This was damning evidence.

House Assassinations Committee members questioned Marina about the photographs in 1978. Marina said they were taken on Sunday March 31st 1963. Dressed in black, Oswald wore a pistol on his belt, holding the rifle in one hand and a recent copy of both "The Militant" and "The Worker", Left-Wing magazines, in the other. Oswald told her he wanted photographs to send to "The Militant".

After his arrest Oswald claimed to Captain Will Fritz of the Dallas Police Department that the Neely Street backyard photographs were fakes-a claim seconded by Conspiracy Theorists ever since. Oswald claimed the photograph shown to him (there was more than one pose) by detectives was a composite made by superimposing his head on someone else's body-a claim made by Oliver Stone in the movie "J.F.K."

As Captain Fritz testified:

"(Oswald) said the picture was not his, that the face was his face, but that this picture had been made by superimposing his face, the other part of the picture was not him at all and that he had never seen the picture before... He further stated that since he had been photographed here at City Hall and that people had been taking his picture while being transferred from my office to the jail door that someone had been able to get a picture of his face and that with that, they had made this picture... (and) that in time, he would be able to show that it was not his picture and that it had been made by someone else."

Had the photos been tampered with in order to create an incriminating image of the accused assassin? If so, such an act in itself would indicate the existence of a conspiracy, as the House Assassinations Committee noted in 1979:

"If the backyard photographs are valid, they are highly incriminating of Oswald because they apparently link him with the murder weapon. If they are fakes, how they were produced poses far-reaching questions in the area of conspiracy. 'Fake' backyard photographs would indicate a degree of conspiratorial sophistication that would almost necessarily raise the possibility that a highly organised group had conspired to kill the President and make Oswald a 'patsy'".

However, Marina Oswald insisted that Oswald ordered her to take the photographs. Moreover, what Oswald did not know was that if someone has a negative of a picture, and a camera, there are individualistic markings by which it is possible to determine whether that negative came from the particular camera to the exclusion of all other cameras in the world. The negative of the picture was found as was Oswald's camera. Scientific evidence presented to the Warren Commission determined that the picture was taken by Oswald's Imperial Reflex camera to the exclusion of all other cameras. Furthermore, the House Assassinations Committee examined the photographs and found them to be genuine. Using sophisticated analytical techniques the panel of experts hired by the committee uncovered a unique mark of wear and tear on the rifle in the photographs that corresponded to a mark on the weapon found in the depository, and concluded that the two weapons were identical. The House Assassinations Committee experts proved that the photographs were genuine by making reference to the unique grain within the photographs.

Robert Groden, most recently in his book 'The Search for Lee Harvey

Oswald' published in 1995, still uses these photographs to infer conspiracy and still maintains they were faked:

Groden wrote: "There are better than a dozen ways to prove that the photographs do not depict an actual occasion, that Lee could not have posed for them, and that they were manufactured prior to the assassination. In proving that these photos are fake, one proves that Lee Oswald was set up well in advance of the assassination as the 'patsy'. The most alarming aspect of the backyard photos is that they were created to frame Oswald before the crime was committed and planted among Oswald's possessions before the murder took place. This and other sophisticated work required to create the photos in the first place could not have been done by amateurs."

In 1997, however, Groden was discredited as a photographic expert during the O.J. Simpson civil trial. G. Robert Blakey, a top University of Notre Dame law professor who was Chief Counsel and Director of the House Select Committee on Assassinations told the National Enquirer that Groden had lied about his credentials:

" Groden's ability to interpret photographs is nil", Blakey said, "Groden's theory (that the Oswald rifle photos were fakes) produced smiles on the faces of those people who know better. The pictures were sent to the best people in the world, bar none, to check them for authenticity-top labs at Stanford University, the University of Southern California and the Rochester Institute of Technology... (who verified the photos were genuine)". We shall return to this aspect in a later chapter when we consider Oswald's interrogation.

Furthermore, recent evidence proving that the photos were seen by someone other than Marina Oswald prior to the assassination was produced when Michael Paine, a friend of the Oswald's, declared that he had seen one of the photos as early as April 1963. This severely undercuts conspiracy scenarios based on the photos.

Oswald had kept his rifle, wrapped in an old brown and green blanket, in a garage at the Irving, Texas, home of Ruth Paine, where Marina Oswald stayed the last eight weeks before November 22nd. When Dallas Police turned up at the Paine house after the arrest of Oswald and asked Marina, through Ruth Paine who interpreted for her, if Oswald had a rifle she replied he had and that it was kept in the garage and was wrapped in a blanket. The blanket looked exactly as it always had as if there was something bulky inside. It was carefully tied with string. As an officer picked it up it hung limp over his arm.

Oswald himself was living in a Dallas rooming house and rarely visited the Paine home on week nights. But on the Thursday evening, the day before the assassination, he hitched a ride to Irving with fellow Book Depository worker, Buell Wesley Frazier. Oswald's explanation was that he wanted to pick up some curtain rods to use in his rooming house. Later investigations indicated that his room was already supplied with curtain rods.

Oswald stayed overnight in the Paine home, and, curiously, never mentioned the curtain rods. He departed in the morning with a bundle with brown paper wrapping. Oswald then placed the package in Frazier's car and casually explained that it contained curtain rods. When Frazier and Oswald arrived at the Book Depository parking lot, Oswald hurried to the building 50 feet ahead of Frazier. He carried with him the package. Frazier would later be puzzled by Oswald's actions. Oswald had never previously walked ahead to the Book Depository but had waited, instead, for Frazier to secure the car and join him.

After the assassination police found a paperbag on the floor. Lt. Day initialled the bag. It was found to be comparable with other brown paper in the Book Depository. Oswald's palm print and a fingerprint were found on the bag.

Conspiracy Theorists have seized on the idea that Oswald's rifle was not capable of firing the bullets to any great degree of force or accuracy. The Warren Commission and the House Assassinations Committee determined otherwise as did Howard Donahue who knew something about the history of the rifle. Bonar Menninger wrote:

"To Donahue this lack of firearms training (He is referring to Conspiracy Theorists) was all too apparent. In none of the books could he find a thoughtful, rigorous analysis of the ballistic evidence. Most of the authors, he believed, instead relied on ballistic generalisations and often outright fallacies to support their arguments..... One example were the terms "Master Rifleman", and "Superb Marksman" mentioned by incredulous writers in connection with Lee Harvey Oswald's performance in Dallas. Donahue knew Oswald's shooting was mediocre at best: The distance Oswald fired from was not that great and out of the three shots he supposedly got off, one missed the presidential limousine entirely.... Yet another misconception... was the belief that the 6.5mm cartridge was a low to medium powered bullet. ..... African Big Game hunter Koromojo Bell had demonstrated the weapon's lethal punch by using a Carcano-type rifle and cartridge to kill scores of elephants with single head shots."

Scientific tests, therefore, have indicated that the Mannlicher-Carcano was a powerful and accurate rifle - accurate enough to allow Oswald to squeeze off three shots, of which at least two found their mark, in the time allowed by the Zapruder film of the assassination. Furthermore, the use of a four power scope was a substantial aid to rapid fire. At the time the first shot struck President Kennedy, the limousine was approximately 180 feet from the window of the Book Depository. Oswald's rifle had a 4 power scope, which made the actual distance appear to be only 45 feet - 15 Yards. The second and fatal shot struck Kennedy when the limousine was only 265 feet from the window of the Book Depository - Approximately 88 Yards. In fact the shots were entirely feasible given Oswald's experience with firearms. Furthermore there is another reason that none of the Conspiracy Theorists have ever considered and that is a 'quirk of fate'; if Oswald's shooting skills were indeed less than adequate the bullets could have hit their target by chance - a ballistics 'hole in one'.

THE SINGLE BULLET THEORY

Much of the controversy about Dallas derives from the confusion and horror that followed the shooting; no one was quite sure whether there were three or four or more shots fired at the limousine.

Richard Warren Lewis and Lawrence Schiller in their book 'The Scavengers And The Critics Of The Warren Report' presented expert Melvin Eisenburg's study of why the acoustics and earwitness evidence in the Kennedy Assassination should be handled very carefully. He said that little credence should be put on witness testimony to the number of shots fired at the scene of a crime. This is for two reasons. Firstly there is the difficulty of accurate perception of the sound of the gunshots and secondly the acoustics of the gunshots. The sound of gunshot is first heard by a witness and he is not ready for it. The same is usually true if further shots are fired immediately after the first shot. Therefore the "memory recording" of such shots is very inaccurate. The perception of the source of the shots is also as unreliable as the number because a loud sound may appear to originate from nearby whereas a weak shot may seem to come from far away.

Eisenburg sounded a cautionary note to earwitness testimony:

The firing of a bullet produces three sounds. First there is the muzzle blast caused by the collision of hot gases which propel the bullet into the relatively stable air at the gun's muzzle. Secondly, the noise of the bullet caused by the shock wave built up ahead of the bullet's nose as it travels through air. Thirdly, the noise caused by the impact of the bullet into it's target. Each of these noises can be perceived as separate "shots" by an inexperienced or confused witness.

Witnesses to gunshots, then, are frequently confused by the direction of the shots because a bullet travels faster than the speed of sound. The acoustics are such that a witness who is standing at right angles to the path of the bullet may perceive the shot to have been fired from a position opposite to him. It is for these reasons that witnesses in Dealey Plaza varied enormously as to the number of shots fired and the direction of the shots.

Conspiracy Theorists cannot have it both ways. Many point to the credibility of witnesses who heard 6 or more shots yet they fall back on the (now erroneous) conclusions of the House Assassinations Committee, which relied on the police dictabelt (audio tape) of the shots fired in Dealey Plaza, which indicated 4. Dictabelt acoustics evidence will be considered later.

The Warren Commission held that the "preponderance of evidence" indicated three shots were fired at the President but there was still no real certainty as to which bullets caused which wounds. As reconstructed from Abraham Zapruder's 8mm film of the assassination, the sequence of events have finally been determined by Failure Analysis Inc's computer model and assassination researcher Kal Korff's computer model. Critics infer that the models are biased towards the lone-assassin theory and biased information was fed to the computers. They are wrong. Even though Failure Analysis' models could prove either theory the single bullet model came out as the most likely examination of the sequence of events.

The sequence of shots, then, can now be established:

SHOT 1. The preponderance of evidence and witness testimony suggests that the first shot was fired shortly after the presidential limousine turned the corner from Houston Street on to Elm Street. Earwitnesses Buell Frazier, Howard Brennan, Barbara Rowland, Royce Skelton, Geneva Hine, Secret Service Agents William Greer and Paul Landis all testified towards this. This bullet then probably struck the branch of the tree in front of the Book Depository, splitting the metal jacket from the lead core. The lead core part of the bullet then continued in virtually a straight line to the area of the overpass, struck the pavement on Main Street, throwing up a piece of concrete which struck James Tague in the cheek. Concurrently, the metal jacket part of the bullet struck an area on Elm Street near the presidential limousine. Virginia Rachley and 4 other witnesses saw the bullet strike; Rachley said "You could see the sparks from it." It is therefore easy to imagine a nervous Oswald firing prematurely as Kennedy appeared briefly through the foliage of the tree and missing his target. When the metal jacket part of the bullet hit the ground near the limousine it is possible that fragments peppered Kennedy and there is some indication from the Zapruder film that Kennedy may have responded to being struck by the metal jacket fragments. This may account for a ricochet fragment appearing on the autopsy x-rays. It is also entirely possible that one of the fragments from the first shot travelled to the area of the Grassy Knoll near the picket fence throwing up dirt which was mistaken for 'puffs of smoke'. Furthermore, Kennedy's response to the first shot would account for the alignment of the back/neck wound and the throat wound (which was in a higher position). Kennedy was hunching forward and beginning to raise his arms as if to protect himself.

David Lui, in 1979, was the first researcher to identify a telling clue as to when the first shot was fired and it occurred at approximately frame 160 of the Zapruder film. Whilst watching the Zapruder film Lui noticed a young girl running to keep pace with the presidential limousine. She stopped abruptly and turned towards the Texas School Book Depository - before any shots were supposed to have been fired. Many years later Lui asked the girl why she had stopped running with the limousine and she replied that she had heard a shot.

SHOT 2. The second bullet was fired and the president was hit in the right side upper back/neck. At first Kennedy's right arm is raised to wave to the crowd but a movement can be detected on the Zapruder film which indicates he is initially responding to the ricochet of the first shot, perhaps Kennedy is guarding his face. As the limousine emerges from behind the road sign Kennedy's arms begin to rise as if he is reaching for his throat. It is likely the second bullet fired has now entered Kennedy's back nicking the spinal cord and producing a reaction known as Thorburn's position - an involuntary movement similar to the reaction produced when the knee is tapped. There are however, disagreements within the medical community as to whether it was a 'Thorburn' response. It is possible, some experts aver, that Kennedy was exhibiting an immediate response to the bullet passing through the base of his right neck; as the bullet enters the pressure cavity it causes an immediate stimulation of all the nerves in the surrounding area, that is the 'brachial plexus', the nerves that supply motor function to the arms. Neural impulses travel very fast, therefore Kennedy would have been expected to react within one frame of the Zapruder film. According to the Zapruder film Kennedy can be seen to be reacting on the right side just before the left side - proof that the bullet passed through the right side of the upper back/neck. It confirms the upper location of the back wound - if the wound had been any lower it would have entered the chest cavity and we would not have seen the peculiar arm movements of Kennedy.

The bullet now exits and there is nowhere for it to go except through Governor Connally who is seated directly in front of the president, especially when we consider that the bullet is travelling at 2000 feet per second. Connally was seated slightly to the left of Kennedy. Conspiracy Theorists have maintained that the bullet could not zig-zag yet ballistics experts have shown that when a bullet tumbles it can change direction. The bullet enters Connally's back sideways - this accounts for the large wound in Connally's back. Exiting his right nipple it travels through his wrist backwards and lodges in his thigh. It is pristine at the sharp end only - the blunt end of the bullet is damaged.

SHOT 3. The third shot enters the top of Kennedy's head and exits to the right temporal side blowing part of his skull away which was later found on Elm Street. The movement of Kennedy to the left and backwards is proof for Conspiracy Theorists that he was shot from the front. As we shall see later, their understanding of the dynamics of the head wound are wrong.

For years Conspiracy Theorists used the Warren Commission's sequence of shots to claim that Oswald could not have fired in the time available. The Warren Commission did not make any definitive judgement as to which shots caused which wounds. It did, however, imply that the first shot could not have been fired until frames 193-198 of the Zapruder film as a tree would have obscured Oswald's view. As we have seen, this idea was spurious. Their claims are now redundant with this new time sequence of the shots - 3 shots fired between frames 160/166 (the first shot) and 313 (the head shot) - a total of 8 to 8.4 seconds and not 6 as originally suspected.

The second shot was probably not fatal. It is entirely feasible that Kennedy could have recovered from this wound to the neck although his recovery would have been difficult and he may have been paralysed, the spine having suffered severe trauma; the third shot was fatal. The time between the two bullets impact was between 4.8 and 5.6 seconds. Connally too had been badly hurt: a bullet had entered into his back, tore across a rib and out his chest, shattered his right wrist and entered his left thigh.

Since tests prove that it took at least 2.3 seconds to operate the bolt action Mannlicher-Carcano rifle, Oswald obviously could not have fired 3 separate bullets - hitting Kennedy twice and Connally once as the Zapruder film time frame indicates. . Conspiracy Theorists, therefore, claim that the timing and the wounds suggest another gunman.

As we have seen the Warren Commission accepted Warren Commission lawyer Arlen Specter's theory that one bullet, fired from behind, hit Kennedy in the base of the neck, exited from his throat, nicking his tie, traversed slightly downwards striking Governor Connally in the right shoulder, exiting his left chest, going through his wrist and lodging in his thigh. However, Governor Connally was "convinced without any doubt" that was not hit by the same bullet that first struck President Kennedy. His recollections of that day have always been totally precise and he knew "every split second of what happened in that car until I lost consciousness".

Volume IV of the "Hearings Before the President's Commission on the Assassination of President Kennedy", however, indicates that Connally contradicted himself. In his testimony Governor Connally had estimated the speed of the presidential limousine at "between 20 and 22 miles an hour" (an error) and the time span between the first and third shots of "ten, twelve seconds" (another error).

The Governor's "total recall" can also be questioned by the following statements made on page 135 of Volume IV: Mr. Specter: Were you conscious of receiving that wound on the wrist at the time you sustained it?

Governor Connally: No sir, I was not.

Mr. Specter: When did you know you were first wounded in the right wrist?

Governor Connally: When I came to in the hospital on Saturday, the next morning, and I looked up and my arm was tied up in a hospital bed, and I said, "What is wrong with my arm?" and they told me then that I had a shattered wrist, and that is when I also found out I had a wound in the thigh.

So Connally, who had no doubt about which bullet hit him had suffered a shattered wrist and a wound in the thigh without knowing it.

A bullet from the Mannlicher-Carcano rifle was found on a stretcher at the hospital where Kennedy and Connally were taken; the Warren Commission had decided that it had fallen out of Connally's superficial thigh wound onto his stretcher. The bullet offered sufficient grounds to make the single bullet theory suspect. The bullet was pristine and only slightly blunted on it's blunt end.

The bullets Oswald used are much more resistant to deformation than most rifle bullets. The major defect in bullet 399 is 'toothpasting' - that is, a small amount of lead has been squeezed out of the jacket base.

According to renowned ballistics expert Duncan MacPherson (author of an authoritative work in his field - "Bullet Penetration: Modelling. The Dynamics and the Incapacitation Resulting from Wound Traumas") a reconstruction of the dynamics of bullet 399 resulted in similar damage sustained by 399 (Conspiracy Theorists have for years maintained that no such reconstruction has been done). He also said that the deformation of bullet 399 is consistent with this bullet having caused all the second shot wounds to Kennedy and Connally.

Advances in scientific techniques should have settled the problem of the shots once and for all but Conspiracy Theorists still refuse to acknowledge or accept them. C.B.S. Television's NOVA team hired computer experts in 1988 to build a computer model of Dealey Plaza to accurate scale. They considered a number of problems related to the shots fired. They concluded that the angle and trajectory of the shots fired from the Book Depository was probably correct as indicated by the Warren Report. Furthermore Failure Analysis INC., produced a computer mathematical model of the trajectory of the 'magic bullet' for the 1992 American Bar Association mock trial of Lee Harvey Oswald in San Francisco. This work was confirmed by Kal Korff who constructed a similar computer model of the bullets trajectories in 1993 which confirms Failure Analysis' model. Furthermore, enhancements of the Zapruder Film frames in 1992 and Failure Analysis' computer model persuaded Governor Connally that he had not been hit by a separate bullet. Connally's belief that he had been hit by a separate bullet has been used by Conspiracy Theorists for over 30 years as proof that there was a second gunman.

In 1978 The House Assassinations Committee convened a medical panel, headed by Chief Forensic pathologist, Dr. Michael Baden, then the medical examiner of New York City. The members of the nine man panel collectively had participated in 100, 000 autopsies. The panel looked at the Zapruder film and concluded that the single bullet theory was correct and Governor Connally did not respond instantaneously to the wound. Baden said that people often do not respond instantly to a wound and that there is not always an instantaneous response. It is plausible, therefore, to conclude that both men were hit by a single bullet.

Dr. Cyril Wecht, in his Conspiracy book "Cause of Death", criticises the single bullet theory. Dr. Wecht was the only dissenting member out of 8 forensic pathologists on the House Assassinations Committee panel. He maintains that a bullet could not do all that damage and still remain pristine.

However there are further scientific reasons why it could remain in a pristine condition. As the bullet passed through President Kennedy's neck it would have slowed down and a bullet that is slowed down is less likely to be deformed. And a full-metal jacket bullet is designed to travel through soft tissue without being deformed. This is the key to an understanding of the 'Magic Bullet'. Furthermore the wound in Connally's back was large thus indicating that the bullet had begun to wobble, changing position and slowing down. A 'slow' bullet does not suffer much damage.

The 'pristine' bullet (Commission Exhibit 399) was also examined to determine if it was chemically identical to the bullet fragments removed from Governor Connally's arm. Conspiracy Theorists were convinced they would not match thus confirming the single bullet theory incorrect. The House Assassinations Committee asked Dr. Vincent Guinn to find out and he used a technique called "Neutron Activation Analysis". The results proved that the fragments matched to the single bullet. It was possible that other bullets manufactured at the same time would have very similar composition and could also have been the source of the fragments but the chance that the same batch of ammunition was used at the assassination scene is too incredulous an hypothesis.

Perhaps the most convincing evidence of all concerning the pristine bullet, or 'magic bullet' as the Conspiracy Theorists call it, was the F.B.I. test that showed marks on the bullet which exactly matched the rifling grooves in the barrel of Oswald's rifle. The results of these particular tests have rarely been mentioned by Conspiracy Theorists.

Conspiracy Theorists, then, have attacked the single-bullet theory for 35 years. Many have used statements issued by some Dallas doctors who attended to President Kennedy.

Dallas doctor, Dr. Shaw was puzzled about the bullet C.E.399 and told CBS' NOVA Team:

"I couldn't quite understand why a bullet going through the President's neck, coming from the right and above, exiting out through his throat, would then zig and zag to strike the Governor who was sitting directly in front of the President. It would seem to me that that bullet would have struck the Governor in the left side of his chest rather than the right side of his chest."

It would appear at first sight, that Dr. Shaw was correct. Photographs of the limousine show Governor Connally seated slightly to Kennedy's left and the location of their wounds suggest they were hit by two separate bullets not by a single bullet fired from the 6th floor of the Book Depository. Dr. Baden, however, maintains that this is entirely consistent if Kennedy was tilting slightly forward when he was struck and Governor Connally was turning slightly to his right and backwards as he said he did when he heard the sound of the first shot. If these occurrences are indeed true as it would seem from the Zapruder frames, C.B.S. and Failure Analysis' computer models which construct an alignment of the shots from the Book Depository, are correct and the single bullet theory, together with other strong circumstantial evidence concerning the location of the shooter is the most likely description of what took place.

Additional reasoning to support the single bullet theory shows that a bullet does not always travel in a straight line after it enters a human body . This fact could also account for the supposedly zig-zag movement of the bullet. These conclusions were supported by National Aeronautics and Space Administration engineer Tom Canning, who gave testimony to the House Assassinations Committee in 1978. He said that a careful study of photographs showed Kennedy was leaning rightward as he waved to the crowd in Dealey Plaza, while Connally was seated toward the middle of the car, making it "almost inevitable" that he would be hit.

Furthermore Canning's testimony is corroborated by photographs published by the Warren Commission but have often been overlooked by Conspiracy Theorists. They show the inside of the Presidential limousine in detail. The jump seats in which Governor Connally and his wife were seated are not directly in front of the rear seats but squeezed some 6 ins. in from the doors of the car. Therefore they show that Governor Connally was not seated directly in front of the President. These facts can be verified by the reader who can view the presidential limousine which is housed at the Ford Car museum in Dearborn, Michigan.

Despite this overwhelming evidence to support the 'Single Bullet Theory' Conspiracy Theorists refuse to acknowledge them. In May 1997 the BBC 'Correspondent' team interviewed German computer scientist, Joachim Marcus and conspiracy author Matthew Smith. Marcus was well known in Germany for his 'photogrammatry' computer techniques, which involved calculating the co-ordinates of 2D photographs and presenting them as 3D models. Marcus' photogrammatry techniques were applied to the Zapruder film of the assassination and a model was constructed. "You can forget the Single Bullet Theory, " Marcus said, "There is no reason why the single bullet (on leaving Kennedy's throat) would change direction again."

David Lomax, the programmes presenter and an eminent 'Panorama' journalist, highlights the problems the media faces when examining this case-they do not refer to superior, authoritative, scientific evidence. At no time did Lomax make reference to previous scientific and computer model evidence, as presented above.

Dr. Baden, interviewed by author Gerald Posner stated:

"One of the silliest arguments critics made over the years is that the bullet came out of Kennedy's neck, made a right turn to hit Connally's shoulder, then made another right when it left his chest in order to strike his wrist and then completely changed directions and made a left to enter his thigh. Some people still believe that, even though photo enhancements long ago showed the Governor was in such a position that his wounds were clearly the result of one bullet passing straight through him."

Speaking on the "Larry King Show" (CNN) in 1992 Dr. George Lundberg, Editor of the "Journal of the American Medical Association", also confirmed the House Assassinations Committee and the Warren Commission's findings that the bullet which went through President Kennedy's neck was one of entry from behind and not the front as some Conspiracy Theorists claim. The evidence for this, he stated, was that the wound on the base of the neck had an "abrasion collar" which is only found in entry wounds. Furthermore Kennedy's shirt collar and tie show fibres projecting outward further supporting that the neck wound was one of exit not entry. Lundberg was speaking about an article written for his Journal by the autopsy doctors, Humes and Boswell, and we shall return to his comments when the evidence concerning the head wound is discussed.

Photos of Kennedy's clothes were also used by Conspiracy Theorists to prove that the bullet wound on Kennedy's back was lower than the 'exit' wound in his neck. Henry Hurt wrote:

" .... the F.B.I. laboratory examined (the President's clothing) and pinpointed to the Warren Commission the exact location of the bullet holes in the back of Kennedy's jacket and shirt. In each instance, the bullet hole was between 5 and 6 inches from the top of the back of the collar and between 1 and 2 inches to the right of the midline of the clothing. This location, of course, was precisely where so many autopsy witnesses, including the President's personal physician, agreed that they were."

The autopsy drawings will be discussed later in this chapter. As far as the bullet holes in the clothing are concerned reference should be made to photographs taken during the motorcade drive from the airport which clearly show the president's jacket 'bunched up' which occurred because of the back-brace Kennedy wore.

The Zapruder film clearly shows the 'shoulder pads' of Kennedy's jacket rising high. However, if this theory of a 'bunched' jacket is rejected, as it is by some Conspiracy Theorists, another rational explanation can be brought into play without reverting to sinister theories. If as I explained earlier, the President's arms are rising in response to the first shot then this movement would account for the jacket and shirt rising. Kennedy was hunching forward in response to the first shot so a wound in the back which was lower than the wound in the front would be consistent. It should also be noted that when Kennedy moves slightly forward after hearing the first shot the body tissues and muscles of the back/neck would be likely to rise thus explaining why the actual wounds in the autopsy photos show the back wound not consistent with the hole in the jacket. This would also explain why the bullet hole in Kennedy's back was lower when he lay flat on the autopsy table. If, as Conspiracy Theorists maintain, the bullet entered the throat and exited the back there would have been damage to the seat or the trunk of the limousine. This would have had to happen if, as Conspiracy Theorists maintain, the shot through the neck was fired from a higher position like a railway overpass or the Grassy Knoll. The bullets were, after all, travelling at a phenomenal 2000 feet per second and would not have slowed down by hitting only tissue and muscle.

Kennedy then was hunching forward in response to the first shot so a wound in the back which was lower than the wound in the front would not have been inconsistent. Furthermore, examination of Kennedy's clothes confirm he was hit from the rear; the bullet pushed the threads forward and spectrographic tests showed residues of copper at the edges of the jacket's hole. JFK's shirt also had one hole in the shoulder/neck region showing threads which were pushed inwards indicating a shot from the rear. The front of the shirt showed threads pointing outward indicating an exit, as does the tie. The position of the bullet wound in the back had been misrepresented by doctors and Secret Service agents. Much of the confusion hinged on semantics - was the bullet wound in the 'back', the 'lower neck' or 'right shoulder to the right of the spinal column'? The autopsy photos show it was slightly down from the base of the neck, in the right shoulder, to the right of the spinal column. As the bullet exited from the front of Kennedy's neck it is not inconsistent to say the 'back' wound was one of entry and the 'front neck' wound one of exit if he had been tilting forward.

Despite every effort by Conspiracy Theorists to discredit the single bullet theory it remains the most logical and reasonable explanation for the wounds to President Kennedy and Governor Connally.

THE HEAD WOUND

The circumstances surrounding the shot to the President's head is important to an understanding of why Conspiracy Theorists believe a shot was fired from the Grassy Knoll which was in front and to the right of the presidential limousine when Kennedy was hit.

If, as Conspiracy Theorists believe, the President was thrown backwards and to the left by the bullet which struck his head then a second shooter would have had to be stationed in the area of the Grassy Knoll. It has been a conventional view that an object striking another object will move the second object in the same direction as the first. Conspiracy Theorists maintain the head wound was caused by a bullet striking the right side of the President's head causing him to be thrown backwards and to the left and that the Warren Commission was wrong when it claimed the head wound was caused by a bullet striking the President from the rear. They claim the Zapruder film shows the president's head snapping backwards after he was shot in the head.

Thus the major controversy surrounding the shot to the President's head is whether the wound was one of exit or entry and why drawings and descriptions by the doctors in Dallas and Bethesda (where the autopsy was performed) clearly differed. The corollary to this, many Conspiracy Theorists believe, was that the President's body was altered to facilitate a cover-up. Conspiracy Theorists have been insisting for 35 years that the Zapruder film of the assassination clearly shows that the President's head shot clearly comes from the right front area.

The best known proponent of these two theories, that Kennedy was shot from the front and the wounds to his body were altered, is David Lifton. His book is flawed and illogical. The author concluded that the backward movement of Kennedy's body could only be explained by a bullet striking him from the opposite direction-the "Grassy Knoll". Many witnesses, as we have seen, thought the shots came from the "Grassy Knoll" and some of the Dallas doctors initially thought they were dealing with an entry wound to the front. Lifton, therefore, concludes that as the X-Rays and autopsy photos show shots from behind, the wounds must have been altered between Dallas and Washington D.C. He contends that all the bullets that struck Kennedy came from the front, and in concealing this fact a large group of conspirators (unnamed) managed to steal Kennedy's body (even though a military aide swears the body was only out of his sight for five minutes) slip it aboard a helicopter after the President's plane reached Washington, alter the body so that it appeared that Kennedy was shot from the rear by Oswald and then take the body back to Bethesda Naval Hospital for the official autopsy. And the evidence for such preposterous allegations? Witnesses who worked at the hospital and describe caskets, towels, body bags etc. many years after the assassination.

Lifton's theory has one important weakness apart from his use of flawed witness statements and what Dr. Michael Baden describes as Lifton's ignorance of pathology- it is the logical reasoning I put in the form of two questions- Why didn't these 'high level' government conspirators destroy the autopsy photographs and X-Rays instead of supposedly altering them ? Are we asked to believe that 'they' were willing to murder a president but were afraid of a Congressional subpoena to produce the Photographs and X-Rays?

Perhaps one of the biggest mistakes made by the Warren Commission was in not releasing to the public the X-rays and photographs of President

Kennedy's body taken during the autopsy at Bethesda Naval Hospital. Instead of submitting the X-Rays and photographs the Warren Commission directed the doctors to furnish their own drawings. As the doctors themselves were to say -they were doctors not artists . Consequently their misplacing of wounds contributed to the popularising of false theories-many of which could have been demolished had the X-Rays and photographs been available. There was no sinister motive blocking their release, as some Conspiracy Theorists have claimed; the decision was made in the interests of good taste and the feelings of the Kennedy Family.

Similarly Conspiracy Theorists point to the President's missing brain as evidence that a cover-up had occurred. After the autopsy was performed all materials relating to it, including X-Rays, slides and the President's preserved brain were turned over to the Secret Service and kept at the White House under the official custody of Dr. Burkley, the White House doctor. In 1965 Senator Robert Kennedy, the President's brother, authorised that the materials be turned over to Evelyn Lincoln, the President's former secretary. Lincoln had an office at the National Archives in Washington D.C., where she was working on the transfer of President Kennedy's papers to the Kennedy Library, which is under the control of the National Archives. Among the materials sent to Evelyn Lincoln was a container containing these materials. In 1966, the materials, including the President's preserved brain, were found to be missing. None who had handled the materials professed knowledge of their whereabouts and thus began the "sinister" theories. It is, however, known that at that particular time Robert Kennedy had expressed concern that the materials could conceivably have been put on display at some later time and he wished to prevent that happening. Accordingly the House Assassinations Committee concluded that "circumstantial evidence tends to show that Robert Kennedy either destroyed these materials or otherwise rendered them inaccessible."

I would venture to take an alternative opinion although I do not have any evidence to support this. I believe the president's brain is interred with the body in Arlington National Cemetery. It would have been a natural procedure for the Catholic Robert Kennedy to carry out.

Dr. Lundberg, the editor of the Journal of the American Medical Association asked Dr. Humes and Dr. Boswell, the autopsy doctors, to write an article for the Journal to clear up these anomalies in their report. They responded with a 14 page article in which they confirmed their original findings. Dr. Humes called the Conspiracy Theorists 'supremely ignorant'. Dr. Lundberg, speaking for all the doctors involved at Parkland, with the exception of Dr. Crenshaw who dissents, confirms that discrepancies arose because they were desperate to save the President's life and did not really examine all the wounds. The autopsy doctors were also under pressure from Jackie and Bobby Kennedy who were impatient with the time taken for the autopsy. Furthermore, in 1988, 4 of the Dallas doctors were invited by CBS' NOVA Television Team to inspect the X-Rays and photographs at the National Archives in Washington D.C. All of the anomalies were dealt with. The doctors' conclusions—no evidence of the alterations of the wounds to what they saw on November 22nd in Dallas. As Dr. Paul Peters commented "(My inaccurate observations about the head wound in 1963) shows how even a trained observer can make an error in a moment of urgency".

Contrary to the claims of Conspiracy Theorists the back of Kennedy's head, as shown in the autopsy photographs and X-rays, is intact with a large gaping wound in the right parietal area. This is consistent with a shot from the rear: this is clearly revealed in the Zapruder film of the assassination. The Zapruder film clearly shows the president's head bursting open in the front and the right. It is also clear that a large flap of scalp hangs down from the large exit wound. When viewed in slow motion it is evident that the shot hit and exited, JFK's head moves forward slightly and then the body and head is whipped back to the left rear. The shot came from the rear and there is no exit wound in the rear of Kennedy's head. The Parkland doctors were misled by the fact that brain tissue pooled at the rear of Kennedy's head as he lay in the operating theatre. Furthermore, the Moorman photograph, taken seconds after the President was shot in the back of the head, also shows the rear of the head to be intact. Therefore the photographs and X-rays taken during the autopsy are consistent with photographs taken in Dealey Plaza. Contrary to the claims of many Conspiracy Theorists there is no credible evidence that the autopsy X-rays and photographs of Kennedy's wounds were faked. And, of course, if the autopsy materials were faked why leave the 'head snap' in the Zapruder movie - a vital piece of evidence which was also handled by Government agencies? If the Zapruder move was tampered with, as some Conspiracy Theorists claim, why leave in movie frames which were guaranteed to cause controversy? Ironically this reasoning that the Zapruder film was altered has surfaced 30 years after

Conspiracy Theorists have been using the Zapruder film to PROVE there was a conspiracy.

Conspiracy Theorists have for years referred to the Dallas doctors' examination of the President's head wound claiming they saw a gaping wound in the 'occipital' region (back of the head) indicating a wound of exit thus proving that a shot was fired from in front. Conspiracy Theorists ignore the concept of 'bevelling' -- when a bullet penetrates the skull bone, it will leave a small hole on the side from which it enters, and a larger dished-out crater on the side that it exits. The existence of 'bevelling' of the bone of Kennedy's skull allowed the autopsists and later a panel of forensic pathologists appointed by the House Assassinations Committee, to establish that the bullet that hit Kennedy in the head entered from behind, with at least one large fragment exiting toward the front.

Furthermore, Conspiracy Theorists have referred to the 'Harper' fragment of bone from Kennedy's skull as proof that the area that was blown out was 'occipital' (rear) thus indicating that the autopsy photographs and X-rays were fake. On November 23rd 1963 William Allen Harper found a piece of John Kennedy's skull in Dealey Plaza. The forensic panel of the House Assassinations Committee accepted the 'Harper' fragment as 'parietal', meaning it came from the side of Kennedy's head which would be consistent with an exit wound from a bullet fired from behind and consistent with the X-rays and autopsy photographs. The anatomical features of the 'Harper' fragment are consistent with it being parietal bone and this finding has been confirmed by a number of medical experts yet Conspiracy Theorists still claim otherwise.

Because the Dallas doctors made conflicting statements about the head wound the 'Boston Globe' was allowed by the Kennedy family to appoint their own panel of experts and became the first news organisation to view the autopsy X-rays and photographs. All four panel experts concluded that there was no evidence of these materials having been tampered with.

Other logical alternative explanations have been given to explain why President Kennedy's head jerks backwards when he is struck by the fatal bullet. Neuropathologist Richard Lindenburg told The Rockefeller Commission (investigating C.I.A. activities and tangentially the possible conspiracy to assassinate President Kennedy) that the movement could have been caused by a violent neuromuscular reaction resulting from "major damage inflicted to the nerve centres in the brain."

Physicist Luis Alvarez experimented by firing a rifle into water melons wrapped with tape. Each time, the melon was propelled backward in the direction of the rifle. Alvarez cited the law of conservation of momentum- as the contents of the melon were driven forward and out by the force of the bullet, an opposite force was created similar to the thrust of a jet engine, propelling the melon in the opposite direction.

Duncan MacPherson, in an interview with researcher Joel Grant, attempted to explain the backward movement of Kennedy's body after the head shot:

"In general, body movement in response to nervous system trauma is a result of contractions in body muscles. This is related to movements of your leg when a doctor raps you on the knee with his little mallet; your leg moves because a nerve induces a muscle contraction, not because it was driven into motion by the force of the tiny rap with the mallet. The slightly peculiar location of Kennedy's arms after the 399 bullet impact is know as Thorburn's position, after a description by Dr. William Thorburn in an 1899 paper on injuries to the area of the spinal cord damaged by bullet 399. In addition to this effect, simulations have shown that bullet strikes to the skull that result in blowing out a significant hole upon exit result in skull recoil towards the bullet entry direction. The dynamics of this are a little complicated, but are more related to the pressure inside the skull cavity created by the bullet passage that to the effects directly related to the bullet movement.

A number of Conspiracy Theorists have claimed there is no evidence to link the Mannlicher-Carcano rifle to bullets or fragments of bullets. Yet a large bullet fragment recovered from the Presidential limousine has been connected by neutron activation analysis to Kennedy's head wound, and, like the "Pristine Bullet", by ballistic tests to Oswald's rifle. No fragments of a third bullet were found.

The most compelling evidence, however, that shows that the bullet which struck President Kennedy from the rear comes from an examination of the autopsy X-rays of Kennedy's skull. The dispersal of bullet fragments comes from the back to the front. Furthermore, as House Assassinations Committee pathologists testified, particulate matter (brain tissue) from the president's head, after the head shot, is spraying forwards as can be seen from a high contrast photo of frame 313 of the Zapruder film.

Dr. Lundberg confirms that the 52 photos and X-rays of the president's body support Humes and Boswell's findings and the House Assassinations Committee panel of forensic pathologists concur.

Together with the evidence which I presented relating to the neck wound it can safely be concluded there was no bullet striking either President Kennedy or Governor Conally from any other weapon or any other direction. A bullet from the "Grassy Knoll" that hit Kennedy and disappeared without trace would have indeed been the true 'Magic Bullet'.

THE GRASSY KNOLL

As well as an examination of the wounds to the President and the House Assassination Committee's acoustics findings there was other evidence presented by Conspiracy Theorists to suggest there was a second gunman firing from the Grassy Knoll. At the time of the shooting there were scores of people running in the direction of the Grassy Knoll and scores were running in the direction of the Book Depository.

Nearly every Conspiracy Theorist cite witness statements which contend that 'puffs of smoke' were coming from the area of the Grassy Knoll. What they fail to inform their readers is the fact that many of the witnesses gave descriptions of what they believed the 'puffs of smoke' were. A number described the smoke as exhaust fumes or steam originating from a nearby steam pipe. A policeman actually burnt his hand on this steampipe. Furthermore it is a myth that modern rifles emit a large amount of smoke.

As a visitor to Dealey Plaza I personally observed smoke rising from the trees at the corner of the wooden fence atop the Grassy Knoll. But it was clearly exhaust fumes from an idling car engine.

One witness, Jean Hill, stated that she saw a 'puff of smoke' from the knoll. However, from Hill's position on Elm Street it is impossible to see anyone running or walking or standing behind a wooden fence. Anthony Summers, in his book 'Conspiracy', circumvents this stark fact by stating that Hill observed someone AFTER she went to the parking lot behind the wooden fence. Clearly this is impossible as Hill can be recognised in photos taken by Wilma Bond - sitting on the ground, dressed in a red raincoat - many moments after the assassination.

One of the most celebrated witnesses to the 'Grassy Knoll shooting' was S.M. (Skinny) Holland who was interviewed by Mark Lane for his book "Rush To Judgement". Holland related how he was standing on the overpass with some colleagues at the time of the shooting. He saw a puff of smoke coming from under the bushes in the area of the Grassy Knoll and picket fence. They ran over to the spot as soon as the shooting was over and found, about 15 feet down from the corner, fresh footprints and cigarette butts. However, Holland's view from the overpass puts the spot where he observed puffs of smoke directly below and in front of the 6th floor window of the Book Depository building. So perhaps both the Warren Commission and Holland were correct. The shots came from the Book Depository but from Holland's perspective the smoke and the report of a gun appeared to come from the Grassy Knoll.

Furthermore, there were two Dallas Policemen stationed on the overpass at the time of the shooting. Police Officer J.W. Foster stood on the east side of the railway bridge over the triple underpass and Police Officer J.C. White stood on the west side. Police Officer Joe E. Murphy was standing over Elm Street on the Stemmons Freeway overpass, west of the railway bridge farther away from the Depository. Two other officers were stationed on Stemmons Freeway overpass, west of the railway bridge farther away from the Book Depository. Two other Police Officers were stationed on Stemmons Freeway to control traffic as the motorcade entered the Freeway. Under the advance preparations worked out between the Secret Service and the Dallas Police, the police were under strict instructions to keep unauthorised people away from these locations. When the motorcade reached the intersection of Elm and Houston Streets, there were no spectators on Stemmons Freeway where Police Officer Murphy was stationed. Immediately after the shots were fired, neither the policemen nor the majority of the 15 spectators standing on the overpass saw anything suspicious. As he ran through the railway yards to the Book Depository Police Officer Foster saw nothing suspicious.

It seems improbable, therefore, that a gunman could have evaded so many pursuers, particularly the railway workers running over from the triple overpass. They had the area behind the fence in view within a few seconds of the final shot and arrived there soon after. Oliver Stone's movie gives a lot of credence to the testimony of Jean Hill, mentioned earlier, who was standing directly across the street from the "Grassy Knoll", and said she saw a man moving rapidly away from the knoll towards the railway lines immediately after the shots rang out. Jean Hill's story has changed so many times over the years her evidence has become suspect. She appears regularly on American 'chat shows' and is now the author of a book 'The Last Dissenting Witness'. Still, none who converged on the knoll from the railway lines or from Elm Street apparently saw this man. And Lee Bowers, who himself related a curious tale of suspicious vehicles moving around before the assassination, and who had a clear view of the area from his position in a railway tower, didn't see him.

Dave Powers, President Kennedy's assistant was riding in the Secret Service car directly behind the president. Powers' statement to the Warren Commission may help explain why some witnesses said they thought the rifle shots came from the underpass and Grassy Knoll area: -

"I commented to Ken O'Donnell that it was 12:30 and we would only be about 5 minutes late when we arrived at the Trade Mart. Shortly thereafter the first shot went off and it sounded to me as if it were a firecracker. I noticed then that the President moved quite far to his left after the shot from the extreme right hand side where he had been sitting. There was a second shot and Governor Connally disappeared from sight and then there was a third shot which took off the top of the President's head and the sickening sound of a grapefruit splattering against the side of a wall. The total time between the first and third shots was about 5 or 6 seconds. My first impression that the noise appeared to come from the front in the area of the Triple Underpass. This may have resulted from my feeling, when I looked forward toward the overpass, that we might have ridden into an ambush."

There is another powerful reason why it is unlikely a second shooter was on the Grassy Knoll. Using more than one rifleman increases the chances that the plot would be unsuccessful. The supposed conspirators must have assumed that the president would be adequately protected by the Secret Service, after the first shot was fired, therefore a second assassin would not be necessary unless it could be guaranteed both assassins fired simultaneously.

The U.K.'s Channel 4 documentary "Who Killed Kennedy?" featured a deaf mute Ed Hoffman who claimed to have seen the assassins, dressed as railway workers, dismantle the rifle and leave the area of the Grassy Knoll. He did not relate his full story until the late 60's and his testimony does not seem credible as no-one else witnessed the events described by him. Hoffman is yet another 'witness' who has benefited financially from his account. He can be seen frequently in Dealey Plaza promoting his book and signing autographs.

Conspiracy Theorists claim to have found at least 6 places in Dealey Plaza where witnesses claim to have detected the origin of shots or the presence of gunmen. One eyewitness, Malcolm Summers, stated:

"As soon as the motorcade passed I waited for about a minute then I came on across to the knoll. When I got there I was stopped by a person in a suit with a coat over his arm. I also believe he had a gun under his arm. It looked like a little machine gun to me."

Malcolm Summers was one of a number of witnesses, including a Dallas policeman, who ran into a number of men claiming to be Federal Officials. Chief Counsel for the House Assassinations Committee, Robert Blakey has said that the movements and whereabouts of every member of the Secret Service and F.B.I. were all accounted for and none were in the Grassy Knoll area. This was one of the most credible, yet puzzling, aspects of the assassination. Speculation in trying to account for this bizarre event was difficult given the credible testimony of the Dallas police officer involved, Officer Joe Smith. Author Gerald Posner attempted to explain these bizarre events and speculated as to what occurred. Posner implied that Officer Smith mistook the credentials of other government workers. There were people from various government agencies in the Dealey Plaza area and it is possible the police officers mistook these government workers for Secret Secret Agents. Posner speculates that the I.D. was misunderstood. Knowledge of Secret Service, F.B.I. or other government agency identification cards was not as widespread as it is today through the medium of television and Hollywood movies. The House Assassinations Committee has recognised that Army Intelligence personnel were in the area of Dealey Plaza at the time of the assassination. It was normal practice for military units to be present in an American city when the president visited, and this may account for the intriguing encounters.

However, I believe that assassination researcher Chris Mills has provided the most logical explanation for these intriguing events.

It would appear that the denials by the head of the Secret Service, that no agent was ever in the vicinity of the 'Grassy Knoll' was wrong.

David Wiegman Jnr., NBC cameraman, told author Richard B. Trask he had ran to the Grassy Knoll and saw a police officer run up the incline:

Wiegman told Trask: "I figured he knows something's up there, so I ran up there. I found myself there with (Secret Service Agent) Lem (Johns) close by, a few feet away. Then I saw people lying on the side, and I saw nothing up there. Lem, sort of, looking around. Couldn't see anything. I knew now I'd better get something. I've got to get some footage. I saw these people lying on the ground and I took them. I saw a body being pulled to the ground...."

Weigman then realises he must go after the presidential limousine and returns to the 'camera car'. Other cameramen have stated that Lem Johns rode in this car to the Trade Mart and rejoined his Secret Service unit.

In his testimony to the Warren Commission Johns stated:

" .... before I reached the Vice-President's car (after he left the Secret Service follow up car responding to the shots) a third shot had sounded and the entire motorcade then picked up speed and I was left on the street at this point. I obtained a ride with White House movie men and joined the Vice-President and ..... Youngblood at the Parkland hospital."

Chris Mills maintains that Lem Johns did not testify to his presence in the area of the picket fence because he knew his actions, although creditable under the circumstances, (he was, after all trying to find any shooters) was against Secret Service procedures thus leaving himself open to any disciplinary action. In his report, 7 days after the assassination, he fails to mention these events and he was not to know that, 8 months later, Officer Smith would testify to an agent on the knoll.

But the fact remains that with the exception of these curious reports, earwitnesses testimony, and "photographic proof" which shall be considered later, nothing in the evidence pointed to a gunman on the "Grassy Knoll".

It was stated in Channel 4's "Dispatches" Television Programme that photographic proof had been uncovered revealing a gunman on the Grassy Knoll. The production team used frames from Orville Nix's movie of the assassination taken from a position directly opposite Abraham Zapruder showing the Grassy Knoll in the background:

"Nix captured the gunman", Chris Plumley states, "We can reveal the previously undetected contents of this film".

Evidently, this is poor research by Channel 4. The picture in question was first publicised by Esquire magazine in 1966 and a story ran in "The Times" November 15th 1966. The enlargement from Nix's film clearly shows what looks like a gunman leaning on a motor vehicle and firing a rifle. However, photo analysis has revealed it was only light and shadows. Moreover, anyone viewing the actual movie film can clearly see that the "gunman" does not move even when the shots were supposedly fired and the Presidential limousine is speeding away. The 'figure' does not move. A conspiratorial gunman, one would assume, would feel the necessity for a quick exit.

Conspiracy Theorists also claimed to detect evidence of this Grassy

Knoll gunman in other photographs. They said one photo revealed the shape of a man with a gun (nicknamed 'Badgeman'). However, Photo Analysts hired by CBS' NOVA, revealed the shape to be a human being but the object which looks like a rifle with a flash suppresser is just a blur induced by the motion of the camera.

Robert J. Groden claims in his 1993 book "The Killing of Kennedy" and his 1995 book "The Search for Lee Harvey Oswald" that conspirators were caught on many photographs taken in Dealey Plaza. His analyses of these photographs have been convincingly shown to be spurious. For example Groden claims there were rifles and conspirators in the Zapruder movie film of the assassination. He stated to the Rockefeller Commission (investigating C.I.A. activities and possible complicity in the assassination) that in frame 413 the shape of a rifle could be seen. It did not. He claimed that in frames 412 to 414 a human head secreted behind a tree and the outline of a rifle are visible. His computer enhancements and colourisation are nothing more than picture making. An assassin stationed where Groden purported him to be would be unlikely to hide himself in a tree 5 feet away from Abraham Zapruder and expose himself to hundreds of people.

In Groden's books conspirators are everywhere in photographs of Dealey Plaza. His photos reveal nothing but lumps of bush, trees and shadows and only with a lot of imagination can they be transformed into sinister gunmen.

The picture of a man holding an open umbrella had puzzled many researchers over the years until the House Assassinations Committee called "Umbrella Man" to its hearings in Washington D.C. Some Conspiracy Theorists said he was a conspirator signalling to gunmen and/or firing a poison dart at the President, paralysing him in order to make Kennedy a better target. The matter was cleared up when the person involved explained that he was simply making a symbolic political statement against Kennedy's "liberal policies" Vis A Vis the Cold War.

Another photograph, taken by Mary Ann Moorman, which purported to show "the gunman" at the instant the shot was fired, was investigated by researchers at the "Polaroid Company" and the Massachusetts Institute of Technology. They concluded that it could be a man but the rifle part of the figure was only light filtering through trees.

In one of the most historic photographs of the assassination Kennedy is seen to grasp at his throat as the first bullet that hits him goes through his neck. In the background can be seen the entrance to the Texas School Book Depository and in the doorway stands a figure curiously like Lee Harvey Oswald . If this is Oswald, Conspiracy Theorists say, then he cannot be the assassin. The picture was taken by press photographer Jim Altgens, who was standing on the South side of Elm Street between the Triple Underpass and the Book Depository. As the motorcade started it's descent down Elm Street, Altgens took the picture approximately 2 seconds after the firing of the second shot. It has been determined that the figure is a Book Depository employee, Billy Lovelady and was so established by the Warren Commission yet is still speculated upon by Conspiracy Theorists.

Conspiracy Theorists have claimed that 3 tramps, arrested in the railway yards behind the "Grassy Knoll", were in fact not tramps but ex-C.I.A. agents E. Howard Hunt and Frank Sturgis of Watergate fame. The photograph, showing their arrest, was examined by F.B.I. photoanalyst Lyndal Shaneyfelt for the Rockefeller Commission enquiry into the activities of the C.I.A., who concluded that the photographs were not of Hunt or Sturgis.

Yet another "analyst" of these photographs said one of the tramps was a notorious Mafia "hitman" Charles Harrelson, whose son Woody Harrelson became famous in the hit T.V. show "Cheers". Experts concluded there was only a passing resemblance. The 3 tramps photograph is a typical example of how the passing of time makes speculation and supposition grow like Topsy. Nearly every Conspiracy Theorist has used these photographs to show collusion, by the Dallas Police or "Government Agents" to suppress evidence of conspiracy. In 1992 the Dallas Police finally put an end to speculation surrounding the photographs by releasing all their files for this period. The 3 Tramps were revealed to be - 3 Tramps, all of whom were named.

Because this was the most photographed murder in history it was inevitable that the stills of movie film and photographs would be poured over and examined in minute detail. "Cognitive Dissonance", that is, the ability to see only what the mind requires or filters through an ideology or committed set of beliefs seems to have been at work for the past 30 years. Any set of photographs of any incident can act like clouds producing changing and curious "outlines of reality". Finally, and at long last, technological advances have provided the answers to the mysterious "gunmen" captured on film and the opening of local and national files on the assassination are slowly but surely putting an end to speculation caused, in the main, by bureaucratic secrecy and inefficiency.

As we have seen the preponderance of evidence shows that 3 bullets were fired, all of them from behind. The House Assassinations Committee agreed that the bullets which hit President Kennedy and Governor Connally were fired from Oswald's rifle. But they did say a fourth shot was fired from the Grassy Knoll and missed, basing many of their conclusions on acoustics evidence from a police tape recording.

The House Assassinations Committee examined the police dictabelt (audio tape) of police messages in Dealey Plaza made at the time of the assassination. It was believed that a motor cycle policeman's radio transmitter stuck on the 'on' position at the time of the assassination, recording the sounds of 4 shots in Dealey Plaza. Acoustics experts working for the Committee said there was a 95 percent probability that one of the 'shots' came from the Grassy Knoll. This persuaded the Committee there was now evidence of a second gunman. It concluded that this second gunman had fired a shot that missed the motorcade completely. But in 1982 a new panel of acoustical experts (It was dubbed the Ramsey Panel after it's chairman, Professor Norman Ramsey of Harvard) re-examined the tape after an amateur assassination buff Steve Barber listened to a published recording of the tape recording and found many anomalies. Two Dallas police channels can be heard on the 'dictabelt' and Barber detected "crosstalk" between the two - specifically, the words of Sheriff Bill Decker a minute after the assassination: "Hold everything secure..." The panel concluded that the sounds on the tape were made one minute AFTER the assassination and that there was no evidence for a second gunman. To be fair to some assassination researchers there are still a number of doubts remaining. As House Assassinations Committee counsel Robert Blakey wrote: "if you discount the evidence of a shot from the Grassy Knoll on its line of analysis, you must also discount the evidence of all 4 shots, which appear as a sequence of spikes occurring at precise intervals on the dictabelt. Were they simply static, random noise? In 1979, I had little doubt about the scientific validity of the acoustics evidence, but the Ramsey report gave me pause. Yet I am inclined to stand by our study. The correlations we were able to make between the timing of the second impressions on the dictabelt and the visual evidence of the shots on Abraham Zapruder's film of the shooting and other data are too close to be coincidence. In addition, another study of "crosstalk" on the dictabelt; he finds "crosstalk" by Sgt. S.Q. Bellah that demonstrates that the 4 spikes came before the Decker Comments, obviously the acoustics evidence now cuts both ways...".

However, most Conspiracy Theorists maintain that the acoustics evidence is definite proof that a second gunman was firing. This raises two questions: If someone did fire from the knoll, where did the bullet go? -- and -- What kind of "Hitman" would miss a relatively easy target from a little over a 100 feet away?

This so called Grassy Knoll bullet did not go into Kennedy's body. As we have seen, the characteristics of both the President's neck wound and the head wound ruled that out. Therefore, the shot must have missed yet none of the spectators in the line of fire along Elm Street was hit by an errant bullet nor did they hear any impact. Nor was the side of the car struck. If a stray bullet coming in from the front and to the right did somehow manage to miss the President, Mrs. Kennedy, the car, and nearby spectators, it may have hit the kerbstone or lawn. It is logical to assume that spectators, police and Federal Agents who were swarming all over this area after the shooting would have found something. They did not. So called 'evidence' that a police detective 'pocketed' a bullet found near Elm Street has never been verified - another example of how Conspiracy Theorists 'choose' their evidence.

There is, then, indisputable scientific evidence that no shots were fired from the Grassy Knoll. There is indisputable scientific evidence that the shots fired at President Kennedy and Governor Connally were from behind and not from in front.

52

CHAPTER 4.

CONSCIOUSNESS OF GUILT.

" The cruellest lies are often told in silence."

Robert Louis Stevenson.

OSWALD'S FLIGHT AND ARREST

As the Presidential limousine left Elm Street and rushed to Parkland Memorial Hospital, policemen were rushing to the Book Depository, alerted by the sounds of the shots and a scattering of pigeons. Marion L. Baker was the first police officer to reach the building. Baker, who heard three shots and was in the Presidential motorcade, wheeled his bike around, parked it at the entrance to the Book Depository and met the building manager Roy Truly at the entrance. Together they raced up the stairs toward the upper floors, where people had reported shots fired. On the second floor landing Baker encountered Oswald but did not arrest him. Less than two minutes had elapsed since the final shots. Baker confronted Oswald and asked Truly if Oswald worked in the Book Depository. Truly replied that he did. Baker lowered his pistol and rushed by.

Henry Hurt, in his book 'Reasonable Doubt' writes:

" (it is) noteworthy that Oswald's demeanour when challenged was certainly different from the struggle he put up when confronted by police about an hour later."

Hurt is implying that Oswald's demeanour was a sign of innocence. However, it is also noteworthy that O.J. Simpson's demeanour, shortly after he murdered two people, was, according to a number of witnesses, very composed and natural.

Conspiracy Theorists maintain that Oswald could not have run that quickly from the 6th floor to the second floor. The Warren Commission asked Baker to re-enact his part and timed him at 90 seconds between the time he left his motorcycle and the time he encountered Oswald. A Secret Service Agent, testing Oswald's timing, moved at a fast walking pace from the sniper's lair to the lunchroom in 78 seconds-without being winded. These timings were confirmed by The House Assassinations Committee in 1979.

The Warren Commission maintained that the last person to see Oswald before the assassination was Charles Douglas Givens-on the 6th floor with a clipboard. Oswald was a warehouse worker who filled book orders. He and the other workers would carry a clipboard to hold the order forms. After seeing Oswald on the 6th floor, Givens left the building to watch the motorcade. The clipboard was not found until 10 days after the assassination. Frankie Kaiser, another Book Depository employee, was searching for a teacher's copy of "Catholic Handbooks", copies of which were stored in the north-west corner of the 6th floor of the Book Depository, near the stairway. Kaiser stumbled on Oswald's clipboard a few feet from where the rifle was found, hidden by book cartons.

After the rifle was found, police started checking all Book Depository employees who had access to the 6th floor. The employees themselves noticed that Oswald was missing. James Jarman Junior, whom Oswald, after his arrest, lied about having had lunch with said, "When we started to line up to show our identification, quite a few of us asked where was Lee. That is what we called him, and he wasn't anywhere around. We started asking each other, have you seen Lee Oswald, and they said no."

Anthony Summers, in his book, "The Kennedy Conspiracy" said he interviewed the last person to see Oswald before the assassination and it was not Givens. Summers interviewed Carolyn Arnold, secretary to the vice-president of the Book Depository, in 1978. She claimed to have seen Oswald 15 minutes before the assassination, on the second floor lunchroom, but even if this were true it in no way detracts from the evidence that by 12.30 Oswald was on the 6th floor shooting at the President.

Conspiracy Theorists imply there is no credible evidence to say that Oswald 'escaped'. Henry Hurt in his book "Reasonable Doubt" writes:

"Though no one testified to seeing Oswald leave the Book Depository, the Warren Commission concluded that he departed about 12.33pm This assumption was based on the knowledge that Officer Marion Baker stopped a man believed to be Oswald a minute or so before this. The Commission decided-without benefit of eyewitnesses-that Oswald walked from the Book Depository seven blocks to the east on Elm Street, in a direction that took him directly away from his rooming house in Oak Cliff. In doing so, he walked past five bus stops .... The testimony from eyewitnesses concerning Oswald's boarding and leaving the bus on Elm Street is so contradictory that it seems virtually useless. The single sliver of concrete evidence was a bus transfer slip supposedly in Oswald's possession when he was arrested."

Other Conspiracy Theorists have given a lot of credence to the testimony of Deputy Sheriff Roger Craig who testified he had seen a man running toward Elm Street and getting into a light coloured car 15 minutes after the assassination. The man he saw getting into the car he said was about 5 feet 8 or 9 inches, 140 to 150 pounds. He later identified the man getting into the car as Lee Harvey Oswald. Deputy Sheriff Craig features in most assassination books. Again it is natural to have conflicting eyewitness reports when a crime of such magnitude occurs. How much credence should we put on Craig's report? Craig left himself open to criticism when he said that Oswald, after his arrest, had told him the vehicle belonged to the Paines, a preposterous statement. It is also quite obvious that Oswald was a very 'ordinary' looking man - the type of person who is frequently mistaken for someone else.

Hurt's statement and Craig's testimony flies in the face of other highly credible evidence. Within a minute after Baker and Truly left Oswald in the 2nd floor lunchroom, Mrs. R.A. Reid, clerical supervisor for the Book Depository, ran into the building after hearing shots and saw and spoke to Oswald who mumbled a reply and proceeded in the direction of the front entrance to the building. From the depository building, Oswald moved on foot looking for a bus.

Oswald found a bus within moments. But the assassination on Elm Street had tied up traffic. The bus was hopelessly stalled. Riding on the bus was Oswald's former landlady, Mary Bledsoe, who recognised him and testified:

"Oswald got on (the bus). He looks like a maniac. His sleeve was out here. His shirt was undone ... he looked so bad in his face, and his face was so distorted ... hole in his sleeve right here."

The Warren Commission reported that:

"As Mrs. Bledsoe said these words, she pointed to her right elbow. When Oswald was arrested in the Texas Theatre, he was wearing a brown sport shirt with a hole in the right sleeve at the elbow. Mrs. Bledsoe identified the shirt as the one Oswald was wearing and she stated she was certain that it was Oswald who boarded the bus. Mrs. Bledsoe recalled that Oswald sat halfway to the rear of the bus which moved slowly and intermittently as traffic became heavy. She heard a passing motorist tell the driver that the President had been shot. People on the bus began talking about it. As the bus neared Lamar Street, Oswald left the bus and disappeared into the crowd."

Henry Hurt further states that: "the testimony from eyewitnesses concerning Oswald's boarding and leaving the bus on Elm Street is so contradictory that it seems virtually useless. The single sliver of concrete evidence was a bus transfer slip supposedly in Oswald's possession when he was arrested."

Hurt's claim is specious. He ignores the testimony of Mary Bledsoe, who was a very important witness precisely because she knew Oswald BEFORE the assassination.

Cecil J. McWatters testified that he gave Oswald a bus transfer ticket before Oswald disembarked. At the time of his arrest Oswald had the ticket on him. The evidence, then, is irrefutable; Oswald left the scene of the assassination and boarded a bus. This action of Oswald's begs the question -- Would a supposedly well-financed conspirator use this method of transport to flee the scene of the crime of the century? And if Oswald was just a 'patsy', as he and some Conspiracy Theorists claimed, why didn't he stay in the building if he was not knowledgeable about his 'involvement'?

After Oswald left the bus he walked to the nearby Greyhound Bus Terminal and hailed a taxi. But as the cab pulled up to the curb Oswald saw that an elderly woman was waiting for a cab too, and he graciously offered his cab to her. The lady declined the offer, Oswald got in and headed off toward the Oak Cliff area of Dallas.

Oswald returned to his rooming house shortly before 1 o'clock, picked up his mail order Smith and Wesson .38 Calibre revolver and left about 1pm

Conspiracy Theorists nearly always relate statements made by Oswald's housekeeper, Earlene Roberts, as evidence that Oswald was somehow linked to Officer Tippit. After she had been interviewed at least four times in the weeks and months after the assassination she suddenly added a new dimension to her testimony. Shortly before Oswald left the rooming house, she now said, a police car pulled up outside the house and 'honked' its horn twice. The implications are clear, certainly to Conspiracy Theorists - a rendezvous had been arranged between the Dallas police, possibly Officer Tippit, and Oswald. However, in her Warren Commission testimony, Mrs. Roberts stated that the police car had two officers in it whereas Tippit was alone in Car 10 on November 22nd. And two witnesses placed Tippit at the 'Top Ten Record Shop' at this time. Are we to believe that these witnesses were also part of the 'cover-up'. Furthermore Mrs. Roberts suffered from cataracts and her eyesight was very poor. It would also have been impossible to observe a police car from where she said she was positioned - as I noted when visiting her rooming house in 1972.

Similarly, some Conspiracy Theorists aver that Officer Tippit may have been 'Badgeman', the supposed Grassy Knoll assassin dressed in a dark uniform standing near the picket fence. A number of theorists, notably Robert Groden, spotted the supposed figure in a photograph taken at the instant President Kennedy was shot. (Expert testimony has dismissed these claims). Tippit's presence in Dealey Plaza at the time of the assassination, however, would have been impossible as it is beyond doubt that witnesses place Tippit at 4100 Bonnie View Road between 12.17 and 12.30pm on November 22nd. The original time for President Kennedy's motorcade to have arrived at Dealey Plaza was between 12.15 and 12.20pm if the planned times were adhered to. It would therefore have been impossible for Tippit to have gone to Dealey Plaza and returned to the Oak Cliff area in the timespan available.

THE MURDER OF OFFICER TIPPIT

Officer Tippit had been alerted about the assassination at 12.45pm and was told to be on the outlook for a suspect with a description based upon a report made by an eyewitness to the assassination, Howard Brennan. At 1.15pm Officer Tippit saw Oswald and called him to his patrol car. Oswald walked over to the window vent and spoke briefly. Tippit got out and started toward the front of the car where Oswald shot him four times with his revolver. Tippit was dead before he hit the ground. At least 12 persons saw the man with his revolver in the vicinity of the Tippit shooting. By the evening of November 22nd five of them had identified Lee Harvey Oswald as the man they saw.

Henry Hurt tries to paint a sinister picture of the Tippet shooting by cleverly pointing out discrepancies in testimony, a natural occurrence in any crime:

" (The Warren Commission) ... had at least two eyewitnesses who claimed in some fashion that they watched Oswald shoot Tippit. Seven eyewitnesses said that Oswald was the man they saw running from the murder scene. However Benavides, who was perhaps in the best location, could not identify Oswald as the gunman. This left the commission with its star witness, Helen Markham."

Hurt's statement is inconsistent with the true facts. There will always be inconsistencies in any eyewitness testimony to a shooting. This is especially so when the criminal involved is less than 15 feet in proximity and the primary concern is one of safety. Conspiracy Theorists have seized on these inconsistencies in support of Oswald's innocence. Eyewitnesses were not compatible in their descriptions of Oswald's clothing, his facial features, and the direction in which he was heading. The preponderance of evidence, however, points towards Oswald's guilt. Although William Scoggins, Helen Markham, Barbera Davis, Virginia Davis, Ted Callaway, and Sam Guinyard differed in the details of what they saw in the vicinity of the murder, they all agreed on one thing-When they were taken to the Police Station to identify the gunman in a line up, every single one identified Lee Harvey Oswald as the gunman.

Most Conspiracy Theorists fail to mention that there were 6 witnesses who were at the scene of the murder of Officer Tippet or saw the gunman running from the scene, gun in hand. As the Warren Commission reported:

"At least 12 persons saw the man with the revolver in the vicinity of the Tippet crime scene at or immediately after the shooting. By the evening of November 22nd, five of them had identified Lee Harvey Oswald in police line-ups as the man they saw. A sixth did so the next day. Three others subsequently identified Oswald from a photograph. Two witnesses testified that Oswald resembled the man they had seen. One witness felt he was too distant from the gunman to make a positive identification".

Furthermore as recently as the late 1980s an assassination researcher, Carl Henry, informed Dallas radio station KLIF that a previously undiscovered witness to the Tippit shooting had been located. The witness, who positively identified Lee Harvey Oswald as the murderer, was laying tiles in a nearby house as Oswald shot Officer Tippit. Oswald fled the scene passing in front of the house the witness was working on.

A taxi driver, William Scoggins, was eating lunch in his cab which was parked on Patton facing the southeast corner of 10th Street and Patton Avenue a few feet to the north. A police car moving east on 10th at about 10 or 12 miles an hour passed in front of his cab. About 100 feet from the corner the police car pulled up alongside a man on the sidewalk. This man, dressed in a light-coloured jacket, approached the car. Scoggins lost sight of him behind some shrubbery on the southeast corner lot, but he saw the policeman leave the car, heard 3 or 4 shots, and then saw the policeman fall. Scoggins hurriedly left his seat and hid behind the cab as the man came back toward the corner with gun in hand. The man cut across the yard through some bushes, passed within 12 feet of Scoggins, and ran south on Patton. Scoggins saw him and heard him mutter "Poor damn cop" or "Poor dumb cop". The next day Scoggins viewed a line-up of four persons and identified Oswald as the man he had seen the day before at 10th and Patton. In his testimony before the Commission, Scoggins stated that he thought he had seen a picture of Oswald in the newspapers prior to the line-up identification on Saturday. He had not seen Oswald on television and had not been shown any photographs of Oswald by the police.

Many Conspiracy Theorists, then, quote Helen Markham who was not consistent in her descriptions of the gunman. They also point to the testimony of Aquilla Clemmons who told investigators she saw two men at the scene of the Tippet shooting. But every other witness disagrees with them.

The Conspiracy Theorists differ in the emphasis they put on various discrepancies in eyewitness testimony but they all make the same omission of not relying on the preponderance of testimony which points to Oswald's guilt in the murder of Tippit. Mark Lane and Henry Hurt, for example, do not mention witnesses Barbara Davis, Virginia Davis, Sam Guinyard and Ted Callaway. Hurt's omission of any references to these crucial witnesses is typical of the methodology of Conspiracy Theorists as we shall see in a later chapter.

Witnesses Domingo Benavides, Barbara Davis and Virginia Davis found the bullets' cartridge cases at the Tippit murder scene and turned them over to the police. The bullets in Tippit's body were too mutilated to be ballistically identifiable, according to F.B.I. experts, although one expert retained by the Warren Commission believed that he could identify one of those bullets as having been fired from Oswald's pistol. The cartridge cases were identified as having come from Oswald's pistol to the exclusion of all other weapons in the world. This is irrefutable ballistic evidence. Many Conspiracy Theorists ignored this conclusive ballistics evidence concentrating, instead, on the 'disappearance' of a police officer's initialised bullet shell and the differences in shell casings found at the scene of the murder- all of which can more logically be attributed to mistakes made by the investigating officers.

After Scoggins witnessed Oswald saying 'poor damn cop' or 'poor dumb cop' T.F. Bowley turned his car east onto 10th Street. He saw Tippit's body lying in the road and pulled over. Inside the police car Domingo Benavides, a mechanic at a nearby Garage, was trying to call police headquarters using the police radio but with no success. Bowley grabbed the microphone and successfully contacted the radio despatcher. Almost immediately sirens whined throughout the area. At this point another report had been received that a man had entered the Texas Theatre, a cinema eight blocks from where Tippit was murdered.

A major puzzle, which has never been satisfactorily answered is - Why did Oswald shoot Police Officer Tippit? The general assumption has been that Oswald panicked and became frightened when Tippit got out of his patrol car and approached the man whose general description fitted the profile of the fugitive. But Oswald could well have bluffed his way out of the encounter although it is unlikely he would have been allowed to walk away if Tippit had found Oswald's concealed pistol - concealing a weapon was, of course, a crime. However a more likely scenario has been overlooked. When the report that a police officer had been shot came over the radio F.B.I. Agent Bob Barret rushed to the scene of the crime and began an inspection. Barret maintains that the police officer in charge of the scene, Captain Westbrook, had found a man's wallet lying near a pool of blood. In it he discovered identification for Lee Harvey Oswald as well as identification for Alek J. Hidell. Westbrook showed the identification to Barret then took the wallet so that it could be listed with other crime scene materials. In the confusion which reigned that day it is likely that the wallet somehow managed to be itemised as being on Oswald's person at the time he was arrested at the Texas Theatre. It is unlikely that F.B.I. Agent Barret would have made the story up, therefore an understanding of why Oswald panicked and shot Tippit becomes clearer. Oswald would definitely have been arrested when Tippit read the two i.d.'s.

OSWALD'S ARREST

Johnny Brewer was the manager of Hardy's Shoeshop on West Jefferson Avenue, a few doors east of the Texas Theatre. On the afternoon of November 22nd Brewer was in his shop listening to reports on the radio about the assassination when suddenly a bulletin cut into the news report that a police officer had been shot nearby. At that moment he heard police sirens and looked out onto the street. He saw a man duck into his doorway.

Oswald's demeanour made Brewer suspicious. He thought he looked "funny". As the police sirens died away, the man walked away from Brewer's shop and towards the Texas Theatre. Brewer saw him walk inside without paying. By now Brewer was highly suspicious. When he had first seen the man he looked as if he had been running. His shirt was untucked and his hair was dishevelled. He looked "scared". For Brewer, entering the theatre without paying confirmed his suspicions so he informed the ticket attendant who called the police.

Oswald sat in the 3rd row of seats from the back of the cinema; I believe this was a conscious decision reflecting Oswald's fascination with the No. 3, and issue we shall return to in a later chapter.

Brewer, meanwhile, walked inside the cinema, told his story to an usher and they both proceeded to check the exits. None appeared to have been used. A dozen or so people were in the cinema. Brewer could not pick out the man but by this time the police had arrived. As the house lights went on Brewer met Officer M.N. McDonald and the other policemen at the alley exit door, stepped out onto the stage with them and pointed out the man who was sitting at the rear of the cinema.

Several Conspiracy Theorists have said that Oswald was "fingered" by a mysterious person who was sitting at the front of the cinema, thus leading to speculation that Oswald was "set up", having gone to the cinema to rendezvous with another conspirator. It is, of course, completely untrue and Officer McDonald has confirmed that the man who pointed out Oswald was, indeed, Johnny Brewer but at the time he did not know his name.

Officer McDonald first searched two men near the front. When he reached the row where Oswald was sitting McDonald stopped abruptly and told the man to get on his feet. Oswald rose from his seat, bringing up both his hands. As McDonald started to search him Oswald said, "Well, it's all over now". Oswald then struck McDonald between the eyes and reached down for his revolver. McDonald and Oswald grappled for the gun. Oswald pulled the trigger but there was only a click; the gun had misfired. Now the other policemen were surrounding Oswald. Detective Bob Carroll, who was standing beside McDonald, grabbed the gun. The question, of course, must be asked— Why would Oswald attempt to murder a police officer if he believed he was innocent of any crime and, one would assume, have attempted to persuade the police officers accordingly?

As Oswald was taken through the cinema lobby, he was heard to shout,

"I protest this police brutality", and "I am not resisting arrest". A large crowd had gathered outside the cinema, and when they saw the policemen emerge with Oswald some of them shouted, "Kill the son of a bitch", and "Let us have him". The policemen hustled Oswald into a police car and drove to police headquarters. Evidently the feelings of the Dallas citizens were running high. Would it, then, have been too incredible a hypothesise to believe that had it not been Ruby who shot Oswald another x number of citizens would have been queuing up to do likewise? As we shall see in a later chapter Ruby's shooting of Oswald is considered by Conspiracy Theorists as further evidence that a conspiracy existed; that Oswald was "eliminated" to prevent him from revealing a conspiracy. As the recent trial of Oklahoma bomber, Timothy McVeigh, has shown there are many members of the public who would be more than willing to take private revenge against the perpetrator of a particularly heinous crime.

Oswald's demeanour inside the police car was arrogant and unflustered.. When a police officer asked him if he had killed Officer Tippit because he was afraid of being arrested, Oswald said he wasn't afraid of anything, and asked "Do I look like I am scared now?" As they drove into the police department basement, Oswald was asked if he wanted to conceal his face from the photographers. "Why should I cover my face?", he asked. "I haven't done anything to be ashamed of." It is noteworthy that Oswald did not say "I didn't kill anyone".

OSWALD'S INTERROGATION

The evidence of Oswald's interrogation is vital to an understanding of the assassination for if Oswald was truly innocent of any involvement in the assassination, as many Conspiracy Theorists claim, then why did he repeatedly lie after his arrest?

Lee Oswald had a history of lying and often astounded his wife by lying about even the slightest things. He lied on job applications and all through their marriage it was Oswald's lying and Marina's telling him off that led to the bitter quarrels between them.

Lee apparently inherited this trait from his mother, according to Priscilla Johnson McMillan who had spent a year with Marina Oswald after the assassination and later wrote her excellent account of Lee and Marina's relationship:

"Neither Lee nor his mother could open up or allow themselves to be vulnerable to anyone. They had to keep others from glimpsing what was inside their minds. And, since they were holding together a view of the world that was not in accordance with reality, they spent a great deal of energy tuning out signals that did not fit. By the age of 4, Robert (Lee's older brother) knew that his mother was deaf to anything she did not want to hear. His brother Lee was the same. As a result neither knew what reality was. Since the truth was weightless and elusive, they felt entitled to play fast and loose with it. Both of them lied, but in this they differed from one another, for Marguerite apparently had enough contact with reality to control her abuse of it. This was not true of Lee. His sense of reality appears to have been so badly impaired that the line between truth and falsehood was wavy, and falsehood was often truer than truth. He lied pointlessly, to no purpose and all the time, even when he had nothing to hide. Marina says Lee told 3 kinds of lies. One was vranyo, a wild Russian cock-and-bull lying that has a certain imaginative joy to it; another was lying out of secretiveness; and still another was lying out of calculation, because he had something to hide. Lying claimed much of Lee's energy and complicated his life a great deal. But he had no choice. He had to keep his reality in and the reality of other people out."

Lee Harvey Oswald was interrogated for 12 hours between his arrival at Police Headquarters and his murder on the Sunday morning. At all times during these interrogation sessions a combination of Police Officers, Secret Service Agents, and F.B.I. Agents were present as well as Postal Inspector Holmes who was there because the rifle and pistol used in the murders of the President and Officer Tippet had been ordered by mail.

Oswald's chief interrogator was Captain Will Fritz of the Dallas Police Homicide Department. Fritz recalled that Oswald would talk to him readily "until I asked him a question that meant something, that would produce evidence," and then Oswald would immediately tell him he wouldn't answer. Fritz thought he seemed to anticipate what he was going to ask. Others who were there also got the impression that Oswald was quick with his answers and that he appeared to have planned what he was going to say.

The fact that there were no recordings or written statements made at the time of the interrogation lead many Conspiracy Theorists to suspect that the Dallas Police, F.B.I. and Secret Service were trying to cover up. They see sinister reasons in not tape recording the conversations between Oswald and the authorities. Oswald's interviews were not recorded, they speculate, because there was a lot to hide and did not want any record of the interrogations.

However, there were less dramatic reasons which prevented the interrogation from being recorded. Captain Will Fritz had been trying for months to obtain a tape recorder for the Homicide and Robbery Bureau, without success. As a result, the only record of Oswald's 12 hours of interrogation during the period from Friday afternoon to Sunday morning, comes from the notes of those who happened to be present.

There were 7 or 8 men moving in and out of the Police Homicide Office and no person was there the whole of the time the interrogations took place. Fritz admits he was violating every principle of interrogation but excuses it on the grounds that numerous Federal and local agencies were involved; there was an atmosphere of chaos within Dallas Police headquarters.

On Friday afternoon Fritz had just begun asking some general questions about Oswald's background when F.B.I. Agents James P. Hosty and James Bookhout entered the Homicide office. When Hosty introduced himself Oswald reacted angrily, accusing Hosty of harassing his wife - a reference to Hosty's calling at the Paine home in Irving to keep tabs on a former Soviet defector. Hosty and Bookhout left it up to Fritz to continue the interrogation as they did not wish to incite Oswald any further.

During his stay in New Orleans the previous summer, Oswald had been questioned by F.B.I. Agents Fain and Quigley and Lieutenant Martello of the New Orleans Police Department. He had told many blatant lies. At the Dallas jail Oswald was now engaging in the same evasions and lies.

When Fritz asked Oswald if he owned a rifle, he replied that he had seen his Book Depository supervisor, Roy Truly, showing a rifle to some other people in his office on November 20th, but he denied owning a rifle himself. He maintained that he had been eating his lunch with two other employees when the motorcade passed by and that afterward he assumed there would be no more work that day, so he went home and decided to go to a movie. The two employees denied it. When he was asked why he took the pistol with him, he said it was because he just wanted to: "Well you know about a pistol. I just carried it." He also lied about buying the pistol in Fort Worth, when, in fact, he purchased it from a mail order house in Los Angeles. At one point F.B.I. agent James Hosty asked Oswald if he had been to Mexico City and Oswald reacted angrily. According to Fritz, he "beat on the desk and went into a kind of tantrum". He said he had never been to Mexico City. The interview was interrupted several times for identification line-ups in which witnesses identified Oswald as the man they had seen shooting Officer Tippit or running away from the scene of the crime.

Later during the day F.B.I. Agent Manning C. Clements asked Oswald for some information concerning his residences. Oswald replied with truthfulness concerning every address he had lived at since his return from Russia with the exception of one-the Neely Street address in Dallas where his wife Marina had taken the photographs of Oswald holding his rifle and pistol. Captain Fritz also asked Oswald about the Neely Street address and found that he was "very evasive about this location".

To his interrogators Oswald denied that he had told Wesley Frazier he was going to Irving to pick up curtain rods. He said the package he brought to work contained his lunch, a preposterous notion considering the size of the package which Frazier described in his testimony to the Warren Commission. Oswald said he had gone to Irving on the Thursday (something he had not done before) because Ruth Paine, the person with whom Marina Oswald was staying, was planning to give a party for the children and he didn't want to be there then. In fact the party had been held the week before. When told that Wesley Frazier and Mrs. Randle had seen him carrying a long heavy package Oswald replied, "Well, they were mistaken."

Oswald also said that when the motorcade passed the Book Depository he had been in the second floor lunchroom with some of his fellow workers, notably Junior Jarman. Jarman testified that he had not seen Oswald in the lunchroom at any time that day. Jarman had finished his lunch before noon and went up to the 5th floor to watch the motorcade with his friends Harold Norman and Bonnie Ray Williams. They heard the shots going off over their heads and heard the sounds of the cartridge cases hitting the floor above them.

Oswald lied repeatedly about owning the rifle. During Saturday's interrogation session Captain Fritz told Oswald of the evidence that he had purchased the rifle under the name "Hiddell". Oswald said it was untrue. Contrary to his wife's testimony he said he had never owned a rifle and that since leaving the Marine Corps he had only fired a . 22 rifle. When confronted with the photographs showing him holding the rifle and pistol, Oswald claimed they were fakes.

Throughout his interrogations, then, Oswald made many statements about his actions on November 22nd that the police and federal agencies knew to be lies. He lied about his whereabouts at the time of the assassination. He consistently lied to hide his ownership of the rifle and pistol. He lied about his flight from the Book Depository. Whenever he could Oswald became tight-lipped when his interrogators raised matters which he could not deny. Oswald's lying did not come as a surprise to his wife as we have seen. It is evident that there was a pattern in Oswald's lies - lying about the circumstances of the murders but honest about his politics.

Conspiracy Theorist Walt Brown writes:

"If Oswald had sought fame he had but to claim it; yet the last 48 hours of his life were filled with denials of wrongdoing, pleas for an attorney and requests to be allowed to shower, hardly the proud harangues of a crazed assassin seeking fame."

Brown fails to understand Oswald's motives in not claiming responsibility for the death of the President but he does highlight a puzzling anomaly. However, in denying guilt Oswald was, arguably from his perspective furthering his ideas of a persecuted left-wing. It is conceivable that Oswald was emulating his heroes - The Rosenburg spies who were found guilty of espionage and executed but who nonetheless denied their guilt up to the moment of execution. Denying guilt and accusing the police of having arrested an innocent man would have exaggerated the image of himself as a martyr for a political cause. Furthermore Oswald had accomplished his goal of becoming a 'heroic' fighter for left-wing causes simply by his arrest. He had the forum he had always longed for.

Those who knew Oswald better than anyone, his brother Robert and his wife Marina, sensed Oswald's guilt when they visited him at the Dallas jail after his arrest. Marina could see it in Lee's eyes. She knew that if Oswald were truly innocent he would be "screaming for his rights" and demanding to see officials at the highest levels. Oswald's compliance was, to Marina, proof of his guilt. Robert believed his brother's demeanour revealed his guilt. As he told author Priscilla Johnson McMillan:

" (Lee) seemed at first to me to be very mechanical. He was making sense, but it was all mechanical. I interrupted him and tried to get him to answer my questions rather than listening to what he had to say. And then the really astounding thought dawned on me. I realised that he was really unconcerned, I was looking into his eyes, but they were blank, like Orphan Annie's, and he knew, I guess from the amazement on my face, that I saw that. He knew what was happening because as I searched his eyes he said to me, 'Brother, you won't find anything there.'" Robert has consistently maintained that his brother was guilty of both murders.

The Secret Service agents, F.B.I. agents and Dallas police who interrogated Oswald have all testified, under oath, to the Warren Commission and the House Assassinations Committee. No-one has yet discredited their testimony. To say, as some Conspiracy Theorists do, that they lied would be tantamount to believing in an incredible and vast conspiracy involving thousands of people, none of whom have come forward in the intervening years to testify to Oswald having been "fitted up". The truth of the matter is quite different. Oswald lied repeatedly during the interrogation. He had a history of lying. And the preponderance of evidence related to the Tippit shooting, Oswald's arrest and his interrogation point to an undeniable "Consciousness of Guilt".

CHAPTER 5

JACK RUBY AND THE MURDER OF LEE HARVEY OSWALD.

" Fame is the spur that the clear spirit doth raise
(That last infirmity of noble mind)
To scorn delights and live laborious days. "

Milton.

The day of the assassination, Dallas night-club owner Jack Ruby, had been at the offices of the Dallas Morning News, checking on an advertisement for his club that would appear in the newspaper. When word reached the building that Kennedy had been shot Ruby, like nearly everyone else in the country, appeared, as one employer remembered, "obviously pale ... and sat with a dazed expression on his face."

Finally Ruby collected himself, made a couple of phone calls, and prepared to leave the building. Ruby may have gone to Parkland Hospital, where he encountered journalist Seth Kantor in one of the corridors. Kantor later remembered that Ruby had tears in his eyes and he later described Ruby as a:

"town character ... (who was) self-seeking and publicity hungry".

Ruby had to be where the action was. If Dallas held any event or there was something exciting happening he would be there. Ruby's friends and acquaintances spoke to authors Gary Wills and Ovid Demaris for their 1968 book 'Jack Ruby'. Andrew Armstrong said:

" ... sometimes he'd be way out in some negro district where there had been a flood or something. I'd say 'What are you doing out there?' 'Oh, nothing, just driving around. '

Another friend, Mitch Lewis said:

" ... he was excited by the cameras and lights. He liked to hang around newsmen. When Marina and Marguerite Oswald came by, (to the police station after the assassination) I was jostled up close to them and so was Jack. I happened to see him when he first looked at them, and his eyes were glazed. I think he was impressed that these frumps ... could suddenly be made the centre of attention."

Barney Weinstein, who knew Ruby well, said:

"He had a wonderful heart. When he hardly knew me, he read about my mother's funeral in the newspaper and came to it. He just had to get into everything, including the excitement of that weekend Kennedy died."

From Parkland Ruby went to the Dallas police station and for several hours loitered in the corridors close to the room where Oswald was denying that he had shot Officer Tippet and the President. At one point Captain Will Fritz emerged and was surrounded by newsmen. Others wanted to know who was being interviewed. Ruby volunteered that it was Captain Fritz and then spelled out Fritz's name. He went home to his apartment early in the evening, made some phone calls, and then headed out again, first to his synagogue, and finally to a cafe near one of his clubs. He bought some sandwiches and soft drinks and announced he was going to bring them to the police, or maybe the employees of a local radio station. He told one of the people in the restaurant that the assassination would be bad for Dallas' convention trade, then added pridefully that he had been the only club owner to close his club in memorium to the president.

Ruby then went back to his car and headed downtown towards the police station. Once again he had no trouble getting straight to where the excitement lay. District Attorney Henry Wade was holding an impromptu press conference for reporters. The DA announced that Oswald would probably be transferred to the county jail at the beginning of the following week. Then Wade began talking about Oswald, mentioning that the suspect had been a member of the "Free Cuba Committee" and a voice at the back of the room corrected him saying it was the "Fair Play for Cuba Committee". It was Jack Ruby.

Conspiracy Theorists use Ruby's statement to infer he had special knowledge of the organisation that Oswald was connected to. However, Oswald's membership in the 'Fair Play for Cuba Committee' had been mentioned in the Dallas newspapers in their early editions after the assassination. Conspiracy Theorists omit to inform their readers there was a chorus of voices correcting Wade's mis-statement to the press.

When the press conference broke up Ruby introduced himself to Wade, put him on a telephone with a reporter, and finally left the police station bound for a local radio station, where he succeeded at last in giving away his soft drinks and sandwiches.

It was now long past midnight, but Ruby was still excited and unable to sleep. He stopped by the Carousel club where he met one of his dancers, Kay Coleman and her boyfriend Harry Olsen, a Dallas policeman. They talked for an hour, Olsen saying:

"They should cut this guy (Oswald) inch by inch into ribbons".

Ruby agreed and cursed Oswald. He then went to the Dallas Times Herald and talked to some of the reporters on the late night shift about the President's assassination. He also joked with them, demonstrating his expertise in balancing on a twistboard, but generally his mood was one of sorrow over the death of the president and the plight of Jackie Kennedy. At 4.30 Ruby drove home to his apartment and awakened his roommate George Senator. At Ruby's insistence they went out, picked up club employee Larry Crafard (who, incidentally, looked like Oswald which may account for the many 'sightings' of Ruby and Oswald conversing at Ruby's Carousel Club) and cruised around Dallas. It was past dawn when Ruby and his companions returned to their homes.

On Saturday afternoon Ruby drove to Dealey Plaza. A television reporter saw him walking by the Book Depository, out by the railway tracks. A police officer, noticing Ruby's interest, directed his gaze to the 6th floor window where the fatal shots were fired. Ruby looked up solemnly then walked to where wreaths had been laid in memorium to the president. He studied them briefly then left. Over the tragic weekend Ruby met many acquaintances and friends. They invariably described his mood as sombre and upset. He made no attempt to hide his feelings.

That evening Ruby visited his sister, Eva Grant. They talked about the assassination and Ruby's feelings came pouring out. He was bitter and angry about the assassination and sorrowful for the Kennedys. He talked of what the assassination had done to Dallas and what it had done to the Jews. Ruby was highly strung and obviously disturbed. To say, as most Conspiracy Theorists do, that Ruby was part of a conspiracy to kill the President and to then calculatedly shoot the assassin, is to ignore those who observed Ruby the weekend of the assassination. Ruby's acting abilities must have excelled Oscar standards.

Exhausted from the last day and a half Ruby did not rise until 9.00 Sunday morning. He watched television for a while and then made breakfast. When he left the apartment at 11.00 he took his pet dachshund with him. Into his jacket pocket he slipped out his .38 calibre revolver he usually carried in his car or, if he was holding takings from the clubs, in his jacket pocket. As his lawyer Melvin Belli noted:

"He was one of those people who are walking collections of pigeon-holes.... partly because he was having income tax problems and didn't want to chance putting money in the bank for fear the government would grab it, partly because he was a packrat by nature, he always walked around with his pockets crammed with money and notes. It was the big reason that he habitually carried a gun-that and the fact that a gun could be worn in Dallas as naturally as a hat."

"He carried a lot of money ... that's why he kept a gun in the bank bag. ... whenever he was carrying money he kept his piece handy," said Bob Larkin, a doorman at Ruby and sister Eva's Vegas Club.

Ruby drove downtown past the Texas School Book Depository and parked his car not far from his destination, the Western Union Telegraph office where he was to wire some cash for one of his dancers. He left his beloved dog Sheba in the car and at 11.17 the Western Union clerk gave Ruby a receipt for his money order. Ruby walked out the door and headed down main street toward the police station. He was 4 minutes away from his historic role in the tragic events of that weekend; the slaying of the president's alleged assassin before a television audience of millions.

There was plenty in Ruby's background to suggest that he was just a pretend gangster trying to avenge Kennedy's death and at the same time bolstering his low self-esteem and craving for "class" and attention. However, the Warren Commission's investigation into his relationships and operations as a night-club owner was less than satisfactory and it was these relationships with unsavoury characters which led to a great deal of speculation that he was controlled by organised crime.

Ruby was born in 1912 to a drunken Russian immigrant and a quiet, gentle woman who was intimidated by her husband and who spent some months in her later years in an Illinois mental home.

Ruby and his brothers and sisters spent much of their childhood in a series of foster homes while their parents were separated. By the time Ruby was 8 or 9 years old he was making money selling shopping bags in the Chicago streets at Christmas time. In his teens he started selling pennants and parking cars. At age 23 he went to California to sell tip sheets at a racecourse. When that didn't work he sold subscriptions for Hearst newspapers.

Until he was drafted into the army in 1943, he continued with these types of petty jobs. He worked as a union organiser, travelled through the eastern states selling punchboards, then opened what he called a legitimate mail order business.

His sister Eva had moved to Dallas and through her, after the war, he got involved in the night-club business there. This testimony contradicts the views of some Conspiracy Theorists who say Ruby was sent to Dallas by the Chicago Mafia. In 1952 a club he ran failed badly and, depressed about it, he retreated to a Dallas hotel and pondered suicide. However he re-emerged to re-enter the club business the following year.

"I was doing some things on the side", Ruby explained, "I made a trip to New York to promote a little coloured boy who could sing and dance. Then I became a distributor for pizza pie and for some medicine. I built some log cabins for a man named Gimble, but we didn't do well. I took over a private club in 1960 but I didn't make a go of it with all the credits involved so I changed it to the Carousel club in 1961". The Carousel club was a sleazy upstairs strip club near the Adolphus and Baker hotels in Dallas. Dallas tolerated it as a convention attraction.

Ruby's medical history shows a series of head injuries. In 1928 when he was selling tickets outside Soldiers Field, Chicago, 2 plainclothes policemen beat him on the head with their pistols. In 1941, in some sort of brawl, he suffered a concussion. In 1955, while he was running the Silver Spur club in Dallas, he got into a fight with 3 customers and a woman ended it by hitting him over the head with a half-gallon jug of wine. Ruby had a habit of carrying a gun and assaulting patrons who wouldn't pay or who bothered women at his clubs. And he loved to play the big shot, bragging of his friends in the Mafia, cultivating friends among the Dallas police and pestering reporters for publicity. Friends and acquaintances have testified that whenever anything exciting happened in Dallas Jack was always there.

Ruby's emotional state the morning he killed Oswald has been well documented. His close friend and roommate George Senator testified to the Warren Commission:

" (Ruby) was mumbling, which I didn't understand. And right after breakfast he got dressed. Then after he got dressed he was pacing the floor from the living room to the bedroom, from the bedroom to the living room, and his lips were going. What he was jabbering I don't know. But he was really pacing."

Ruby himself described his actions that fateful Sunday morning:

"... Sunday morning ... I saw a letter to Caroline (JFK's daughter), two columns about a 16 inch area. Someone had written a letter to Caroline. The most heartbreaking letter. I don't remember the contents ... alongside that letter on the same sheet of paper was a small comment in the newspaper that, I don't know how it was stated, that Mrs. Kennedy may have to come back for the trial of Lee Harvey Oswald ... I don't know what bug got ahold of me. I don't know what it is, but I am going to tell the truth word for word. I am taking a pill called Preludin. It is a harmless pill and it is very easy to get in the drugstore. It isn't a highly prescribed pill. I use it for dieting. I don't partake of that much food. I think that was a stimulus to give me an emotional feeling that suddenly I felt, which was so stupid, that I wanted to show my love for our faith, being of the Jewish faith, and I never used the term and I don't want to go into that-suddenly the feeling, the emotional feeling came within me that someone owed this debt to our beloved President to save her the ordeal of coming back. I don't know why that came through my mind."

Ruby often acted impulsively. Perhaps due to his head injuries he also had a propensity to violence. A stripper named Penny Dollar, who once worked at Ruby's Carousel Club testified at Ruby's trial in 1964. She told the jury that she had seen Ruby throw a man downstairs and beat his head repeatedly on the pavement, then rise in bewilderment and say, 'Did I do this? Did I do this?'.

His sister Eva Grant has testified to the emotional turmoil Ruby was in during the weekend of the assassination:

"He was sick to his stomach ... and went into the bathroom ... He looked terrible ... He looked pretty bad ... I can't explain it to you. He looked too broken, a broken man already. He did make the remark "I never felt so bad in all my life even when Ma and Pa died ... someone tore my heart out."

Cecil Hamlin, a longtime friend said Ruby was "very emotional ... very broken up". Buddy Raymon, a comedian, remembered that when Ruby telephoned him, "he was crying and carrying on: "what do you think of a character like that killing the president?" George Senator said "it was the first time I ever saw tears in his eyes".

After the assassination Ruby visited the synagogue and cried. His brother Hyman said "They didn't believe a guy like Jack would ever cry. Jack never cried in his life. He was not that kind of guy to cry." To many players in the events of that weekend Ruby was observed with tears in his eyes.

Ruby's rabbi Hillel Silverman, who had known Ruby for 10 years, said that one day in 1963 Ruby suddenly appeared on his doorstep with half a dozen dogs. Ruby was crying and said that he was unmarried but, pointing to one dog, described it as 'his wife'. He then pointed to the other dogs and described them as 'his children'. According to Rabbi Silverman, Ruby was sobbing and crying and seemed to be 'a very emotional, unstable, erratic man'.

Melvin Belli, who became Ruby's lawyer after he shot Oswald wrote: "There was one weird trait. Unfailingly, at the mention of a member of President Kennedy's family, tears would start to course down his cheeks. It could even be a casual mention-later we tested his reaction by saying things like, 'Too bad Jack Kennedy won't be able to see the Giant's play'- and the tears would just flow out of there. It was too spontaneous to be an act. I am convinced of the sincerity of this affection, although I am just as convinced, because of the circumstances of the Oswald shooting and the way Ruby talked about it, that the affection could not have been a preconceived motive for the killing."

Still there were many signs that Ruby was not just an unstable, erratic and emotional man who killed Oswald out of a need for attention and grief over the assassination. The investigation into his background was shallow because the Warren Commission had to rely on the F.B.I. which interviewed hundreds of his acquaintances but did not fully investigate his underworld connections and his trips to Cuba. Two attorneys assigned to investigate Ruby for the Warren Commission wanted to explore rumours that he was a payoff man between the local mob and the Dallas police. They were also suspicious about his handling of large amounts of cash and his Cuban connections. They requested the C.I.A. for any material it had on Ruby. However, the C.I.A. ignored them until 11 days before the Warren Report was issued in September 1964. Then it replied that a search of its files had provided no information on Jack Ruby or his activities. Such actions by Government agencies only fuelled later claims that there was a cover-up. The real reason, however, was that the C.I.A. like other elements of the 'Bureaucracy' have always been notoriously unwilling to release data fearing their sources or intelligence gathering techniques would be compromised. These reasons are not, ipso facto, sinister.

One of the most intriguing of the unanswered questions concerned Ruby's travel to Cuba in 1959. The House Select Committee on

Assassinations later determined that he had made at least 3 trips to Havana that summer and that he had visited a safe deposit box in Dallas in the meantime. Ruby's lawyer Melvin Belli wrote:

"It came out in one of our earliest interviews that he had tried to arrange some sort of deal with Cuba soon after Fidel Castro overthrew the Batista regime. But that, Ruby would insist, was when Castro was considered something of a hero in the United States. Now Castro was considered a Russian-supported communist, and Ruby was mortified to think that anyone might get the wrong impression of the deal. 'When Castro first came in he was considered a hero', he said, 'and I thought maybe I could make a deal in selling jeeps to Cuba. He was still a hero at the time; his brother was the first one to turn. Steve Allen and Jack Parr (T.V. entertainers) and Jake Arvey's son were all interested then in making deals with him. I had been associated with a very high type of person, but a gambler, Mack Willie, who ran a club in Cuba, so I went there for eight or ten days.' People would say he had planned to give guns to Cuba, Ruby fretted; they would think he wasn't a good American. He insisted that we telephone all over the place to try to set the record straight on this, although I got the impression, frankly, that the deal had been primarily the figment of his imagination."

That same year the F.B.I. contacted Ruby 9 times trying to recruit him as an informant. But J. Edgar Hoover, head of the F.B.I., withheld the information from the Warren Commission. Later it was disclosed that Ruby, because of his advantageous position as a Dallas night club owner, had given F.B.I. Agent Charles Flynn information about thefts and similar offences. In November of 1959 Flynn recommended that no further attempt be made to develop Ruby as a PCI, potential criminal informant, since his information was useless.

The C.I.A. failed to disclose a report that Ruby may have visited Santos Trafficante, mob boss of Florida, while he was jailed in Cuba at the time. The House Assassinations Committee later investigated these reports but did not place any credence upon them. There were other tantalising reports that Ruby was smuggling prisoners or gambling assets out of Cuba. But the most plausible explanation is that Ruby was attracted to any moneymaking schemes that came his way. He told the F.B.I. in December 1963 that he had had in mind "making a buck" by possibly acquiring some jeeps but that nothing had come of it.

Ruby did make many telephone calls to his underworld contacts in the months before the Kennedy assassination. But there is no evidence they were conspiratorial in nature. He wanted help in persuading the union representing his dancers to crack down on rival clubs using amateur talent. The Warren Report stated:

"Breck Wall testified that Ruby called him to determine whether or not the American Guild of Variety Artists (AGVA), which represented striptease dancers in Dallas, had met concerning a dispute Ruby was having with the union. Ruby's major difference with AGVA's failure to enforce against his two competitors, Abe and Barney Weinstein, AGVA's ban on 'striptease contests' and performances by 'amateurs'. As recently as Wednesday, November 20th, Ruby had telephoned an AGVA representative in Chicago about that complaint and earlier in November he had unsuccessfully sought to obtain assistance from a San Francisco gambler and a Chicagoan reputed for his heavy-handed union activities."

The calls can certainly not be used as evidence of a conspiracy to kill President Kennedy since most of the calls were made before the President's trip to Dallas was even announced, much less before the motorcade route was set. Journalist Seth Kantor speculated that Ruby borrowed money from the mob and that the mob later called in the debt by asking him to silence Oswald. But an analysis of the events of that tragic weekend fails to produce any hard evidence that these underworld contacts played any role in Ruby's actions.

Conspiracy Theorists rightly point to Ruby's association with Dallas mob bosses Civello and Campisi but fail to put it in the right context. Ruby's world consisted of night-clubs, betting and socialising with people who were in the same 'business'. As the McClellan Senate Investigatory Committee recognised in the 1950's no city in the United States was immune to Mafia control of off-track betting, gambling and night-club entertainment. It was the milieu in which Ruby operated. At the same time Ruby entertained many Dallas police officers at his club. One such police officer was Joe Cody who stated that Ruby was often seen with Joe and Sam Campisi because they were part of Ruby's social scene. Ruby ate at the 'Egyptian Lounge' and Cody often joined Ruby and the Campisis. But there was no criminal connection.

In a sense he was a police 'groupie' often giving them free drinks and arranging dates for them with his 'girls'. It was inevitable that Ruby would associate with characters who could be linked in some way with the underworld. But it is illogical to assume, as some Conspiracy Theorists do, that there MUST have been mob involvement in Ruby's actions that tragic weekend. The evidence indicates otherwise.

"It is so ludicrous to believe that Ruby was part of the mob, "Tony Zoppi, a close friend of Ruby's, told author Gerald Posner, "The Conspiracy Theorists want to believe everybody but those who really knew him. People in Dallas, in those circles, knew Ruby was a snitch. The word on the street that you couldn't trust him because he was telling the cops everything. He was a real talker, a fellow who would talk your ear off if he had the chance. You have to be crazy to think anyone would have trusted Ruby to be part of the mob. He couldn't keep a secret for five minutes. He was just a hanger on, somebody who would have liked some of the action but was never going to get any."

In an interview with Posner former Dallas Assistant District Attorney Bill Alexander stated: "It's hard to believe ... that I, who prosecuted Ruby for killing Oswald, am almost in the position of defending his honour. Ruby was not in the Mafia. He was not a gangster. We knew who the criminals were in Dallas back then, and to say Ruby was part of organised crime is just bullshit. There's no way he was connected. It's guilt by association, that A knew B, and Ruby knew B back in 1950, so he must have known A, and that must be the link to the conspiracy. It's crap written by people who don't know the facts."

James Leavelle, the homicide detective who was handcuffed to Oswald when he was shot and who also transferred Ruby to the County Jail, has said that he asked Ruby why he shot Oswald and his answer was simple: "I wanted to be a hero. It looks like I fouled things up." It is the most obvious and logical explanation for his act given the nature of the man and the way he operated and felt.

Leavelle's reasoning for Ruby's actions are confirmed by many of Ruby's friends who believed he shot Oswald to become a hero. And Ruby, in the days after the shooting believed he would soon be out of jail and running his night clubs as usual. Andrew Armstrong, Ruby's bartender, visited Ruby regularly in jail to report on the Club's affairs. When interviewed by authors Ovid Demaris and Gary Wills, Armstrong and many of Ruby's friends and acquaintances had little doubt as to Ruby's motives:

"Jack talked as if it would be no time before he was back running things." An attorney who visited Ruby in jail said Ruby "never expected to spend a night in jail."

Many of Ruby's friends agreed with this reason. "At the club, after the first shock," said Carousel Club drummer Bill Willis, "we all said, 'Well, it figures. Jack thought while he was downtown he might as well kill Oswald too." Max Rudberg, a Ruby friend said, "Well, everyone was saying the sonovabitch needs killing, and Jack was anxious to please ... he was bound to poke his head in and see what was happening. Wherever there was a crowd, he couldn't possibly pass it by." Milton Joseph, a local jeweller, had no doubt that Ruby killed Oswald to be in the limelight.

Bill Roemer, the F.B.I. agent in charge of investigating the Chicago Mafia in the 1960's, agrees, as he told author Gerald Posner, - "Ruby was absolutely nothing in terms of the Chicago mob. We had thousands of hours of tape recordings of the top mobsters in Chicago, including Sam Giancana (the Godfather), and Ruby just didn't exist as far as they were concerned. We talked to every hoodlum in Chicago after the assassination, and some of the top guys in the mob, my informants, I had a close relationship with them - they didn't know who Ruby was. He was not a front for them in Dallas."

Roemer knew what the Mafia was like. He arrested many Mafia members and part of his duties was to keep surveillance on Chicago boss Sam Giancana. Roemer knew that if the Mafia hired anyone for a 'hit' they would choose someone who had not only a track record of killing but who would remain 'tight lipped'. None of these features applied to Ruby.

Roemer's observations about Ruby and the possibility he had ties to the Mafia are confirmed by a memo, released by the F.B.I. in 1978. Back in 1963 the F.B.I. spent months digging into the background, character and motivations of Ruby. They interviewed mobster Frank LaVerde of Chicago, whose insight into the claims of Conspiracy Theorists is telling:

"It's not logical to send a guy in to hit a guy (Oswald) who's stood up for 25 hours. You know you can trust a guy who can stand up for 25 hours, but how do you know you can trust the guy you send in to hit him?"

There is a certain inherent logic in LaVerde's statement.

Ruby certainly knew many people who had police records. "It was the nature of his business, " says Bill Alexander. "Running those types of night-clubs, he came across plenty of unsavoury characters. The police had a pretty good idea of what happened at Ruby's club, and there was no dope and he certainly didn't allow any of the girls to do anything illegal from the club, because that would have cost him his licence. Ruby was a small time operator on the fringe of everything, but he never crossed over to breaking the law big time."

Mark Lane in his conspiracy book "Rush to Judgement", Oliver Stone in his movie "J.F.K.", and Henry Hurt in his book 'Reasonable Doubt' examine Ruby's 1964 testimony to the Warren Commission which, they say, proves Ruby's involvement in a conspiracy. After Ruby had been convicted of Oswald's murder and sentenced to death, Warren Commission members Earl Warren and Gerald Ford questioned him at the Dallas jail. For many months there had been rumours that Ruby was a hit man whose job had been to silence Oswald. According to Lane and Stone, Ruby seemed eager to disclose his part in a conspiracy. According to Lane:

"Ruby made it plain that if the Commission took him from the Dallas jail and permitted him to testify in Washington, he could tell more there; it was impossible for him to tell the whole truth so long as he was in the jail in Dallas." I would like to request that I go to Washington and ... take all the tests that I have to take. It is very important ... Gentlemen, unless you get me to Washington, you can't get a fair shake out of me."

Henry Hurt writes: "Ruby recited his story to the Warren Commission which took his testimony in a small kitchenlike room in a Dallas courthouse. But throughout his testimony, Ruby exuded signals-some subtle, some direct- that given the opportunity there was a great deal he would like to tell the commission. Scattered through his testimony are statements that are a variation on one direct plea he made to Chief Justice Warren: ' I want to tell the truth, and I can't tell it here.' ... Ruby must have spent those months living in terror for his life. But, as always, Ruby seemed to toady to authority, to try to ingratiate himself as he had spent so many years doing with the Dallas Police Department. It was not really surprising that there were signs that under certain circumstances he would like to co-operate, after a fashion, with the Commission. To what degree he might have co-operated is anyone's guess."

After quoting similar statements by Ruby, Lane wrote:

"Representative Ford asked, not a little redundantly, "Is there anything more you can tell us if you went back to Washington?" Ruby told him that there was, and just before the hearing ended Ruby made one last plea to the Chief Justice of the United States":

RUBY: But you are the only one that can save me. I think you can.

WARREN: Yes?

RUBY: But by delaying minutes, you lose the chance. And all I want to do is tell the truth, and that is all.

Lane's account is misleading. It appears that Ruby was begging to be allowed to reveal the conspiracy but he could not do so in Dallas, fearing for his life. And the Chief Justice would not let him be sent to Washington, bringing into suspicion the Federal Government who may have been afraid Ruby would implicate the F.B.I., C.I.A. etc.

What Lane did not say was that the 'test' Ruby wanted to take was simply a lie detector test; and the reason Ruby wanted to take one was to prove he was not part of a conspiracy. Ruby also states in his testimony that he believes his family is in danger because of the act he committed: "There is a 'John Birch Society' right now in activity ...". He also reveals the real reason he shot Oswald- because he saw " a small comment in the newspaper that ... Mrs Kennedy may have to come back for the trial of Lee Harvey Oswald. That caused me to go like I did; that caused me to go like I did. I don't know Chief Justice but I got so carried away. And I remember prior to that thought, there has never been another thought in my mind; I was never malicious to this person. No one else requested me to do anything." Later in his testimony he states, "I am in a tough spot and I do not know what the solution can be to save me ... I want to say this to you ... The Jewish people are being exterminated at this moment. Consequently, a whole new form of government is going to take over our country, and I know I won't live to see you another time."

Television documentaries on the assassination which suggest conspiracy usually contain the news footage of Ruby declaring his wish to be taken to Washington D.C. where he will 'reveal the truth about the assassination'; Ruby is seen claiming that 'no one knows the true facts'. Conspiracy Theorists arrange these statements with careful cutting, splicing and editing and playback the picture of a Ruby who infers conspiracy.

Gary Wills and Ovid Demaris were the first to interpret Ruby's statements within the right context:

"He told them his family was in danger. They (Warren Commission) asked why. For standing by a man the world holds guilty of the president's death: (RUBY) 'Well assuming that, as I stated before, some persons are accusing me falsely of being part of the plot-naturally, in all the time from over six months ago, my family has been so interested. ' Friends have been sympathetic, too, and put themselves in danger. (RUBY) 'That sympathy isn't going to help me, because the people that have power there, they have a different verdict. They already have me as the accused assassin of our beloved president.' If the world believes that, how can it fail to exterminate the Jews? And people were trying to convince President Johnson of this, so his power would be used to further the extermination. That is why Jack (Ruby) has to get to Washington and convince Johnson it is all lies."

Ruby, then, wanted to tell about a conspiracy - a conspiracy to murder the Jews. Earl Warren, the Commission's chairman told author Merle Miller: "I went down and took Jack Ruby's testimony myself- he wouldn't talk to anybody but me. And he wanted the F.B.I. to give him a lie detector test, and I think the F.B.I. did, and he cleared it all right. I was satisfied myself that he didn't know Oswald, never had heard of him. But the fellow was clearly delusional when I talked to him. He took me aside and he said, 'Hear those voices, hear those voices?' He thought they were Jewish children and Jewish women who were being put to death in the building there."

Melvin Belli his lawyer, quoted Ruby as saying: "If I go on (the witness stand) I'm liable to get a lot of people in trouble." This had nothing to do with the discredited "plot" theory. He was referring to his friends and top Jews all over the world. By that time the belief that he was bringing shame and destruction on the Jewish people was beginning to unhinge him. As he sank deeper and deeper into disorientation toward the trial's close, the aberration became stronger and stronger.

After his arrest, Ruby had been diagnosed as a 'psychotic depressive'. His testimony to the Warren Commission indicates that he believed he was a victim of a political conspiracy by right wing forces in Dallas. He suggested that the John Birch Society was spreading the falsehood that he, a Jew, was implicated in the President's death in order to create anti-Jewish hysteria. 'The Jewish People are being exterminated at this moment', Ruby insisted. 'Consequently, a whole new form of government is going to take over our country.' To foil this supposed plot, Ruby repeatedly asked to be given a lie detector test. At various points in their conversation Ruby told Warren:

" No subversive organisation gave me any idea. No underworld person made any effort to contact me. It all happened one Sunday morning... If you don't get me back to Washington tonight to give me a chance to prove to the President that I am not guilty, then you will see the most tragic thing that will ever happen ... All I want is a lie detector test ... All I want to do is tell the truth, and that is all. There was no conspiracy."

The following month Ruby was allowed to take a polygraph test in his jail cell, and he showed no signs of deception when he denied being part of a conspiracy. Because of the doubts of his sanity, however, the results were considered inconclusive. Yale psychologist Roy Schafer had given Ruby 10 psychological tests after his arrest and said Ruby gave a weighty indication of emotional instability. However, if Ruby was part of a conspiracy plot he would not have taken the test against the advice of his lawyers.

According to the test results, which were administered by one of the ablest in his field, F.B.I. polygraph administrator Bill P. Herndon, Ruby answered honestly to the following questions:

Q. Did you know Oswald before November 22nd 1963?

A: No.

Q. Did you assist Oswald in the assassination?

A: No.

Q. Between the assassination and the shooting, did anybody you know tell you they knew Oswald?

A: No.

Q. Did you shoot Oswald in order to silence him?

A: No.

Q. Is everything you told the Warren Commission the entire truth?

A: Yes.

Q: Did any foreign influence cause you to shoot Oswald?

A: No.

Q: Did you shoot Oswald because of the influence of the underworld?

A: No.

Q: Did you shoot Oswald in order to save Mrs. Kennedy the ordeal of a trial?

A: Yes.

Q: Did you know the Tippet that was killed?

A: No.

There is another reason apart from Ruby's testimony which proves that Ruby was acting alone when he shot Oswald. Oswald was scheduled to be transferred from the city jail in the police station to the county jail at 10.00am on Sunday November 24th. Before the scheduled transfer, he was to undergo further interrogation by Captain Will Fritz, the head of the homicide section of the Dallas Police, and representatives of the Secret Service and F.B.I.

Oswald's interrogation was extended on Sunday morning because Postal Inspector Harry D. Holmes arrived. He had helped the F.B.I. trace the money order that Oswald used to buy the rifle with which he killed President Kennedy. Holmes had also helped the F.B.I. trace the ownership of the post-office box number to which Oswald's rifle and pistol were sent. How did Holmes happen to be there that Sunday morning? In his testimony to the Warren Commission he said:

"On this morning I had no appointment. I actually started to church with my wife. I got to church and I said 'You get out, I am going down to see if I can do something for Captain Fritz. I imagine he is as sleepy as I am.'

" So I drove directly on down to the police station and walked in, and as I did, Captain Fritz motioned to me and said, 'We are getting ready to have a last interrogation with Oswald before we transfer him to the county jail. Would you like to join us?'

"I said 'I would'."

After Fritz, the representative of the Secret Service, and an F.B.I. agent finished their interrogation of Oswald, Fritz turned to Holmes and asked whether he wanted to interrogate Oswald. The invitation was unexpected but Holmes accepted. It was for this reason the interrogation continued for another half hour or so.

Ruby shot Oswald approximately 5 minutes after he left the Western Union office. Had Holmes continued on to church with his wife that morning, the length of interrogation would have been shortened and Jack Ruby would never have had the opportunity to kill Oswald.

However, notwithstanding these circumstances, David Scheim in his book "The Mafia Murder of President Kennedy" builds his conspiracy case by extracting two sentences from Jack Ruby's Warren Commission testimony to 'prove' Ruby had assistance in shooting Oswald:

"Who else could have timed it so perfectly by seconds. If it were timed that way, then someone in the police department is guilty of giving the information as to when Lee Harvey Oswald was coming down."

Contrast this seemingly "conspiratorial" statement with the true context of Ruby's testimony to the Warren Commission: -

RANKIN: "I think, Mr. Ruby, it would be quite helpful to the Commission if you could tell, as you recall it, just what you said to Mr. Sorrels and the others after the shooting of LHO. Can you recall that ... ?"

RUBY: "I spent an hour with Mr. Hall, Ray Hall. And I was very much broken up emotionally, and I constantly repeated that I didn't want Mrs. Kennedy to come back to trial, and those were my words constantly repeated to Mr. Hall ... ".

RANKIN: "There was a conversation with Mr. Sorrels in which you told him about the matter. Do you remember that?"

RUBY: "The only thing I ever recall I said to Mr. Ray Hall and Sorrels was, I said, 'Being of Jewish faith, I wanted to show my love for the president and his lovely wife. After I said whatever I said, then a statement came out that someone introduced Mr. Sorrels to me and I said 'What are you, a newsman?' Or something to that effect. Which is really- what I am trying to say is, the way it sounded is like I was looking for publicity and inquiring if you are a newsman, I wanted to see you. But I am certain- I don't recall definitely, but I know in my right mind, because I know my motive for doing it, and certainly to gain publicity to take a chance of being mortally wounded, as I said before, and WHO ELSE COULD HAVE TIMED IT SO PERFECTLY BY SECONDS. IF IT WERE TIMED THAT WAY, THEN SOMEONE IN THE POLICE DEPARTMENT IS GUILTY OF GIVING THE INFORMATION AS TO WHEN LEE HARVEY OSWALD WAS COMING DOWN. I never made a statement. I never inquired from the television man what time is Lee Harvey Oswald coming down. Because really a man in his right mind would never ask that question. I never made the statement 'I wanted to get 3 more off. Someone had to do it. You wouldn't do it.' I never made those statements ... Anything I said was with emotional feeling of I didn't want Mrs. Kennedy to come back to trial."

Conspiracy Theorists raise all kinds of similar conspiratorial questions about Jack Ruby, in trying to prove he was part of a plot. Virtually everyone fails to mention the testimony of Ruby's Rabbi, Hillel Silverman. Rabbi Silverman had visited Ruby in prison frequently. Rabbi Silverman is convinced Ruby was not part of a conspiracy.

According to Rabbi Silverman, at his first meeting with Ruby on the day after the shooting of Oswald, Ruby told him that "had I intended to kill him (at a press conference on the Friday evening), I could have pulled my trigger on the spot, because the gun was in my pocket." Lonnie Hudkins, a newspaper reporter, confirms this statement in an interview with BBC 'Timewatch' researchers:

"I asked him if he was packing a pistol at that midnight press conference and he said 'yes'. I asked him, 'Why didn't you plug him then?' and he said 'I was frightened of hitting one of you guys.' "

These are important statements because the time to shoot Oswald would have been the Friday night press conference. It was pure coincidence that Ruby had an opportunity to kill Oswald on the Sunday morning.

According to Silverman, Jack Ruby told him that on Saturday morning, November 23rd, he had viewed a T.V. broadcast from New York city in which a Rabbi Seligson was talking about President Kennedy and the assassination. Ruby became emotional, so he drove to the site of the assassination. Ruby then told Silverman that on the next morning, November 24, he read in the newspaper that Jacqueline Kennedy might have to come to Dallas to testify in Oswald's trial. He said this greatly upset him.

Ruby's true motives were announced in the seconds after he fired the shot into Oswald's abdomen. He remarked to his police interrogators "I was afraid that Mrs. Kennedy would be asked to return to the trial." His lawyer, Melvin Belli wrote that after Ruby's arrest and imprisonment:

"One of these guards gave Ruby a Bible and got in the habit of talking religion with him. Ruby became more and more obsessed with his faith as the days droned on. His conversation with us often touched on people he thought were being nice to him, and he would mention Sheriff Decker, then, more and more, this guard who talked religion and read the Bible to him. I kept hearing about this religious solace without ever getting to meet the guard who was providing it. At the same time I was getting the impression that somehow (District Attorney) Henry Wade and his men were hearing a lot more about Ruby than they should have. One day it came to me-the guard might be their source. I asked Jack, 'What have you told him?' 'I told him everything, Mel.' He stared at me innocently. 'I must have told him what happened when I shot the gun and about Jackie and the children.'

The final word by Ruby on his possible involvement in a conspiracy came shortly before he died in January 1967. Ruby made a deathbed statement using a tape recorder, secreted in an attaché case, which was smuggled into his hospital room by his brother, Earl Ruby. Ruby was questioned by his lawyers. The tape recording was later incorporated in an L.P. record entitled 'The Controversy'. The interview lasted 12 minutes but was edited down to 3 minutes for the recording. Ruby said that it was pure chance in meeting Oswald at the Dallas police headquarters:

"The ironic part of this is I had made an illegal turn behind a bus to the parking lot. Had I gone the way I was supposed to go-straight down Main street-I would've never met this fate, because the difference in meeting this fate was 30 seconds one way or the other ... All I did is walk down there, down to the bottom of the ramp and that's when the incident happened-at the bottom of the ramp."

Some Conspiracy Theorists, in attempting to prove that Dallas police allowed Ruby to enter the Dallas basement through an unlocked door and not the ramp fail to mention an important witness who actually saw Ruby descend the ramp. The witness was an ex-Dallas police officer named Napoleon Daniels. Daniels, a college educated African-American had been a member of the segregated Dallas police force who had left prior to the assassination. Daniels had observed Ruby descend the ramp when the police officer guarding the entrance. Roy Vaughn, was distracted by a car trying to manoeuvre into the basement entrance. Vaughn had to walk into the middle of the street to divert the car. Daniels thought the man entering the basement was a police detective and did not tell Vaughn. He did, however, notice a bulge at the person's waist that could only be a holstered handgun. The Dallas police tried to discredit Daniel's testimony possibly because he was black but also because his testimony revealed the incompetence of the Dallas police Department.

Another authoritative source has gone on record as late as March 1997 which confirms that Ruby, in the confusion which surrounded the Police station that Sunday morning, did not have any assistance in entering the basement. Paul McCaghren, a retired police lieutenant who was not present at the time but later investigated the shooting of Oswald said that Ruby's access to the basement was just lucky timing on his part. He said that in hindsight things should have been done differently but it was a situation that had never occurred before. According to the report of the investigation an armoured truck was to be used to transport Oswald to the County Jail from the City Jail. But, according to the report, police decided that "an unmarked police car would be better from the standpoint of both speed and deception... Such a car, bearing Oswald, should follow the armoured truck". But the police lieutenant driving the squad car was forced to go the wrong way on a ramp at police headquarters to pull in front of the armoured car because the exit was blocked. Another police officer, guarding the area, the report said, was surprised when the lieutenant pulled in and blasted his car horn to hold pedestrian traffic. McCaghren said this is when Ruby slipped into the basement, went immediately down the ramp and shot Oswald. Jim Ewell, a former reporter with the Dallas Morning News maintains that the idea that the Dallas Police Department had a hand in assisting Ruby is not true and that Dallas Police Department officials would have done things differently in the transfer of Oswald but top city officials overruled them. He believes they would have made the media stand in the street had they been given their way. The city officials wanted to make sure the world knew that Oswald was not being mistreated. Furthermore, during the transfer of Oswald, many officers were blinded by the high intensity television lights which accounted for the fact that Ruby was able to move amongst them without being challenged.

Ruby denied that he knew Oswald and said he had never been in his club. Rumours that Ruby and Oswald knew each other have been repeated over and over again since the time that Ruby shot Oswald. Many Conspiracy Theorists, most recently Robert Groden in his 1995 book 'The Search for Lee Harvey Oswald', state flatly that Oswald recognised Ruby just before Ruby pulled the trigger in the Dallas police basement. The Warren Report investigated numerous specific allegations that Ruby knew Oswald but found none which merited credence. Although it would be impossible to investigate all of these 'sightings'- all of which are uncorroborated and unsubstantiated-a clue why they arose in the first place may be gleaned from the Commission's investigation of one particular 'sighting':

"The testimony of a few witnesses who claim to have seen Ruby with a person who they feel may have been Oswald warrants further comment. One such witness, Robert K. Patterson, a Dallas electronics salesman, has stated that on November 1st., 1963, Ruby, accompanied by a man who resembled Oswald, purchased some equipment at his business establishment. However, Patterson did not claim positively that the man he saw was Oswald, and two of his associates who were also present at the time could not state that the man was Oswald. Other evidence indicates that Ruby's companion was Larry Crafard. Crafard, who lived at the Carousel Club while working for Ruby from mid-October until November 23rd, 1963, stated that sometime in late October or early November he accompanied

Ruby to an electronics store in connection with the purchase of electronic equipment. Ruth Paine testified that Crafard's photograph bears a strong resemblance to Oswald."

As Marina was to say :

" How could Lee have known Ruby? ... He didn't drink, he didn't smoke, he didn't go to night-clubs and, besides, he was sitting home with me all the time."

Conspiracy Theorists have also tried to link Ruby with Officer Tippit. Many are confused because they misread Ruby's recognition of the name 'Tippit'. Ruby initially thought it was an acquaintance, Police Officer Gayle Tippit, who had been shot.

In the final recording of Ruby's voice he was asked if he knew the time Oswald was supposed to have been moved, Ruby replied "He was supposed to be moved at 10'o'clock." Ruby explained he always carried a gun because he often had large sums of money.

Ruby was, of course, found guilty of murder. In his summing up District Attorney Henry Wade said, Don't tell me it takes guts to shoot a man who is manacled ... This is a wanton killing. Ruby felt he could kill Oswald and be a hero, make money and become famous ... You have a cold-blooded killing that could not be more malicious. If you turn this man loose you'd set civilisation back to the lynch laws ... I ask you to show Jack Ruby the same mercy, compassion, and sympathy that he showed to Lee Harvey Oswald in the police department." Ruby was sentenced to die.

His conviction was appealed and, because of mistakes in his trial he was about to be given a second one, but he died in prison.

For 32 months, since the time he shot Oswald, Ruby was locked in a windowless cell on the Dallas County Jail's corridor 6-M. A 'suicide watch' guard looked in on him around the clock-a single naked light bulb glared over his bed. Ruby could not tell night from day. He read every newspaper he could lay his hands on, eagerly sifting them for his name. He read dozens of books, including Perry Mason novels and the Warren Report, played cards with his guards, did physical exercises-and seemed out of his mind most of the time according to jail staff.

Ruby was clearly tipping over the edge in his psychoses and paranoia. He rammed his head against the plaster walls and raved over and over about the suffering Jews who were being killed as revenge for his crime.

When he became ill Ruby screamed that his prison guards were piping mustard gas into his cell. Later, when his doctors discovered that he was suffering from adenocarcinoma - a cancer that had spread swiftly through most of his cavities, ducts and glands of his body, Ruby accused them of injecting him with the disease-a medical impossibility, contrary to the claims of many Conspiracy Theorists.

Almost from the arrival at the hospital on December 9th 1966, Ruby's condition was considered hopeless. Contrary to the claims of Conspiracy Theorists Jack Ruby died telling the truth and he was not the masterly co-conspirator he is now portrayed. Ruby was a small time wheeler-dealer who could never have been a participant in a complex conspiracy-who could have trusted such an incompetent small timer to play a leading role in a cunning conspiracy? Nearly everyone who knew Jack Ruby testifies to this fact.

Ruby expired in the same hospital where Kennedy and Oswald died.

CHAPTER 6

WAS OSWALD AN AGENT FOR THE KGB?

— OR THE MILITARY?

— OR CASTRO?

— OR ANTI-CASTRO CUBANS?

— OR THE C.I.A?

"I would never believe that any government would be stupid enough to trust Lee with anything important."
George De Mohrenschildt, Lee Harvey Oswald's best friend in Dallas.

To the Warren Commission the rumour that Oswald had been an intelligence agent was problematic. International problems could follow if the rumours were true. After the assassination, America's leaders feared that the American people would demand retaliation for the murder of their president. The leadership worried that the Cold War would heat up if it was found that the president had been murdered either by Castro's agents or the KGB. If Oswald had been working for the Cubans there would be an outcry from the American people for another invasion of Cuba. If the Russians were responsible for the assassination the world could be on the brink of nuclear war. The leaders of the nation quickly decided that they must convince the country that the president's death was the result of a single madman, not of some vast communist plot. Accordingly the Warren Commission failed to pursue many leads opening up unanswered questions which were immediately obvious to much of the American public. The Warren Commission was not given full information by the F.B.I. and C.I.A. about possible leads suggesting Oswald had not acted alone. Did Oswald work for military intelligence? And if he did what would be the repercussions from this? Was Oswald working for the C.I.A. and if so did the C.I.A. hire Oswald to kill Kennedy? These were the considerations by the new president, Lyndon B. Johnson, when he appointed the Warren Commission to investigate the assassination in December of 1963.

To the Conspiracy Theorists the rumours about the ex-marine and

Marxist's stay in the Soviet Union and his visits to the Cuban and Soviet Embassies in Mexico City, as well as his contacts with anti-Castro Cubans and Mafia-linked characters, real or imagined, were confirmation of conspiracy. Doubt had been planted and denials from the State Department, F.B.I., the Cuban Government and C.I.A. were not believed. The American public were slowly becoming convinced that Oswald was working for a government agency, foreign or domestic.

MILITARY INTELLIGENCE/ C.I.A. LINKED INTELLIGENCE.

Stories that Lee Harvey Oswald was an agent of some sort spread almost from the moment of his capture and it was inevitable considering Oswald's background. Here was a 24 year old ex-marine who defected to the Soviet Union who hinted to Soviet Authorities that he had something valuable to peddle in exchange for the granting of permission to stay in that country.

The story behind these rumours began with Oswald's enlistment in the United States Marine Corps on October 24th 1956, six days after his 17th birthday. After basic training at San Diego and Camp Pendleton, California, Oswald reported to the Naval Air Technical Training Centre in Jacksonville, Florida, for a six week course in the basics of radar control. Advanced instruction followed, and Oswald eventually was given an MOS (military occupational speciality).

Oswald went to Japan, assigned as a radar operator to the First Marine Aircraft Wing, based at Atsugi. Oswald's job was to direct aircraft to their targets by radar, communicating with the pilots by radio. Atsugi was more than an ordinary air station. It was also one of the largest C.I.A. bases in the world.

By the time Oswald was transferred back to the United States to a duty assignment at El Toro Air Station, California, he was reading Russian newspapers and impressing his colleagues with a command of the Russian language. It was this fact that led New Orleans District Attorney, Jim Garrison, to suspect that Oswald was being 'sheep dipped', that is, trained for intelligence work. In his book "On the Trail of The Assassins", he wrote:

" I thought about the Russian examination Oswald had taken at El Toro and began to look into his earlier Marine service for hints of possible intelligence work. By now I knew that Oswald possessed the characteristics the military looks for in it's intelligence recruits."

Jim Marrs in his book 'Crossfire', quotes Gerry Patrick Hemming, who served with Oswald in Japan and was himself recruited by the C.I.A. whilst a Marine. Hemmings claims that Oswald never said he was an agent but Hemmings had a 'hunch' he was. This is the total sum of Marrs' evidence that Oswald was recruited as an intelligence agent.

Another former C.I.A. agent, actually a C.I.A. finance officer, James B. Wilcott, claimed that, while serving in Japan after the assassination, he heard that Oswald had worked for the C.I.A. The House Assassinations Committee found his testimony "Not worthy of belief".

In short, there is no evidence at all that the military considered Oswald's learning Russian suspicious or attempted to recruit him as an intelligence agent. Oswald's superiors considered Oswald peculiar but harmless. The House Assassinations Committee considered the proposition that Oswald was being trained for intelligence work whilst in the marines and found the allegations groundless.

KGB

Shortly after Oswald joined the Marines colleagues were referring to him as Oswaldskovitch. Oswald, in turn, was addressing them as 'comrade'. Oswald was clearly infatuated with the Soviet Union. Some conspiracy theorists claim there was a sea change after his period in the Marine Corps, hinting that Oswald may have been recruited as an intelligence agent for future espionage activities in the Soviet Union. They ignore the fact that Oswald had been attracted to communism since he was a teenage boy and had been acquiring knowledge of Soviet affairs and ideology since that time.

After requesting to leave the Marine Corps Oswald left for the Soviet Union. He arrived in Moscow around the time of his 20th birthday, in October 1959. Shortly thereafter he told his Government guide that he wanted to become a Soviet citizen. Turned down he made a dramatic attempt at suicide. The ploy worked, at least for a while. After being released from the hospital Oswald was transferred to another hotel although his tourist visa had expired. His diary claims he was interviewed by a new set of Soviet officials the same afternoon. They, too, denied Oswald's request to remain in the Soviet Union considering him to be unstable. Eventually he got what he wanted and was allowed to stay, securing employment at a factory in Minsk.

The House Assassinations Committee decided that the Soviets had no part in the President's murder. One of the difficult tasks they faced was to assess the bona fides of KGB defector Yuri Nosenko. The Warren Commission knew about him but did not make his defection public in 1964. Nosenko, who claimed to have been Oswald's case officer, met secretly with the House Assassinations Committee at C.I.A. headquarters in Langley, Virginia. They decided that Nosenko had actually been sent by the KGB to assure the US Government of Soviet innocence in the assassination.

However, as Tom Mangold has made clear in his excellent biography of C.I.A. counter espionage chief, James Jesus Angleton, published in 1991, that assessment by the Committee was wrong. Nosenko was a bona fide defector who was correct when he said there was no Soviet involvement in the assassination and Oswald was not a KGB agent. The details of Mangold's investigation are complex and far too onerous for a book this size— suffice to say that Nosenko's legitimacy is now accepted by most writers on intelligence activities (e.g. Christopher Andrew, Evan Thomas and Peter Grose). Furthermore, Nosenko's credentials were confirmed by a top KGB defector to the U. K., Oleg Gordievskiy, who corroborated Nosenko's story (that Oswald was not recruited by the KGB) after his own defection in the 1980's.

Oswald was never recruited as an agent, Gordievskiy has explained, "Oswald was, of course, known to the KGB, but he was never recruited as an agent. It appears that our people deemed him useless."

Gordievskiy's observations about Oswald's abilities were recognised by Oswald's friend in Dallas, George De Mohrenschild, when he told the Warren Commission:

"I would never believe that any government would be stupid enough to trust Lee with anything important. An unstable individual, mixed-up individual, uneducated individual, without background. What government would give him any confidential work? No government would. Even the government of Ghana would not give him any job of any type.... knowing what kind of brains he had, and what kind of education, I was not interested in listening to him (talking about his Marxist principles) because it was nothing; it was zero."

There is little doubt that Oswald was questioned by representatives of the KGB but this was not unnatural. There is also evidence that Oswald was secretly 'bugged' and followed by security police during his stay in the Soviet Union and fellow factory workers were requested by the KGB to inform on Oswald. However, since the end of the Cold War former KGB agents have revealed the truth behind their interest in Oswald. They initially thought he was a spy and they didn't know what to make of the 'arrogant' 20 year old who offered to tell them everything he had learned in the Marines.

"He had no contacts we were interested in, no information we did not have already," former KGB chief Vladimir Semichastny said in an interview with BBC's 'Timewatch' researchers in 1993. "There were conversations but this was such outdated information. The kind who say the sparrows have already chirped to the entire world and now Oswald tells us about it. Not the kind of information that would interest such a high level organisation like ours. . . . We concluded that he was not working for U.S. Intelligence. His intellectual training and capabilities were such that it would not show the F.B.I. and C.I.A. in a good light if they used people like him."

Oswald soon became disillusioned with the Soviet system which he saw as a perversion of Marxism. He made 2 makeshift grenades-possibly to blackmail the Russians into letting him leave. That wasn't necessary. When Semichastny heard of his request, he said, "Thank God!. . . Let him go."

It is reasonable to assume Semischastny is telling the truth. The Cold War has ended and ex-KGB agents have not been restricted by totalitarian state secrecy acts. It would have been in Semichastny's interest had there been a KGB conspiracy to kill Kennedy as the world rights to his revelations would have netted millions of dollars.

It is extremely unlikely that Kennedy was the victim of a Russian state-sponsored assassination. Kruschev was trying to make peace with Kennedy in 1963, not kill him. The KGB regarded Oswald, as we have seen, as a neurotic nuisance, and was happy to see him go when he re-defected to the United States in 1962.

Moreover, in the rules of the cold war, his character traits were questionable; his life was loose and undisciplined and he stood out from his environment unlike those KGB 'moles' who adapted to American society. Oswald's strange life-style and Russian wife only invited examination by the people and government agencies in every place he lived in the year prior to the assassination. Oswald was not the sort of person spying agencies build intelligence networks around.

One of the most compelling reasons why the KGB did not assassinate President Kennedy was that Kennedy's successor, Lyndon Johnson, was anathema to the Russians. As Johnson was a southerner he was considered to be a racist, anti-Soviet and anti-communist to the core; a reactionary right-winger who was associated in their minds with belligerent and militaristic solutions to the growing Soviet arsenal.

C.I.A. AGENT

The Warren Commission counsel, Lee Rankin was very concerned that Oswald may have been working for American Intelligence during the time he spent in the Soviet Union. The rumour was started by Oswald's mother who was obviously embarrassed and could not come to terms with her son's defection. After the assassination Mark Lane represented Marguerite Oswald and she had repeated the same tales when Oswald defected. Rankin said, "We have a dirty little rumour that is very bad for the Commission, very damaging to the agencies that are involved in it and must be wiped out insofar as it is possible to do so by this commission." The following exchange occurred between one member of the Commission, Hale Boggs, and another, Allen Dulles, former Director of the C.I.A., about C.I.A. practice:

Boggs: "The man who recruited him would know, wouldn't he?"

Dulles: "Yes, but he wouldn't tell."

Boggs: "What you do is. . . make our problem utterly impossible because you say this rumour (about Oswald as an agent of the F.B.I. or C.I.A.) can't be dissipated under the circumstances."

Dulles: "I don't think it can unless you believe Mr. Hoover, and so forth and so on, which probably most of the people will ... I think Mr. Hoover would certainly say he didn't have anything to do with this fellow."

This portion of testimony was to lead to all kinds of speculation that the truth would never be arrived at because the F.B.I. and the C.I.A. would always lie.

However, notwithstanding the fact that Allen Dulles' first allegiance was to the C.I.A. it is unlikely his lack of veracity had anything to do with the assassination. As Peter Grose, states in his recent biography of Dulles:

"(He) sought with the utmost subtlety to neutralise the impulses of his fellow commissioners to pursue lines of enquiry that might expose C.I.A. operations, even though they had nothing to do with the Dallas shooting."

The C.I.A. withholding of files from the Warren Commission and House Assassinations Committee was to possibly save themselves from embarrassment. After Oswald's return from the Soviet Union it is possible he was entered on a C.I.A. 'Watch List' involving illegal mail openings and surveillance. They may also have been aware that he possibly offered to kill Kennedy when he visited the Cuban and Soviet embassies in Mexico City in September of 1963. Accordingly, bureaucratic bungling may have prevented the Secret Service from being alerted when the President's trip to Texas was organised. In this scenario the C.I.A. became culpable, to a certain extent, and their fears may have led to a 'cover-up'.

These bureaucratic positions could do nothing but feed conspiracy ideas that the agencies were hiding incriminating evidence of C.I.A. involvement in the assassination. . The bureaucratic urge to protect sources and methods forced intelligence agencies to ask that not everything be released. In this sense there was a cover-up. The Warren Commission conclusions were sound but their manner of investigating all possible leads was, at the very least, inadequate. As Arthur Schlesinger put it:

"The Chief Justice and his colleagues had perforce to depend greatly on the intelligence agencies. They did not know that the agencies had their own secret reasons to fear a thorough inquiry. If it came out that the putative killer might have had intelligence connections, domestic or foreign, that F.B.I. agents should have had him under close surveillance, that C.I.A. assassins might have provoked him to the terrible deed, the agencies would be in the deepest trouble."

In the aftermath of the assassination, then, top officials were more concerned with safeguarding their own agendas than they were in discovering all the facts relevant to the investigation. The attitude towards secrecy was different 30 years ago. At the C.I.A. 'plausible deniability' was the game. Agents, operating with almost limitless funds were allowed to do as they pleased as long as their bosses were free to deny it. The top men at the F.B.I. and C.I.A. had worried that their operations would be publicised through the Kennedy assassination investigation.

During the 50's and 60's the F.B.I. and it's Director J. Edgar Hoover frequently violated the rights of American citizens with illegal wire-taps and break-ins, while the C.I.A. was earnestly enlisting the help of the Mafia to eliminate Fidel Castro.

At the time of the assassination relations between President Kennedy and Castro, were at an all time low. Because of the threat to American interests the Kennedy brothers inundated the C.I.A. with demands for containing or removing Castro. There were 2 possible solutions- the assassination of Castro by a hired killer or his removal by a Cuban uprising, initiated and supported by an invasion of the island by anti-communist Cuban emigres, most of whom were living in the Miami and New Orleans districts.

The C.I.A. set about hiring the Mafia to organise the murder of Castro. Claiming they were representing a group of businessmen who wanted to see Cuba liberated they approached Mafia member Johnny Rosselli, who in turn secured the support of Chicago Mafia Boss Sam Giancana and Florida Mafia Boss Santos Trafficante.

But plans to kill Castro came to nothing and the C.I.A. decided to concentrate on it's second plan to assist in the invasion of Cuba. The 'Bay of Pigs' invasion ended in failure. The C.I.A. was blamed for the disaster and it's chief Allen Dulles was forced to resign along with Richard Bissel, his deputy.

Immediately afterwards President Kennedy ordered the C.I.A. to organise a more determined and highly secret operation to overthrow Castro, it was given the code name 'Operation Mongoose'. Hundreds of C.I.A. agents and contract agents were assigned to the task. It was overseen by Robert Kennedy.

Robert Kennedy's biographer, Arthur Schlesinger Jnr. argues that Robert Kennedy was innocent of trying to kill Castro—that the murder plots were initiated by the C.I.A. during the Eisenhower administration and continued after JFK took office in January 1961. In 1967 when stories of the murder plots began to emerge in the press Robert Kennedy angrily told his aides:

"I didn't start it. I stopped it.... I found out that some people were going to try an attempt on Castro's life and I turned it off."

In February 1963 the C.I.A. terminated its contract with Rosselli and began negotiations with Rolando Cubela, a Cuban Minister and friend of Castro. He was given the code name 'Amlash'. On the very day that President Kennedy was killed a C.I.A. agent handed him a specially designed ballpoint pen that could inject it's user with a lethal poison.

However, there is no credible evidence the plots had anything to do with trying to kill JFK, contrary to the claims of some Conspiracy Theorists who say that a "secret cabal" of renegade C.I.A. agents, the F.B.I., Mafia and anti-Castro Cubans hired Oswald to kill Kennedy or set him up to take the fall. There is no corroborated or credible evidence to support the theory that Kennedy was killed as revenge for 'betrayal' in the Bay of Pigs fiasco when the president refused to give air support for the invasion, allowing hundreds of anti-Castro Cubans to be either captured or killed. Apart from non-corroborated hearsay and 'confessions' by individuals with less than stable backgrounds, there is no corroborated evidence which proves they did commit the murder of the President. A number of anti-Castro Cubans, like Antonio Veciana, have stated that they saw Oswald with C.I.A. agents but their stories were investigated by the House Assassinations Committee and were found to be without credence.

Possible C.I.A. involvement in the Kennedy assassination had first been investigated, on a government level in 1975, before the HSCA was set up. The Rockefeller Commission, named after the commission's chairman, then Vice-President Nelson Rockefeller, dismissed theories that the C.I.A. was somehow involved in the assassination. The report rejected as 'far-fetched' speculation the claim that the agency had connections with either assassin Lee Harvey Oswald or Jack Ruby. Similarly the commission dismantled the theory that former C.I.A. agents E. Howard Hunt and Frank Sturgis, both of 'Watergate' fame, had participated in the assassination. As evidence, proponents of the C.I.A. theory cited photographs of the '3 tramps' which were discussed in an earlier chapter. At the commission's request, F.B.I. photoanalyst Lyndal Shaneyfeldt studied the photographs and determined that they were not of Hunt or Sturgis. Moreover the panel found no evidence the two men were in Dallas that day. Nor could the commission find any evidence that Hunt and Sturgis had known each other before 1971. One unidentified witness said that Sturgis, born Frank Fiorini, had taken his name from the fictional character Hank Sturgis in Hunt's 1949 novel 'Bimini Run'. But the commission found court records that Sturgis had changed his name in 1952 at the request of his mother, who had divorced his father and married a man named Ralph Sturgis. Thus the web of associations continue in conspiracy thinking.

Although the Rockefeller Commission could not assess all the monumental Kennedy assassination records and evidence, the panel agreed that Oswald had acted alone and had no assistance from the C.I.A.

Conspiracy Theorists show little understanding of the C.I.A. as an institution and the motivating factors that agents embrace. They see C.I.A. personnel as shadowy figures who are out of control and frequently ignore the instituted chain of command within the Agency. To Conspiracy Theorists C.I.A. agents are not dedicated and professional men and women but untrustworthy 'spooks'.

Evan Thomas, who interviewed more than 66 former C.I.A. agents for his book "The Very Best Men" wrote that far from the popular notion that C.I.A. agents were reactionary and sinister, they were in fact, in the 1950's and 1960's, very liberal in their views:

"(Men like Frank Wisner, Richard Bissell, Tracy Barnes and Desmond Fitzgerald were) Patriotic, decent, well-meaning, and brave. . . they were also uniquely suited to the grubby, necessarily devious world of intelligence. 'They were innocents', said John Bruce Lockhart, a senior official in the British S.I.S. who knew the four men from his service as. . . liaison to the C.I.A. in the 1950's and as chief of operations in Europe, the Middle East and Africa. By "innocent", Lockhart meant incapable of wickedness and naive about the difficulties and risks of what he called "a life in secrets."

William Colby was also a dedicated professional. He was a brave OSS officer during the second world war and later transferred to the newly created C.I.A. after it was instituted in 1947. In the 1970's he was appointed head of the Agency. Colby was a practising Catholic whose probity and moral perspective is unquestioned. He dealt with the rumours of C.I.A. involvement in the assassination of President Kennedy in his memoirs published in 1978:

"I ... had no inkling then (November 22nd 1963) of the impact it (the assassination) would have on the C.I.A., forcing it to defend itself against paranoid conspiracy theories that it had a role in the assassination. The intense investigations of later years showed that it had no such role, and I am satisfied from my own knowledge of the C.I.A. and it's dedicated American officers that no such activity took place or was even possible. And as for the allegation that C.I.A.'s actions against Castro stimulated the Cuban dictator to retaliate in this fashion, I have never seen anything but the most far-fetched circumstantial reasoning that could support such a theory. The fact of the matter is that the C.I.A. could not have had a better friend in a President than John F. Kennedy, he understood the Agency and used it effectively, exploiting it's intellectual abilities to help him analyse a complex world and it's paramilitary and covert political talents to react to it in a low key."

Conspiracy Theorists will no doubt respond with - 'Well, he would say that, wouldn't he?'. But I find Colby's statement believable precisely because he wrote his memoirs after leaving office and his professional reputation is firmly established within the United States. Furthermore it was William Colby who insisted on the release of all information about the Castro assassination attempts to the U.S. Congress further enhancing his integrity. Indeed, he was severely criticised by many of his C.I.A. colleagues for releasing the information.

After his brother's death in Dallas, Attorney General Robert Kennedy confided his suspicions of C.I.A. involvement to a family friend, C.I.A. Director John McCone. Robert Kennedy said later, "You know, at the time I asked McCone ... if they had killed my brother, AND I ASKED HIM IN A WAY THAT HE COULDN'T LIE TO ME, AND THEY HADN'T."

Evan Thomas, an expert on C.I.A. activities and an accredited historian, wrote:

"The many conspiracy theories notwithstanding, there is no evidence that the C.I.A. itself somehow became sucked into a plot to kill JFK."

After the movie 'JFK' was shown in 1991 there was an outcry for the release of C.I.A. files on the assassination. John Newman, who researched the files after they were released under the 1992 JFK Records Act, wrote in his book 'Oswald and the C.I.A.':

" ... we have yet to find documentary evidence for an institutional plot in the C.I.A. to murder the president. The facts do not compel such a conclusion. If there had been such a plot, many of the documents we are reading - such as C.I.A. cables to Mexico City, the F.B.I., State (Department), and Navy - would never have been created."

But Newman did find reasons why the C.I.A. were not as forthcoming as they should have been. After researching released C.I.A. files after passage of the 1992 JFK Records Act, Newman believes that the C.I.A. erred in not opening a '201' file when Oswald offered to give the Russians radar secrets when he 'defected'. Oswald's C.I.A. file, he believes, is linked to the betrayal of the U2 spyplane by a C.I.A. 'mole' and the handling of Oswald's file was part of an operation to hunt out the 'mole'. This may explain the anomalies arriving out of the C.I.A.'s unwillingness to present their files to the Warren Commission and the House Assassinations Committee. Furthermore both the C.I.A. and the F.B.I. were engaged in illegal operations against the 'Fair Play For Cuba Committee' seeking to discredit the FPCC in a 'foreign country' at the time of Oswald's visit to

Mexico City. The C.I.A. may also have known that Valeriy Kostikov, a Soviet official with whom Oswald spoke during his Mexico City visit, worked for the KGB assassinations department. Such revelations would have severely embarrassed the C.I.A. exposing their incompetence and ineptitude. And, as stated earlier, the C.I.A. may also have known of a possible threat to kill Kennedy during his visit to the Cuban embassy and did not pass the information on to the F.B.I. and Secret Service. If all this is true it would have been a 'nightmare' at the C.I.A. headquarters in Langley, Virginia, in the days and weeks following the assassination.

ANTI-CASTRO AGENT

Oswald's whole life had been dedicated to Marxist principles and he became enamoured with the Cuban revolution even during his time in the Marine Corps. Yet there were some curious activities during Oswald's stay in New Orleans in the summer of 63 which would suggest he was playing the role of an anti-Castro agent. During this period he was actively promoting his own chapter of the Fair Play for Cuba Committee on the streets of New Orleans. On one occasion he was known to attempt to infiltrate an anti-Castro group and visited one of it's leading members who had a store in New Orleans. His name was Carlos Bringuier. Bringuier talked to Oswald who offered to pass on his military experience to Bringuier's group. Later Bringuier saw him passing out Pro-Castro literature on the streets and confronted Oswald which led to an altercation. A number of people were arrested and Oswald eventually paid a fine. So far the story is straightforward- it is likely Oswald had been trying to build up his credentials as a dedicated supporter of Castro and it is also feasible to assume he was to use the publicity that was created to impress the Cuban authorities when the time came for him to fulfil his fantasy of joining the Cuban revolution.

Yet someone who had important connections to anti-Castro groups in New Orleans, Miami and Dallas came forward to say that Oswald had visited her and offered to shoot Kennedy in retaliation for his betrayal of anti-Castro Cubans at the 'Bay of Pigs'. It seemed to be the most compelling piece of evidence linking Oswald to anti-Castro Cubans. The woman who was 'visited' by Oswald was Sylvia Odio, a member of the Cuban Revolutionary Junta, or JURE, an organisation which had a lot of credibility with Cuban emigres, and her story has been used by just about every

Conspiracy Theorist. She told the House Assassinations Committee, after they had called her to testify before its hearings, that she had been visited, in late September 1963, by 3 men who asked for help in preparing a fundraising letter for JURE. The House Assassinations Committee tells us Mrs. Odio stated that 'two of the men appeared to be Cubans', although they also had characteristics that she associated with Mexicans. The two individuals, she remembered, indicated that their 'war' names were 'Leopoldo' and 'Angelo'. The third man was an American called 'Leon Oswald', and she was told he was very much interested in the anti-Castro cause.

The House Assassinations Committee reported:

"Mrs. Odio stated that the men told her that they had just come from New Orleans and that they were about to leave on a trip. The next day, one of the Cubans called her on the telephone and told her that it had been his idea to introduce the American into the underground 'because he is great, he is kind of nuts'. The Cubans also said that the American had been in the Marine Corps and was an excellent shot, and that the American had said that Cubans 'don't have any guts because President Kennedy should have been assassinated after the 'Bay of Pigs', and some Cubans should have done that, because he was the one that was holding the freedom of Cuba actually'. Mrs Odio claimed the American was Lee Harvey Oswald. Mrs. Odio's sister, who was in the apartment at the time of the visit by the 3 men and who stated that she saw them briefly in the hallway when answering the door, also believed that the American was Lee Harvey Oswald."

The Warren Commission did not believe Sylvia Odio or her sister, claiming that Oswald was on his way to Mexico City by bus when the incident was alleged to occur:

"During the course of it's investigation. . . the Commission concluded that Oswald could not have been in Dallas on the evening of either September 26 or 27, 1963. It also developed considerable evidence that he was not in Dallas at any time between the beginning of September and October 3, 1963. On April 24, Oswald left Dallas for New Orleans, where he lived until his trip to Mexico City in late September and his subsequent return to Dallas. Oswald is known to have been in New Orleans as late as September 23, 1963, the date on which Mrs. Paine and Marina Oswald left New Orleans for Dallas. Sometime between 4pm on September 24 and 1pm on September 25, Oswald cashed an unemployment compensation check at a store in New Orleans; under normal procedures this check would not have reached Oswald's postal box in New Orleans until at least 5am on September 25. The store at which he cashed the check did not open until 8am Therefore, it appeared that Oswald's presence in New Orleans until sometime between 8am and 1pm on September 25 was quite firmly established ... In spite of the fact that it appeared almost certain that Oswald could not have been in Dallas at the time Mrs. Odio thought he was, the Commission requested the F.B.I. to conduct further investigation to determine the validity of Mrs. Odio's testimony. The Commission considered the problems raised by that testimony as important in view of the possibility it raised that Oswald may have had companions on his trip to Mexico. The Commission specifically requested the F.B.I. to attempt to locate and identify the two men who Mrs. Odio stated were with the man she thought was Oswald. In an effort to do that the F.B.I. located and interviewed Manual Ray, a leader of JURE who confirmed that Mrs. Odio's parents were political prisoners in Cuba, but insisted that he did not know anything about the alleged Oswald visit. The same was true of Rogelio Cisneros, a former anti-Castro leader from Miami who had visited Mrs. Odio in June of 1962 in connection with certain anti-Castro activities. Additional investigation was conducted in Dallas and in other cities in search of the visitors to Mrs. Odio's apartment."

Sylvia Odio was re-interviewed by the House Assassinations Committee in the late 1970's. Her story helped to convince the Committee that there was a conspiracy to assassinate President Kennedy and found her to be a credible witness when she appeared before them at their hearings in Washington. An investigator Gaeton Fonzi called her story "convincing". Anthony Summers in his bestselling book "Conspiracy" said it was "The strongest human evidence of a conspiracy". Sylvia Meagher, another Conspiracy Theorist, called it, "The proof of the plot."

F.B.I. Agent James Hosty believes that his fellow agent Wally Heitman discovered the true identity of one of the trio. Heitman maintained that he was Loran Hall, a half-Indian who frequently passed as hispanic. The other two men were Larry Howard and William Seymour and together with Hall visited Odio's home to collect money for a JURE rival group Alpha 66. Hall had described Seymour as an ex-Marine who frequently 'popped off' about President Kennedy. However, in the 1970's Hall retracted his statement that he and his companions were the men who visited Odio. He refused to testify regarding what he told the F.B.I. back in 1964 about visiting Odio's home. This was entirely understandable as Hall had committed a grave mistake - identifying another member of this underground terrorist group and saying that Seymour had 'popped off' about Kennedy which led to drastic reductions in donations to the movement after the assassination.

Sylvia Odio and her sister came to Dallas after the Castro Revolution in Cuba. Her parents had been imprisoned in Cuba for opposing Castro. This incident and the fact that her husband had abandoned her predisposed Sylvia to a mental illness and she frequently suffered 'fainting spells'. She underwent treatment by a psychiatrist.

Odio was still active in the anti-Castro underground, however, and was in contact with the leaders of JURE. She was also active in negotiating arms deals for the organisation.

The true story behind the 'Odio affair', according to Ray and Mary LaFontaine, is that it was made up. Even though I disagree with the Fontaines overall conspiracy thesis I believe their explanations for this curious event are sound and they convincingly demonstrate Odio did it as a ploy to help her anti-Castro friends avoid blame for the assassination. As the LaFontaines describe it Oswald may very well have visited her in Dallas when she held her meetings for the emigre anti-Castro community and Oswald may have joined them at such a meeting proclaiming that the detested Kennedy, who betrayed the anti-Castro Cubans, should be killed when he visited Dallas the next month. This was Oswald's way of acting as a daring agent provocateur as he did in New Orleans the previous summer. This meeting was more likely to have occurred in October when Oswald had returned from his Mexico trip. Continuing, then, his one-man 'revolutionary' infiltration operations and claiming that Kennedy should be killed Odio became fearful after the assassination. She suspected that the president's murder would be blamed on anti-Castro Cubans in Dallas. She had to invent an official story declaring herself innocent and by extension her emigre friends because she believed the story of Oswald's non-conspiratorial visit had leaked out after the assassination.

She chose to put the Oswald connection in the context of a hallway meeting that occurred in June with three men named Rodriguez, Cisneros and Martin. She then 'persuaded' her sister Annie that the meeting took place with Oswald and two others. Apparently Odio had tripped herself up when she admitted to a Catholic priest that one of the names of the sinister group was a man called "CISNEROS".

F.B.I.

Many Conspiracy Theorists state flatly that Oswald was an informant or agent for the F.B.I.. They offer no concrete proof and the F.B.I. assassination files, as examined by the House Assassinations Committee, show no such link. The supposition that Oswald was an agent or informant stems from 2 connections Oswald had with the F.B.I.-surveillance of the pro-Castro, ex-defector, by the Dallas office of the F.B.I. and an interview with F.B.I. agents in New Orleans that Oswald requested.

The question of whether or not Oswald was an F.B.I. informant has plagued the Bureau ever since the assassination. If Oswald had been an informant the possibility of his manipulation by a government agency would lend credence to conspiracy theories.

Robert Groden quotes supposed former C.I.A. and F.B.I. agent Harry Dean as alleging that:

"... the agency is not going to send an agent to talk to an individual who has been thrown into jail for simply disturbing the peace. The F.B.I. knew that Oswald was an agent..."

Less sinister motives, however, can be gleaned from the New Orleans incident. It was likely Oswald knew sooner or later the New Orleans office of the F.B.I. would learn about his FPCC activities. He had previously lost a number of jobs because, he believed, the F.B.I. informed the employers that Oswald was a pro-Soviet ex-defector. Contacting the F.B.I. to explain his activities could, in a way, pre-empt any investigation of his activities which would involve questions asked at his place of work. Furthermore, no undercover agent would 'blow' his cover by summoning an agent to a police station. It was also F.B.I. procedure to grant interviews to anyone who requested one.

Conspiracy Theorists also use the fact that Oswald had F.B.I. agent, James Hosty's telephone number in his address book - proof, they say, that Oswald was an informant. Oswald obtained Hosty's number from his wife, Marina whom Hosty had visited when she lived with the Paines. Oswald was living in Dallas at the time and Hosty did not interview him. It was natural for the F.B.I. to 'track' any former defector to the Soviet Union and this fact is not suspicious contrary to Conspiracy Theorists' claims.

Hosty was asked directly by CNN reporter Larry Woods, in 1993, if Oswald had been an F.B.I. informant. He replied:

"Never. Jack Ruby was for a short period of time and that's where the confusion came about. The reporters who wrote that story about Oswald being an informant have now admitted that article was a hoax."

Conspiracy Theorists have questioned the veracity of the F.B.I. and the truthfulness of Agent Hosty ever since the Warren Report was released. Hosty had been told, in the spring of 1963 to investigate Oswald, a former defector to the Soviet Union, as a potential security risk. But he was not allowed to confront Oswald with the fact that later that year Oswald had been secretly filmed by C.I.A. cameras outside the Soviet and Cuban embassies in Mexico City. Letting Oswald know what the C.I.A. and F.B.I. knew about his Mexico trip might reveal that the American government was bugging an embassy thus causing a scandal. It is not unusual for agencies to protect their sources rather than prevent a crime. But in this instance Hosty had no way of knowing what Oswald was up to so he questioned his wife Marina about Oswald's whereabouts.

When Oswald heard about Hosty's visit he delivered a note to Hosty, care of the Dallas F.B.I. office, warning him to stop harassing his wife. The note has been a prized item for Conspiracy Theorists. F.B.I. receptionist Nanny Lee Fenner managed to read the note and she said it contained threats of violence. The note was later destroyed as J. Edgar Hoover was worried that it may have been construed as F.B.I. ineptitude in not keeping track of an obviously unstable individual during the period of the President's visit to Dallas. Conspiracy Theorists claimed that the note may have indicated a deeper relationship between Oswald and the F.B.I. or a threat to the president.

Agent Hosty remained silent on the issue but broke his self-imposed silence to CNN reporters in 1993:

" (The note).... was a complaint, not a threat ... it dealt with the fact that I had interviewed his wife without his permission and something about 'come talk to me directly... I'll report you for this'... At the time the note was unsigned and I wasn't sure who it was from. (I only knew it was Oswald) when I interviewed him at the police station (after the assassination)."

If Oswald had worked for the F.B.I., why was he constantly suffering a shortage of finances? One New Orleans landlady has said that Oswald used to go up and down the street placing his garbage in neighbour's bins.

He took a bus to Mexico and he looked for the cheapest accommodation in whatever place he was living.

The two people who have seen all the F.B.I. and C.I.A. files relating to the assassination state there is no 'smoking gun' that can come to light regarding unreleased files. House Assassinations Committee Head Counsel Professor Robert Blakey and Warren Commission Counsel David Belin deny the files contain any information that would incriminate the F.B.I. (or, indeed, elements of the C.I.A.). They both say there is no information which would prove 'conspiracy'.

CASTRO AGENT

Fidel Castro played an important role in the life of Lee Harvey Oswald and Castro's revolution became, for Oswald, the most important event of his times.

Castro was born on August 13th 1926 in the rural eastern part of Cuba. In 1952 he ran for parliament but Cuba's ruler Batista cancelled the elections. Thereafter Castro made it his life's aim to rid Cuba of the corrupt dictator.

With a small band of men Castro made his first assault on Batista's regime by attacking the Moncada Barracks. The attack was a disaster, half his men were caught, tortured and killed and Castro was put on trial. Sentenced to 15 years in prison Castro was released after 22 months, fled to Mexico and began reorganising his guerrilla fighters.

On December 2nd, 1956 Castro and 82 men sailed to Cuba on a yacht named the 'Granma'. Batista's soldiers were waiting in ambush. Only 12 men, including Castro escaped to the Sirra Maestra mountains where he began his guerrilla campaign which resulted in victory in 1959. With a triumphal march into the capital, Havana, Castro proclaimed his revolution successful.

Castro became 'Jeffe Maximo', the maximum leader, and set about reconstructing Cuban society along socialist lines. He instituted a massive welfare state for the Cuban people and nationalised the sugar industry, seizing millions of dollars of U.S. property. He also set about ridding the island of U.S. Mafia corruption represented by the large gambling casinos and bordellos, robbing the crime syndicates of their lucrative takings.

Gradually, within 2 years, Castro came to believe, not without reason, that the United States was unable to accommodate his radical socialistic efforts and so he looked to the Soviet Union for economic assistance. The

United States isolated Cuba by cutting off the sugar markets and oil supplies and enlisted the C.I.A. to train Cuban exiles for an invasion of the island. This resulted in the ill-fated 'Bay of Pigs' invasion. The C.I.A. continued to organise anti-Castro groups after the disaster and financed hundreds of covert operations against Cuba, (Code name 'JM/WAVE', later 'Operation Mongoose') The Kennedy Administration eventually became so frustrated with the C.I.A.'s poor results that the Kennedy brothers badgered the C.I.A.'s leadership to get rid of Castro at all costs.

Castro was naturally embittered by the many Cuban exile attempts on his life and in September 1963 he stated to Associated Press reporter Daniel Harker a warning to the United States against "aiding terrorist plans to eliminate Cuban leaders." Castro stated, according to Harker, that U.S. leaders would be in danger if they promoted any attempt to eliminate the leaders of Cuba.

However there is strong evidence that Castro was, at the same time, trying to bring about an accommodation with Kennedy. As Robert E. Quirk, in his masterly biography of Castro, put it:

"Kennedy has the opportunity, said Castro, to become the greatest president in the history of the United States, a leader who could, at last, understand that there could be co-existence between capitalists and socialists, 'even in the Americas'. He was someone you could talk with. Castro refused to retract his criticisms of the past. But Kennedy had learned a lot in recent months, and the Cubans could live with him. 'In the last analysis, I'm convinced that anyone else could be worse'. Flashing 'a broad and boyish grin', Castro added: 'If you see him again, tell him that I'm willing to declare Goldwater my friend if that will guarantee his re-election'. Would Jean Daniel, (foreign editor of 'L'Express') serve as his 'emissary of peace'? As a revolutionary, Castro said, the present situation did not displease him. 'But as a man and as a statesman, it is my duty to indicate what a basis for understanding could be.' Castro added that he had found 'positive elements' in what the Frenchman reported about Kennedy. He asked Daniel to stay a few days longer so they could continue their discussions."

Castro was having lunch with Daniel when the news came that Kennedy had been shot. According to Daniel, Castro had been saying good things about Kennedy. Then a phone call came. As Robert E. Quirk wrote:

"As Castro put the receiver to his ear, his face clouded over. 'Wounded?'

His voice seemed strained. He paused. 'Very seriously?' He listened intently, then returned to the table and sat down. 'It's bad news', he said. 'The American president had been shot in Dallas'. He speculated: 'Who could have done it? Perhaps it was the work of a madman? Or a Vietnamese? A member of the KU Klux Klan?' Vallejo (Castro's assistant) tuned the radio to the NBC station in Miami, and they listened in troubled silence to a series of bulletins on the stricken Kennedy's condition. Then came the report that the president had died. Castro stood up. 'Well,' he said, 'there is the end of your mission of peace. Everything is changed'. He thought the assassination could affect the lives of millions in every part of the world. And especially the lives of Cubans. As he invariably did when he was agitated, he paced the floor. 'I'll tell you one thing', he said. 'At least Kennedy was an enemy to whom we had become accustomed. This is a serious matter, a very serious matter'. He reminded Daniel that in the Sirra Maestra he had always opposed assassinations, even of Batistianos."

When news came that Lee Harvey Oswald had been arrested for the crime Castro's suspicions that the assassination would be blamed on Cuba came true. Oswald's connections to Cuba were prominently spread throughout the American press.

"(Oswald never had) 'any contacts with us' Castro contended. 'We never in our life heard of him'."

When Oswald's activities in support of Fidel Castro were first known there was a fear that Oswald may have been hired by Castro to kill Kennedy. Those who knew of the assassination attempts against Castro by the C.I.A./Mafia were afraid that the assassination may have been an act of retaliation.

But the American government knew otherwise. The National Security Agency, which intercepts communications, pulled out all stops to decipher intercepts of conversation, cable traffic, radio and telephone communications at the highest levels of the Soviet and Cuban governments. Together with information from human sources, the intercepts clearly show that both Soviet and Cuban leaders were ignorant of the assassination and were fearful of receiving blame.

When Rolando Cubela's meeting with the C.I.A. was revealed by the Senate Intelligence Committee (otherwise known as the Church Committee after Senator Frank Church, the chairman) in 1975, some Conspiracy

Theorists speculated that Cubela was a double agent who was 'turned' by Castro to kill Kennedy. However, by then, Cubela had been arrested by Cuban Counterintelligence and was imprisoned. Were he a double agent he would have been unlikely to be sentenced, as Cubela was, to death.

In 1978 Fidel Castro was asked to testify before the House Assassinations Committee, in Havana. He said it would have been 'tremendous insanity' for him to have ordered Kennedy's assassination. He noted that murdering Kennedy brought to office a man (President Johnson) who would have been expected to be tougher toward Cuba. Richard Helms, Deputy C.I.A. Director, commented, "We would have bombed Cuba back into the middle ages."

There is, however, the possibility that Castro had known of Oswald's intent to kill Kennedy when Oswald visited the Cuban Embassy in Mexico City in September 1963. Castro may have been told it was the rantings of a lunatic and because of the adversarial relationship between the U.S. and Cuba the Cuban leader did not pass on the information. Castro gave a speech on November 27th 1963 and mentioned Oswald making a 'provocative statement' when he visited the Cuban Embassy. And there may have been tacit encouragement of Oswald by Castro's agents in Mexico City. Strong evidence, only released in the 1990's, shows that Oswald offered to kill Kennedy for the Cubans when he visited their Embassy. Such a scenario would have Kennedy shot in Dallas and Oswald fleeing to Mexico where he would have received safe haven by the Cubans and immediate departure for Cuba. Credible witnesses have said that Oswald met with not only KGB agents but with Castro agents as well (specifically Cuban Intelligence agents Luisa Calderon, Manuel Vega y Perez and Rogelio Rodriguez y Perez) but they may not have taken him seriously. If they had we would not have seen a virtually penniless Oswald trying to make ends meet in the 2 months prior to the assassination. Whilst this evidence does not necessarily prove that Oswald was hired by Russia or Cuba it is tantalising in that it suggests that Oswald may have offered to kill Kennedy as a way of proving his worth to them but the Soviets and Cubans adopted a 'wait and see' position. There is no evidence that Cuban or Soviet agents were directly involved in the assassination.

A more compelling scenario is that Oswald read about Castro's threat to retaliate against C.I.A. attempts to kill him. Oswald saw this as an opportune moment to fulfil his revolutionary fantasies by taking unilateral action. An article with Castro's statement was prominently displayed in the New Orleans Times-Picayune on a day when Oswald was in the city and Oswald was an avid reader of newspapers. In his deluded state, he might have thought that killing Kennedy was one way to win Castro's appreciation.

How, then, can we be certain that Oswald was not working for American intelligence (C.I.A./F.B.I.) or a similar government agency? I believe we must depend upon the logical conclusion that, in order to be plausible, a theory must fit the available evidence into a reasonable chronology of events. Oswald was creating his own role of agent provocateur to further his own agenda in supporting the Cuban revolution. In attempting to assassinate right-winger General Walker (evidence for this is both circumstantial and the evidence presented by his wife, Marina) Oswald was willing to risk his life to fulfil his political ideals. Most Conspiracy Theorists reject the theory that Oswald was working for the KGB or Castro. The consensus of opinion is directed towards either the Mafia or elements of the C.I.A. working in conjunction with anti-Castro exile groups. They argue that Oswald was merely posing as a left-winger. In order to accept this hypotheses we must accept the idea that from the age of 16 or younger Oswald's beliefs were a fraud and he was merely posing as a left-winger and that all of his actions and political statements to his American and Russian friends, his acquaintances, his brothers, mother and wife were bogus. Conspiracy Theorists cannot overcome this hurdle no matter how hard they try.

CHAPTER 7

MAFIA ASSASSIN

"Organised crime is a society that seeks to operate outside the control of the American people and their governments. It involves thousands of criminals, working within structures as complex as those of legitimate governments. It's actions are not impulsive but rather the result of intricate conspiracies, carried on over many years and aimed at gaining control over whole fields of activity in order to amass huge profits.

The core of organised crime activity is the supply of illegal goods and services - gambling, loansharking, narcotics and other forms of vice - to countless numbers of citizen customers. But organised crime is also extensively involved in legitimate business and in labour unions. Here it employs illegitimate methods- monopolisation, terrorism, extortion, tax evasion- to drive out or control lawful ownership and leadership to exact illegal profits from the public. And to carry on it's many activities secure from governmental interference, organised crime corrupts public officials."

Task Force Report on Organised Crime, 1967.

If the idea that Oswald was working for an intelligence agency did not persuade Warren Commission and House Assassinations Committee investigators there were, at least, intriguing hints at Mafia involvement in the assassination of President Kennedy. In 1979 the House Assassinations Committee gave the Mafia theory a boost with it's conclusion that Kennedy's death was probably the result of a conspiracy and that Mafia leaders had the 'means, motive and opportunity to kill the president'. Part of the Committee's findings were based on the acoustics evidence that has now been challenged and, I believe, disproven (see Chapter 3). The motive was probably to get Bobby Kennedy off the backs of the Mafia leaders and their ally Teamsters Union President, Jimmy Hoffa. The House Assassinations Committee Chief Counsel Robert Blakey followed up with a book 'The Plot to Kill the President' blaming the Mafia for President Kennedy's assassination.

The House Committee, in its special volume on organised crime, relates that:

"Up to the 1960's the ... groups of organised crime were in an enviable position. They had an organisation that few believed existed and about which little was known. Its leaders - and hence the organisation itself - were protected by low-level members who actually performed the criminal acts many of which federal and other agencies considered to be beyond their purview or legislative mandate. At best, organised crime was assigned a low priority of state and local levels of law enforcement, and even this was easily nullified by corruption and politics. At the Federal level, even where there was concern, effective action was hampered by inadequate enabling legislation."

"The only major national investigation to be conducted during the period from prohibition until the late 1950's was that of the Senate Select Committee to Investigate Organised Crime in Interstate Commerce chaired by Senator Estes Kefauver. The Committee held its hearings in major cities across the country. It built up a substantial body of knowledge that indicated that there was a national and highly successful syndicate known as the Mafia, involved in a wide range of criminal activities throughout the United States and abroad. Violence was a key to its success, as was corruption, and it was completely ruthless. As a result of the Committee's findings Congress passed some gambling legislation similar investigations were precipitated at the State and local levels and in 1954 the Federal Government took further action by setting up the organised crime and Racketeering Section in the Department of Justice. Its main function was to co-ordinate the effort against organised crime, but it found little co-operation from other agencies."

In the Kennedy Administration the attitude of agencies towards the Mafia changed: As the House Assassinations Committee stated:

"The zeal of the Kennedy brothers signified the roughest period for organised crime in Department of Justice history. . . The Attorney General (Robert Kennedy) focused on targets he had become acquainted with as counsel for the Rackets Committee. He was particularly concerned about the alliance of the top labour leaders and racketeers as personified by Teamster President James R. Hoffa." Accordingly the pursuit of Hoffa was an aspect of the war against organised crime.

The House Assassinations Committee organised crime volume went on to state: "Santos Trafficantes gambling operations in Florida were in trouble. . . Sam Giancana's concern could be readily understood. For some time he had been the subject of intense coverage by the F.B.I. By the spring of 1963 it had become "bumper to bumper", almost 24 hours per day - while driving, on the golf course, in restaurants, wherever he was ... As a consequence, Giancana was staying away from his home base in Chicago to a significant degree, and it was creating problems. Later in July, on two weekends Sam Giancana and Phyllis McGuire, the singer, were together at the Cal-Neva Lodge on Lake Tahoe, Nevada. One of these weekends Frank Sinatra, who owned 50 percent of the Lodge was with them ... Later that month, the F.B.I. learned of rumbling in the higher echelons of organised crime in Chicago over Giancana's absenteeism and bad publicity."

Other La Cosa Nostra leaders were experiencing difficulties... including Carlos Marcello. The House Assassinations Committee stated:

"The F.B.I. determined in the 1960's that because of Marcello's position as head of the New Orleans Mafia family (the oldest in the U. S., having first entered the country in the 1880's) the Louisiana organised crime leader had been endowed with special powers and privileges not accorded to any other La Cosa Nostra leaders. As the leader of the 'first family' of the Mafia in America, according to F.B.I. information, Marcello has been the recipient of the extraordinary privilege of conducting syndicate operations without having to seek the approval of the national commission."

After Marcello appeared as a witness before the Kefauver Committee in the 1950's Senators were astonished that he had not been deported as an illegal alien. When Robert Kennedy became Attorney-General in 1961 he deported Marcello but Marcello re-entered the United States surreptitiously shortly afterwards.

In all, 116 indictments were handed out between 1960 and 1964 against Mafia members throughout the United States. It was this volatile climate of hostility that persuaded many that the Mafia was behind the assassination of President Kennedy. They had the motive, the means and the will to carry out the crime.

The F.B.I.'s investigation of an organised crime connection in the assassination of the president was 'severely limited' according to the House Assassinations Committee report. "I know they sure didn't come to see me," says Courtney Evans, who was the head of the special-investigations unit set up by Hoover to watch over the Mafia. Released F.B.I. files make clear that the Warren Commission failed to pursue F.B.I. leads linking Oswald's own assassin, Jack Ruby, to the Mafia. Ruby had ties to mobsters in Chicago, New Orleans, Los Angeles and Dallas. Nor did the Commission act on evidence that Ruby, 12 days before the assassination, asked a notorious Teamster Union racketeer from Chicago, Barney Baker, to 'straighten out' a union dispute at Ruby's Dallas night club. There is no evidence that organised crime had anything to do with the Kennedy assassination, despite claims by authors like David Scheim, but the Warren Commission's failure to investigate the possibility left a fertile field for Conspiracy Theorists.

Yet Conspiracy Theorists have for years used Oswald's uncle Charles F. (Dutz) Murret, as a conduit for Oswald's alleged mob links. David E. Scheim writes:

"Murret, a criminal operative in the empire of New Orleans boss Marcello, had in fact had a lifelong influence on his nephew".

This statement can be challenged by the people who knew the circumstances of Oswald's relationship with his uncle- Charles Murrett's family. In all of the evidence they have given to the Warren Commission and House Assassinations Committee there is no indication whatsoever that Charles Murret engaged his nephew, Lee, in any nefarious or suspicious activities or meetings. From the testimony of Marina Oswald we can see how Lee's time at the Murret's home was fully accounted for.

F.B.I. Agent William Roemer insists that if the Mafia planned to kill Kennedy, he would have heard about it as he listened to Chicago Boss Sam Giancana (who helped the C.I.A. plot to kill Castro) and other members of the Mafia's National 'Commission' scheme and brag.

The House Assassinations Committee, unlike the Warren Commission, investigated New Orleans Mafia Boss Carlos Marcello as Oswald spent the summer of 1963 in that city. They interviewed Edward Becker, a speculator in the oil business, who stated that Marcello, in reference to Robert Kennedy, said to him:

"Livarsi 'na pietra di la scarpa!" (Sicilian for "Take the stone out of my shoe") and spoke of using a 'nut' for an assassination. Becker said Marcello added, "If you want to kill a dog, you don't cut off the tail, you cut off the head."

However, another man present, Carl Roppolo, denied Marcello ever said anything like that, and was not even sure if there was a meeting with Becker. The House Committee concluded that it was extremely unlikely that Marcello, who knew he was under Federal investigation, would discuss a plot to kill the president with anyone but his close colleagues. The Committee also discovered that Becker had a "questionable reputation for honesty and may not be a credible source of information."

Hubie Badeaux, the former New Orleans police intelligence chief who was personally acquainted with Marcello, told author Gerald Posner:

"Carlos doesn't talk like that. He talks with 'dees and dems and dose', just like in Brooklyn. Carlos wouldn't know what the s*** you are talking about. He's not even from Sicily, for God's sake, he's from North Africa, Tripoli. I don't even know if he speaks Sicilian worth a damn. If he was going to talk about Kennedy, there is no way on this earth he would talk to a geologist about that. What the hell is the geologist going to do but get him in trouble? He doesn't need his help. And for Carlos, who hardly ever talks, that would have been a goddamn oration. That story doesn't fit Carlos Marcello. You have to know Marcello and know how he talks to understand how stupid that story is."

Florida Mafia Boss Santos Trafficante also came under suspicion from the House Assassinations Committee. Traficante had been the boss of gambling operations in Cuba before the revolution of 1959. Jailed by Castro shortly afterwards, he had been bailed out by Rolando Cubela, the Cuban military official who later became the C.I.A.'s AM/LASH, the code name for one of it's agents hired to kill Fidel Castro. In the summer of 1963, Trafficante, like Marcello, expressed contempt for the Kennedys, and said that the president was going to be 'hit', according to Jose Aleman, a prominent Cuban exile. Before the House Assassinations Committee, however, Aleman offered a more innocent explanation-he was going to be hit with a lot more votes from the Republican Party in the 1964 election.

Both John H. Davis and David Scheim popularised the Mafia theory in their books, respectively 'Mafia Kingfish: Carlos Marcello and the Assassination of John F. Kennedy' and 'Contract on America: The Mafia Murder of John F. Kennedy'. These two books helped make the 'Mafia Did It', school of assassination theories grow all the more persuasive in the 1980's. In the 1990's the American public became convinced of Mafia involvement with the publication of 'Double Cross-The Story of the man who Controlled America'. It was written by Sam Giancana's younger brother and nephew and revealed the confessions of Sam Giancana who supposedly said the Mafia killed Kennedy. True to form the 'conspirators' are no longer living therefore cannot confirm the story. As the Giancana's tell it, Dealey Plaza was filled with conspirators shooting at the president. In the first printing of their book they named one of the 'assassins' as Jack Lawrence, a Christian Minister who was totally innocent of any involvement in the assassination merely one of the Dealey Plaza witnesses. Realising their mistake his name was eventually omitted.

In 1992 the Mafia theory received some credence with the publication of Frank Ragano's book. Ragano was Jimmy Hoffa's and Florida Mafia Boss Santos Trafficante's lawyer. Ragano was also a close friend of Carlos Marcello. Based on Ragano's conversations with journalist Jack Newfield, the following critical events led to the assassination of President Kennedy. In August of 1962 Teamsters Boss Jimmy Hoffa (a corrupt Union Boss who was being pursued by Attorney General Robert Kennedy and who later was convicted and sent to prison) spoke with Ed Partin about possible plans to kill both Robert and John Kennedy. In September of 1962 Carlos Marcello discussed 'killing' Kennedy with Edward Becker (as discussed above). In February of 1963 Jimmy Hoffa sent his lawyer, Frank Ragano, to enlist two friends, Santos Trafficante and Carlos Marcello, in helping Hoffa get rid of the Kennedy brothers. The way the two Mafia bosses responded lead Ragano to believe that Hoffa's request would be granted. In December 1963 the first time Hoffa saw Ragano after the assassination, Hoffa told him, "I'll never forget what Santos did for me." Almost 24 years later, on the occasion of a reunion between the lawyer and his old client, Trafficante told Ragano, "Carlos f***ed up. We shouldn't have gotten rid of Giovanni. We should have killed Bobby."

The big question is Ragano's credibility. Could he be believed? It is interesting to note that Ragano made his claims less than 3 weeks after the movie 'JFK' had created a national fervour on the subject and at a time when he was coincidentally trying to sell his autobiography. There is no corroboration for his tale and no corroborating witness to his February 1987 conversation. Both Marcello and Trafficante are now dead. There is evidence that Ragano may have born a grudge against Trafficante and this was his way of extracting revenge.

Marcello and Trafficante both make intriguing villains. But in addition to the lack of credible and corroborated evidence, there are two big problems with these accusations. The two men lasted as dons for decades in part by being cagey, not trying to kill the president of the United States. As F.B.I. Agent Bill Roemer told Gerald Posner:

"The mob would never go after someone as high ranking as JFK and RFK. They don't go after judges, they don't go after reporters, they don't go after F.B.I. Agents or cops-they will only go after these people when they have stolen money from them and double-crossed them. It's counterproductive. It would be the end of the Mafia if they went after the Attorney General or the president and anything went wrong. It's not the way these businessmen would have acted. The risk would be far too great."

Conspiracy Theorists introduced another intriguing aspect to the 'Mafia Killed Kennedy' theory when it was revealed, in the 1970's, that President Kennedy and Chicago Mafia boss Sam Giancana shared a mistress, Judith Campbell Exner. There were also statements made by mob-linked figures that Kennedy was having an affair with Marilyn Monroe and the Mafia had tape recordings of their illicit rendezvous.

First of all the question must be asked-Why would the Mafia decide to kill President Kennedy when, one would assume, they held incriminating evidence linking the president with the mistress of a mob boss? Secondly-Why would the Mafia kill Kennedy if they could get rid of him in a much 'cleaner' way-by releasing the 'supposed' audio tapes confirming his relationship with Marilyn Monroe? The information about these scandalous activities would have doomed Kennedy's chances for re-election in 1964. Kennedy's close friend, ex-Washington Post Editor Ben Bradlee, has said the revelations would have led to Kennedy's impeachment by Congress. For the first time in the history of the U.S. Mafia mob bosses had a president who was in their 'hip-pocket'. Why on earth would they risk organising a vast conspiracy knowing they would be putting their own positions at extreme risk?

Another drawback to the 'Mafia Did It' school of thought is Oswald himself. It is hard to think of a more unreliable, unlikely professional hit-man than a paranoid loser like Oswald. If he was working for the Mafia why did he take a shot at Retired General Edwin A. Walker six months before he killed Kennedy? His job at the Book Depository was very convenient. But he got the job BEFORE the motorcade route was selected. There is no trail of phone calls between Oswald and the Mafia in the days before the assassination nor any evidence to suggest the Mafia placed Oswald in the very convenient Book Depository.

None of the books linking the Mafia with the assassination of John Kennedy are credible and rely on hearsay and second hand accounts, speculation and obscure connections between the various and nefarious characters who dot the landscape of assassination literature. The 'Mafia Did It' school of authors need to explain how and why the violent threats against the Kennedy brothers would have been voiced before such low-level figures as Aleman or the Marcello informant if a plot had actually existed. At most these books have established that the Mafia hated the Kennedys, talked about killing them, and wanted them out of their lives but the leap in believing there is credible evidence that they carried out their wishes simply lacks inherent logic.

Conspiracy Theorists might also explain how some of the world's most hardened criminals might let the weight of an incredibly hazardous plot fall on an unknown quantity of the likes of Oswald. What does not seem to add up is how other conspirators might have picked someone as unstable as Oswald to carry out their plot. Conspiracy Theorists may reply that Oswald was a 'patsy' so did not know what was going on. We must then look at many of the questions and anomalies that were considered earlier—why did he leave the scene of the crime?—why did he shoot Tippet?— and so on and so forth. We can realistically conclude, then, that there is no credible evidence of Mafia involvement in the assassination of President Kennedy.

CHAPTER 8

NEW ORLEANS

"We must all watch out and speak out. Otherwise, in twenty years people will be asking, How did Jim Garrison ever get this far? And the answer will be : We let him."

James Kirkwood,
"American Grotesque"

In 1991 the Movie Director, Oliver Stone, co-wrote and directed "JFK" and it became a landmark in the history of the Kennedy Assassination. 'JFK' played to audiences numbering in the millions in cinemas across America. The movie, which depicted New Orleans District Attorney, Jim Garrison, as a hero and had conspirators using Lee Harvey Oswald, did what no conspiracy book was quite able to do—persuade the American public that their government either assisted in the assassination or covered it up. There was a 'backlash' in the American press but how could their words compete with an exciting and dramatic visual experience? The movie alarmed even some of the conspiratorially-minded members of the assassination research community.

The movie stands, for many Americans, as the definitive account of what happened in Dealey Plaza on November 22nd 1963. Polls taken after the movie's release revealed that an absolute majority of Americans believed President Kennedy was killed as the result of a conspiracy. It still has the potential to become the accepted version of this historical event even in the late 90's.

One of the reasons the movie had such an impact was Stone's casting of the very credible Kevin Costner in the central role of Jim Garrison, a controversial New Orleans District Attorney, who, years after the assassination, read the 26 volumes of the Warren Commission Findings and decided that his city played a pivotal role in the 'conspiracy'. In 1969 Garrison attempted to convict a former New Orleans businessman, Clay Shaw, of conspiracy to assassinate the president.

The jury, in the 6 week trial, reached a verdict of not guilty in less than an hour but Garrison held firm, until his death in 1993, to his theory that Clay Shaw was part of a coup engineered by the covert action wing of the

C.I.A.. His 1988 book, 'On The Trail of the Assassins', along with Jim Marrs' 'Crossfire', was the basis for the movie 'JFK'. Garrison insisted that the cast of characters involved in the conspiracy or cover-up ultimately included the C.I.A., the Secret Service, President Johnson, Earl Warren, the Dallas Police and just about everybody else except Lee Harvey Oswald, who he claimed was busy that day being framed. As Garrison said:

"Lee Oswald was totally, unequivocally, completely innocent of the assassination, and the fact that history. . . . has made a villain of this young man who wanted nothing more than to be a fine marine is in some ways the greatest injustice of all."

Jim Garrison did indeed take the world by surprise when he revealed that he had proof and the names of culprits in his investigation of the Kennedy assassination and his statements reflected Warren Report criticisms which were popular at the time because of Mark Lane's 'Rush To Judgement' and Edward J. Epstein's 'Inquest'. But the world and the world's press were, as yet, unfamiliar with this New Orleans District Attorney who had a penchant for publicity.

Garrison served as an artillery officer and as a pilot of an unarmed spotter plane in World War II. He joined the F.B.I. after his discharge, became bored and eventually re-enlisted rising to the rank of lieutenant-colonel in the National Guard. Since his election as District Attorney of New Orleans in 1961, Garrison had conducted a running battle with the city's judicial and legal establishment, a position that only raised him in the estimation of most New Orleanians. He was loud and reckless and even before the Kennedy case his exploits had made him renowned.

What was not so well known was that in 1951 Garrison had been relieved from active duty, and discharged in 1952, for what Army doctors diagnosed as chronic, moderate anxiety reaction, manifested by chronic hypochondriasis, exhaustion syndrome, gastro-intestinal discomfort, and an allergy to lint.

"Look" magazine which reported these findings after the Clay Shaw trial, reported that:

"He was also found to have a mother dependency. He was diagnosed as totally incapacitated for military service and moderately impaired for civilian life. Long term psychotherapy was recommended."

In September 1967 Life magazine completed it's own investigation of Mafia activities in New Orleans and published it's findings. The articles, entitled 'The Mob' and 'Carlos Marcello: King Thug of Louisiana' revealed much about Garrison's character.

"State authorities, for the most part", Life said, "take the view that Marcello and his gang aren't there. 'I'm thankful we haven't had any racketeering to speak of in this state', says Governor John McKeithen."

Then the article quoted Garrison as saying, "I don't have to worry about things like that. I've cleaned up the rackets in this town." The article went on to point out that 3 times since 1963 Garrison had had his hotel bill at the Sands Club in Las Vegas paid for by Carlos Marcello's lieutenant Mario Marino, who had moved from New Orleans to Las Vegas 10 years earlier. Life said that on his last trip to Las Vegas in March of that year, Garrison had also been granted 5000 dollars credit at the cashier's cage. Garrison told the Life reporters that he believed it was customary for casinos to pick up the hotel bills of prominent public officials. Garrison's response to the Life articles was to state that he would resign if any evidence of the Mafia was found in New Orleans. He did not resign in the face of what was considered by Federal officials to be "overwhelming evidence of Cosa Nostra activities".

The Garrison assertions that there were no organised crime activities in New Orleans were at a time when the scale of Mafia operations ran to over one billion dollars a year. The flurry of vice arrests in the early sixties that won Garrison his popularity as a 'rackets-buster' were all low level operators of prostitution and gambling. Their removal from the scene helped Carlos Marcello consolidate his hold on the city's vice and narcotics. Garrison enjoyed considerably less success against Marcello. Between 1965 and 1969 Garrison managed just two convictions and five guilty pleas in cases the New Orleans police department made against Marcello's organisation. He dismissed 84 cases, including 22 gambling charges, one of attempted murder, 3 of kidnapping, and one of manslaughter.

At the time of the Shaw trial Marcello, as we saw in chapter 7, a convicted drug dealer and associate of Meyer Lansky and Frank Costello, was regarded by law enforcement officials as one of the most powerful organised crime figures in America, dominating an area that spread across the southern parts of the United States. Garrison, however, told a national television audience that Marcello was a 'respectable businessman'.

'Life' magazine also revealed that Garrison also "even managed to hush up the fact that last June (1969), a Marcello bagman, Vic Corona, died after suffering a heart attack during a political meeting held in Garrison's own home."

Garrison began investigating two days after the assassination after hearing reports that Oswald had spent some time in New Orleans the previous summer. Garrison's short investigation might have ended there except for a conversation he had with Senator Russell B. Long and Joseph M. Rault, Jr., a wealthy New Orleans oilman, in November 1966. Long remarked that the Warren Commission was full of holes and Garrison now had the kind of publicity-generating case every D.A. dreams of.

Garrison re-opened his investigation in 1966 and put a purported getaway pilot in the 'conspiracy', David William Ferrie, under round the clock surveillance. Cameras were installed in front of Ferrie's house. Meanwhile Garrison set about checking old leads. One of them was a story told by a New Orleans lawyer named Dean Adams Andrews, the character played by John Candy in the movie 'JFK'. Shortly after the assassination Andrews informed the Secret Service that Oswald had come to his office several times during the summer of 1963 looking for help in converting his 'undesirable' discharge from the Marine Corps to an honourable one. The day after the assassination, Andrews added, he received a phone call from a man requesting he go to Dallas and defend Oswald. The lawyer's name, Andrews said, was Clay Bertrand.

That was one version of Andrews's story. In another, he told the F.B.I. the whole thing had been a hoax. Garrison chose to believe the first version of the story and decided that 'Clay Bertrand' was an alias for Clay Shaw, the director of the New Orleans Trade Mart. There was no evidence to substantiate such a conclusion but some Conspiracy Theorists continue to quote the Shaw trial witness, police officer Habighorst, who claimed that Shaw gave the alias 'Bertrand' when he was booked. It was a vital piece of evidence in Garrison's case against Shaw.

However, Conspiracy Theorists omit to mention the fact that Habighorst's testimony was discredited by 3 members of the New Orleans police department who were present at the time of Shaw's booking. Much later Andrew's finally admitted that 'Clay Bertrand' was a pseudonym he heard at a 'fag' wedding and that he invented other parts of his story to 'get on the publicity gravy train and ride it to glory ... I was just huffing and puffing. I let my mouth run away with my brain.'

Ex-C.I.A. employee Victor Marchetti has for years tried to link Clay Shaw with the intelligence organisation. He first made his claims in 'True' magazine and in 1993 appeared on nationwide American television in the documentary "The JFK Conspiracy - Final Analysis" Narrated by actor James Earl Jones. In the documentary Marchetti implied that C.I.A. Director Richard Helms and his close aides knew that Shaw had been working for the C.I.A. and wanted the agency to assist Shaw in any way they could and that Jim Garrison's revelations would be harmful to the Agency. The Agency was afraid that Garrison would 'misconstrue' the relationship it had with Shaw.

But what kind of relationship did Shaw have with the C.I.A.? Marchetti implies that the relationship was of a sinister nature - that Shaw was a C.I.A. operative plotting to kill Kennedy. The facts of the matter are entirely different. What Marchetti was reporting was Shaw's cooperation with the Domestic Contact Service of the C.I.A. whose job was to seek the assistance of Americans in all walks of life to learn about the activities of foreign governments and their citizens, an activity entirely acceptable and common during the period of the Cold War. There is no evidence that Shaw did any more than inform the Domestic Contact Service of statistics pertaining to shipments through the port of New Orleans. This is, of course, consistent with Shaws job as Director of the International Trade Mart. A C.I.A. memo of 29th September 1967 reveals the dismay of the C.I.A. at the antics of Garrison in trying to link the C.I.A. with the assassination of President Kennedy. And why didn't the C.I.A. respond to Garrison's claims during the period of the New Orleans investigation? Apparently they were in a difficult position and their quandary is revealed in the September 29th 1967 memo:

"Shaw himself was a contact of the Domestic Contact Service's New Orleans office from 1948 to 1956 and introduced General Cabell, then Deputy Director of Central Intelligence, when he addressed the New Orleans Foreign Policy Association in May 1961. In view of this dilemma, the Department of Justice has so far taken the position that if any effort is made by either the prosecution (Jim Garrison) or defense (Shaw's lawyers) to involve C.I.A. in the trial, the Government will claim executive privilege. This, too, can be turned by Garrison into a claim that it is part of the whole cover-up by the establishment and particularly C.I.A..

"No alternative to the claim of privilege appears to be available, however.

To protect the Government's position on privilege, it would appear that the Government cannot take any action publicly to refute Garrison's claims and the testimony of his witnesses, as the Louisiana judge would almost certainly take the position that any such public statement would negate the privilege."

It would seem that secrecy, albeit in most cases benign, took precedence above all other considerations.

Garrison had acted on a tip that Ferrie was the getaway pilot. He arrested him for questioning but released him for lack of evidence. Just two months before his announcement that he had a break in the case, in March 1967, Garrison had brought in Clay Shaw for questioning. Then Ferrie was found dead. It was sensational news and the publicity took off.

"My staff and I solved the assassination weeks ago", Garrison claimed. "I wouldn't say this if we didn't have evidence beyond a shadow of a doubt. We know the key individuals, the cities involved, and how it was done."

The more publicity Garrison got the wilder his charges became. In May 1967 Garrison issued a subpoena for C.I.A. Director Richard Helms, demanding that Helms produce a photograph showing Oswald in the company of a C.I.A. agent in Mexico City. Garrison apparently reasoned it this way - The C.I.A. had never produced a photograph of Oswald taken by their surveillance cameras stationed outside the Cuban and Russian embassies. Therefore, they must have taken a photograph that showed Oswald in the company of someone whose identity they did not want revealed. Who could Oswald's supposed companion be? Obviously a C.I.A. agent.

By this time the American press was calling the Garrison investigation a farce. In June 1967 an hour long documentary was broadcast by NBC charging Garrison with attempting to bribe and intimidate witnesses and using other questionable tactics. When NBC gave Garrison broadcast time to reply on July 15th, Garrison once again asserted that Oswald was without question, "in the employ of intelligence agencies." He did not, however, produce any evidence.

The crime Clay Shaw was accused of was not murder but conspiracy. According to Garrison, who not only leaked details of the case, but presented his findings on the 'Johnny Carson Show', the men Shaw supposedly conspired with constituted a fair representation of New Orleans 'lowlife'. The dramatis personae of the plot included not only Ferrie and Oswald but also a Cuban exile named Carlos Quiroga, W. Guy Banister, a former F.B.I. agent and private detective involved in anti-Castro activities, and Edgar

Eugene Bradley, a Californian whose only apparent offence was having a name like Eugene Hale Brading, the reported organised crime associate who was found in the Dal-Tex building after the assassination.

It was Ferrie, however, who first attracted the attention of Jim Garrison. Under any circumstances David William Ferrie would have been hard to overlook. He was a character out of a comic strip with his stuck-on eyebrows and flaming red wig, a victim of alopecia. He was a would-be priest who was thrown out of two seminaries for 'erratic behaviour' (Ferrie was a sexual deviant) before making himself a 'bishop' in the Orthodox Old Church of North America, a church of his own creation. It was this man, Jim Garrison would say later, who would be remembered as 'one of history's most important individuals'.

Garrison's case grew more sensational when, on February 22nd 1967, the day after his release from questioning, Ferrie was found dead in his apartment; the result, the coroner later determined, of a cerebral haemorrhage caused by the rupture of a blood vessel. Within the week Garrison placed Shaw under arrest and called his press conference.

The day of the assassination Ferrie was in a New Orleans courtroom, looking on as his employer of the moment, Carlos Marcello, was being cleared of charges that had resulted in his deportation 2 years before. In 'celebration' of Marcello's victory, Ferrie and two friends, Alvin Beauboeuf and Melvin Coffey, decided to drive a thousand miles to Texas to go ice-skating and 'do some goose hunting.' They set off, drove all night and arrived at a Houston ice-rink. Conspiracy Theorists made much of this event, linking it to the assassination. Ferrie was alleged to be the getaway pilot for the Dallas conspirators and he travelled to Texas on the day of the assassination to 'await further instructions'.

In order to believe the Conspiracy Theorists we have to also believe that Alvin Beauboeuf was also a 'conspirator' who has been hiding the truth of the Ferrie trip for 30 years.

"It wasn't even Dave's idea to go to Houston," Alvin Beauboeuf told Gerald Posner, "It was my idea. I used to competitively roller-skate for years, and I had never ice-skated. So I told Dave, 'You are from Ohio, you ice-skate, and I would like to go.' And it was just like Dave to say, 'Let's go.'"

Garrison's tip that Ferrie might have been the pilot of a getaway plane for Oswald came from a New Orleans private detective and friend of Banister's,

Jack Martin, who in a later interview with the F.B.I. claimed he had invented the entire story. The following is an extract from a United States Secret Service report filed by Special Agents Anthony E. Gerrets and John W. Rice:

"On the night of 11-29-63 SAIC Rice and reporting agent interviewed Jack S. Martin at length in his small run-down apartment located at 1311 N. Prieur Street, New Orleans, which he shares with his wife and 6 year old son. Martin, who has every appearance of being an alcoholic, admitted during the interview that he suffers from 'telephonitis' when drinking and that it was during one of his drinking sprees that he telephoned Assistant District Attorney Herman S. Kohlman and told him this fantastic story about William David Ferrie being involved with Lee Harvey Oswald. He said he had heard on television that Oswald had at one time been active in the Civil Air Patrol and had later heard that Ferrie had been his Squadron Commander. Martin stated that Ferrie was well known to him; that he recalled having seen rifles in Ferrie's home and also recalled that Kohlman had written an article on Ferrie and that Ferrie had been a Marine and had been with the Civil Air Patrol. Martin stated that after turning all those thoughts over in his mind, he had telephoned Herman S. Kohlman and told his story as though it was based on facts rather than on his imagination."

Martin seemed very credible to Garrison but not only was he an alcoholic he had received treatment for mental illness. Hubie Badeux, the former chief of the New Orleans police intelligence division told Author Gerald Posner:

"He was goofy to begin with and lied all the time" ... Badeux said Martin had a reputation for "wild and crazy stories." The part of Martin was dramatised by the actor Jack Lemmon in Stone's movie 'JFK', giving credence to the character.

Conspiracy Theorists have made much of the roles played by Martin, Banister and Ferrie in the murky world of New Orleans. Oswald, in his pro-Castro activities on the streets of New Orleans had been passing out handbills with the address 544 Camp Street stamped on them- Guy Bannister's office address. But there are several innocent reasons why Oswald was using this address. His weekly visits to the employment exchange took him past that address and he could easily have seen the 'For Rent' signs displayed on the small corner building. There is evidence that Oswald may have attempted to rent the office but his meagre income prevented it. . It is also possible that Oswald may have used this address, which was used at one time as an office for an anti-Castro group, as a way to embarrass his anti-Castro opponents.

And it is unlikely that Oswald's 'pro-Castro' activities were a scam, as some Conspiracy Theorists claim. Their theory has been that Oswald was acting as an anti-Castro agent to support the anti-Castroites Ferrie and Banister in their efforts to discredit the Fair Play for Cuba Committee. But Oswald's first pro-Castro demonstration occurred before he arrived in New Orleans. In early April 1963 Oswald staged his first Pro-Castro demonstration in Dallas with a placard on his chest saying 'Hands off Cuba! Viva Fidel!' and handing out FPCC leaflets on the streets. Two police officers later reported seeing the demonstration and Oswald himself reported these activities to the New York office of the FPCC.

Conspiracy Theorists miss the point that these New Orleans characters were not overlooked in the original F.B.I. investigation. The F.B.I. checked Ferrie's plane and found it had not been airworthy since 1962. At the time of the assassination Ferrie was questioned by the F.B.I. and asked him if he had ever lent Oswald his library card. This issue has been raised by Conspiracy Theorists for 30 years, many of whom state categorically that Ferrie loaned Oswald his library card. This was clearly false as Ferrie produced the library card for F.B.I. agents when he was interviewed on November 27th 1963.

The story originated with Ferrie's friend Layton Martens and Marten's assertion that he was told about it by Ferrie's lawyer and employer, G. Wray Gill. Gill, in turn, told the F.B.I. that he had heard about it from a man named Hardy Davis who in turn had learned about it from Jack Martin who in turn had simply guessed that Oswald would have used the card as he believed Ferrie knew Oswald. Incredibly Conspiracy Theorists have had a field day peddling similar items of hearsay, innuendo and supposition resulting in sinister conspiracy links.

Conspiracy Theorists also continue to publish purported photographs of Ferrie, Shaw and Oswald together at a party in New Orleans. In one photograph, recently published by Robert Grodin in his book "The Search for Lee Harvey Oswald", the tall figure in the background is clearly Clay Shaw. However, it takes a considerable stretch of the imagination to identify the supposed Oswald and Ferrie characters and there is no mention of a source for the photographs.

Anthony Summers, in his book 'Conspiracy', tells the story of Guy Banister's secretary Delphine Roberts 'finally' confessing to seeing Oswald, Ferrie and Banister together at Banister's offices 544 Camp Street. Evidently Summers did not make any judgement as to Roberts' mental stability therefore her statements about Oswald are not credible. She told author Gerald Posner she had:

". . . read the sacred scrolls that God himself wrote and gave to the ancient Hebrews for placing in the Ark of the Covenant. . . I think I have been the last person to see them." Roberts also told Posner that the reason she told Summers the story was because she was paid money.

Garrison's efforts were directed at making his hypothesis stick. In his search any evidence that led away from Shaw was discarded, while testimony from dubious sources was accepted as fact. Given those ground rules, which are remarkably similar to the methodology many Conspiracy Theorists adopt, it was not too difficult to turn up leads. Ironically, some of them came from the Warren Commission itself, which had also looked briefly into the backgrounds of Ferrie and Guy Bannister.

Garrison produced a number of witnesses who claimed to have seen Bannister, Ferrie, Oswald and Shaw together. Most of these witnesses could not, eventually, withstand the light of day and disappeared from sight; except for the 6 Clinton, Louisiana, witnesses who said they saw Shaw, Ferrie and Oswald together in the summer of 1963. The 'Clinton Episode' is mentioned by most Conspiracy authors and many use it as 'proof' that Oswald conspired with others during his time in New Orleans. The witnesses were found by Jim Garrison in 1967 and gave evidence in the 1969 trial of Clay Shaw. They claimed that Shaw, Oswald, Ferrie and possibly Banister arrived in town at the time of a black voter registration drive. They assumed they were F.B.I. agents. The House Assassinations Committee found their testimony credible and significant. Gerald Posner, however, obtained affidavits, handwritten statements and summary memoranda to Garrison regarding the initial stories the Clinton residents told and found they contradicted testimony they gave at the Shaw trial. The evidence suggests their disparate stories only became consistent after coaching by Garrison's staff. It is also noteworthy that the witnesses did not come forward until years after the assassination.

Ray and Mary LaFontaine, like most of the Conspiracy Theorists, believe the Clinton witnesses and they ridiculed Posner's research. But I believe

Posner's explanations are valid and are supported by Newsweek's Hugh Aynesworth's understanding of this curious event and I quote him in full as his descriptions of the Clinton residents and the events that were witnessed that day are vital to an understanding of what occurred:

"Sometime around mid-January I was in Dallas, running down a rumour that Clay Shaw's name had been found in old papers of Jack Ruby's. . . . the wire services had used the story directly from the Dallas Times-Herald without checking. It said that in Ruby's papers was the notation 'Opening for Shaw'.

I got up there, found the guy who had the stuff and looked at the page in question. It said simply 'Opening of Show'. On the same page were names and addresses of show business characters and contacts Ruby had. That is a perfect example of how irresponsible most of the press was in the matter.

Anyway while in Dallas I checked with a few well-placed contacts, informers and the like ... and lo and behold, a guy I hardly knew called me and told me he could supply me with a list of all the witnesses Garrison was planning to use. Was I interested, he asked? Well, yes and no. I had run down about 75 to 100 similar 'tips' and usually had found they were worthless-figments of somebody's vivid imagination or false. But at this point I felt Garrison had such an advantage I had to take a look-see.

There on a three page sheet were the names, addresses and planned testimony (capsuled) of more than 20 Garrison witnesses. Most of them I recognised, but a few were completely new. Most of the new were from the Clinton-Jackson area.

I had heard several months before, that Garrison's investigators were supposed to have found that Lee Harvey Oswald had sought a job at the state mental hospital at Jackson. Upon checking the dates and checking Oswald's whereabouts, on those days, I found the odds about 100-1 that Lee Harvey Oswald could have been there. But, this was 1969 and after watching Garrison's behaviour for better than 18 months, I knew that logic, fact or common sense had no place in Big Jim's strange world.

I asked Bill Gurvich ... to go with me. About two-thirds of the names on the list were unknown to Gurvich also. In other words they had come forth more than five months after the Preliminary hearing of Clay Shaw, and about six months after 'the Giant' had bragged that he knew all the names, places and etc.

Gurvich and I drove to Clinton in his car, following a visit with a top Louisiana State Police official in Baton Rouge. We learned enough from the State Police official to let us know that the whole thing was a hoax, but we decided to visit several of the witnesses anyway-in the belief that if we could talk with them, and tape-record the conversation, we would probably find flaws in their stories. 'It's for sure they'll never be able to tell the same wacky story twice,' said Gurvich. This turned out to be true.

John Manchester, the town marshall, was the first witness we encountered. He was shocked that we knew that he was to testify. Manchester, a foul-talking, dirty and scruffy man who looked like the only way he could whip a man was to kick him in the groin, wouldn't comment on his testimony at first, but he kept saying, 'Ain't no way that son-of -a-bitch (Oswald) coulda fired all them shots. Ain't no way.'

Manchester told me he recognised Oswald at that time-the day Oswald shot Kennedy, adding, 'And I told several people about it.' I pressed him to give me the names of those people he had mentioned this to, but beyond a stammer or two, he couldn't come across. 'You probably still run around with the same guys now you did then, don't you?' I taunted the skinny racist. 'Damn right,' he replied, 'when I got a friend he's a friend'. He said he worked with and drank coffee with most of the same people in 1963 and 1968, but when I kept asking him who he mentioned seeing Oswald in Clinton to, he just grinned that brown smile and changed the subject. Once he said I reminded him of a guy he knew in the Air Force or the Army. 'I got enough of that shit real fast,' he added, 'and I'm gettin' enough of these questions of yours too.'

Some of his cronies were kidding Manchester that when Irv Dymond (Shaw's lawyer) 'got a hold of him, he'd shake loose and tell everything he knew.' Manchester wiped mud from his cowboy boots and snapped, 'Sheeit. ... ain't nobody gonna make me do nothin'.' They told him he'd have to dress up when he appeared in court. 'Sheeit ... I'll wear just what I got on. If that ain't good enough for 'em, screw 'em,' he said.

Gurvich, who is a well-known and respected referee at State Police (and other law enforcement) shooting matches, got to telling Manchester how Oswald shot Kennedy. Manchester said he couldn't believe it, that Oswald had help and that probably they 'was plannin' the whole thing when they's up here that summer.'

I kept talking to him about his early (November of 1963) identification of Oswald as having been there and he got angry and told me how he had 'knocked the Hell out of a reporter' at a recent trial in Clinton. 'He tried to come over that bar, towards the jury, you know, and I jes let him have it. He might still be pukin'. He added, 'I don't mess around with these rabble rousers. . . . the press. You or anyone else messes with me, I'll cut 'em a new asshole.'

We went to see Corrie Collins, but were told he had left town. A deputy took us to his house and barged right in and sat down in the living room as Collin's father, Emmet 'Snowball' Collins, looked at the three of us with fear in his eyes. It was just after dark and he knew we weren't there to watch T.V. he told us his son now lived in Baton Rouge and worked at the Post Office there. The white-haired man of 70 told us he didn't know anything about the case and didn't know what his son knew.

We left and drove to Baton Rouge, where about 11pm we just missed him at the Post Office, but we found that he was working there under an assumed name. We tried to find his home, but to no avail. We never found Corrie, but it was simple to see how he HAD to testify to what Manchester and the other scrub-nuts wanted him to. His father was simply terrified by three white men barging into his house after dark. In short, being a negro in Clinton -a hotbed of the red-neck and the Klan - is not much fun.

Henry Burnell Clark, a clerk at the Stewart and Carroll Store in Clinton, was supposed to have identified Ferrie and Shaw on the Clinton main drag. He didn't want to talk about it. 'Go 'way, man,' he winced. 'I don't know what you're talking about.'

We didn't get around to the others up there. It wasn't the most pleasant town to be in and we figured we'd come back another day. But Manchester soon called Garrison to complain about us and within days Garrison had sent Alcock to complain publicly at a press conference that Kent Biffle, Gurvich and I had been talking to witnesses. They weren't sure, said the little punk, Alcock, but there was a possibility that we were trying to bribe them. Of course, nothing ever came of it-except that Garrison dropped some of the witnesses.

Manchester, you'll recall, testified that he had spent two minutes talking to Clay Shaw that summer of 1963 and Dymond asked him how he could be so sure-to have only seen a man for two minutes five years before. 'I don't forget faces,' Manchester snapped. 'I may not remember names, but I remember faces. It's my job to.' More importantly, perhaps, three to four weeks after I'd spent one to two hours with the man discussing the very subject he was concerned with, Manchester did not recognise me when I went up to talk to him following his testimony on the stand. 'Newsweek, eh,' he said. 'Yeah, I met a feller from there not too long ago, and ...' One of the assistant D.A.'s pulled him away - him, still not recognising a man with a 12 inch scar on his face whom he had threatened a few days before. Quite a memory has mister Manchester!

Many people have asked me about the Clinton-Jackson witnesses. Were they mistaken? Who did they see? How could so many be wrong? And so on. I honestly cannot explain how it happened, though I have some small insight into how it could have occurred. First I think John Manchester and a State Policeman... put it all together. I'm certain that there were many out-of-towners-F.B.I., press, etc. - during that 1963 Voter Registration Drive in Clinton. And I feel certain every damn one of them was resented. And remembered. Maybe one of them looked something like Shaw or like Oswald. Funny though that nobody came forth after Oswald's face was plastered all over the world, November 22-24, 1963, when their memories should have been ultra-sharp.

The most important witness in the trial of Clay Shaw was Perry Raymond Russo and Garrison's case was built around Russo's testimony. Garrison's first contact with Russo had come in a letter Russo wrote to the District Attorney stating that he had known David Ferrie and possessed interesting information about him. In late February, 1967, Garrison sent his chief assistant to Baton Rouge to interview Russo. During the two hour interview Russo quoted Ferrie as hinting how easy it would be to shoot a president and flee to Mexico or Brazil and that one day he would 'get' Kennedy. Russo, however, made no mention of a plot. That came only after Garrison had jogged his memory, first with truth serum, under whose influence he supposedly recalled meeting with a man named 'Bertram', and later under hypnosis when at long last the details of the 'plot' emerged. During his trance Russo recalled having attended a party at Ferrie's apartment in September 1963. At the party three men supposedly discussed the details of the forthcoming assassination, the need for an appropriate scapegoat and possible means of escape. The three men, according to Russo, were Ferrie, a tall white-haired man named 'Clay Bertrand' and Lee Harvey Oswald.

A number of questions should have been satisfactorily answered by Garrison but they weren't. To date there has been no answer to the question

- Why would Clay Shaw, David Ferrie and Lee Harvey Oswald discuss the assassination within earshot of a virtual stranger? Furthermore, if Russo were a part of the 'conspiracy' what possible motive would he have in coming forward to testify for Jim Garrison? Ferrie and Oswald were dead and the only two 'co-conspirators' left were Russo and Shaw. Russo was home free; the 'conspiracy' had succeeded. In fingering Shaw how would he know that Shaw wouldn't finger him? - then they would both go to prison.

James Phelan was the first reporter to see through Russo's story. Phelan discovered the vast discrepancies in Assistant District Attorney Andrew Sciambra's memos about the Russo interviews. It was clear to Phelan that Russo was changing his story about Ferrie and Shaw in each telling.

Author, James Kirkwood, interviewed Russo against the wishes of Garrison:

" Russo said, 'Oh, the hell with it. If we do it (The interview), it'll get back to Garrison and Garrison'll clobber me.' ... The real reason I didn't want to see Shaw was that I knew if I sat down in a room with him, talked to him, listened to him, that I'd know he's not the guy and then all I could do is go on the run, go to Mexico or go out to California and become a beatnik but I couldn't run from myself ... They asked me a lot of questions (Garrison's staff) and I'm a pretty perceptive guy I was able to figure what they wanted to know from the questions they asked. And when they got through asking me questions, I asked them a lot of questions, like 'Who is this guy? Who is that guy? Why is this so important?' ... In addition I read every scrap of stuff that was in the papers about the case."

Kirkwood said that in the interview Russo told him he was:

" 'caught up in the middle on this thing', that if he stuck to his story, Shaw and his friends and lawyers would clobber him. If he changed his story, then Garrison would charge him with perjury and chuck!- there would go his job with Equitable Life. He told me all he was concerned about was his own position, that he wished he'd never opened his mouth about it, wished he could go back to the day before he shot off his mouth up in Baton Rouge...... He said 'I no longer know what the truth is. I don't know the difference between reality and fantasy'."

At the time of the Shaw trial Russo had second thoughts about his testimony and refused to repeat the fabrication about the Ferrie party. He gave Shaw's lawyers a tape recording confessing that Garrison's assistants had told him what to say. Russo confessed:

"It was sort of a script and I was playing my part. I guess I played too good one, huh?.... I never dreamed he (Garrison) only had me. I guess I always knew he (Shaw) had nothing to do with anything.... (Garrison said) that after Shaw was convicted we'd all be rich...... (Garrison) told me about people who had been convicted of perjury and said mine would be worse because a lot of people had been affected by what I said."

Reporter, James Phelan, who also interviewed Russo, was asked by James Kirkwood if he felt sorry for Russo:

"Oh, I felt sorry for him at the onset, but -That thing he said about not being able to run from himself, that was the only instance in all the times I spoke with him that he expressed any kind of concern for what he'd done. The rest of the time it was 'What's going to happen to me? What's going to happen to me?' I talked to him about justice, the truth, the objective truth, and what he was doing to Shaw, if his story was phoney. He asked me once if I'd heard about the Dreyfus case. He said, 'What was it? I hear people talking about it.' I said, 'Well, it's a famous case, an instance of an innocent man getting railroaded into prison, Devil's Island, down in the Caribbean, a French guy accused of selling out his country. It was a famous case.' I said, 'He was finally sprung by a writer by the name of Emile Zola, who wrote a pamphlet called 'J'accuse.' I said, 'It's interesting that you raise this, because if your story is false and if Clay Shaw is innocent - you're going to go down as a little footnote in history as a piece of S... that turned Clay Shaw into another Dreyfus.' He said, 'Oh! Oh!' But after a while I lost any sympathy I had. I really did. I think what he's done is too enormous. I'm sorry for him that he's capable of doing such a thing-but I think he ought to be in jail. I think it's a monstrous thing."

Since the movie 'JFK' was made Russo, who was given a small part as a patron of a New Orleans bar, has reverted to his original story. He was sought after by numerous authors and documentary makers riding the success of the Stone movie.

By the time Shaw finally came to trial in 1969 the case was in shreds. Garrison, himself rarely turned up in the courtroom and the 'secret evidence' that Garrison had promised was not forthcoming. Instead his assistants called a parade of 'witnesses' to the stand, many who proved more beneficial to the defence.

One witness at Shaw's trial appeared clad in a toga, and when asked for his identity, replied, "Julius Ceasar". Yet another 'witness', Charles

Spiesel, a New York businessman, claimed he had seen Ferrie and Shaw together at a New Orleans party and that someone had said, in reference to President Kennedy, "somebody ought to kill the son of a bitch." Speisel was destroyed by the defence when they got him to admit that he had fingerprinted his own daughter to prove it was the same girl who returned from college. He claimed he had been hypnotised by maybe fifty or sixty people.

The Shaw jury was out only 50 minutes before they returned a 'Not Guilty' verdict. The Garrison investigation into the assassination of President Kennedy and the subsequent trial of businessman Clay Shaw had proved nothing. But Garrison's reckless investigation had far reaching effects on Shaw. Drained of the experience he died a few years later.

The author, James Kikwood, believed that an innocent man had been hounded to death. Kirkwood interviewed Shaw on a number of occasions whilst Shaw was awaiting trial. Shaw's protestations of innocence stand forever against the scandalous nature of Garrison's charges:

"I'm no authority to judge and it's difficult to sift through all that's written about the Warren Commission, the C.I.A., the F.B.I., the Attorney General, the Right and the Left, the Cuban situation and so forth. I only know I had no part in any plot. But I do feel many people believe in a conspiracy. . . . I suppose the knowledge of my innocence has been the great sustaining factor. . . . It's gone on too long, the pressures are as great in this limbo I've been in, going on two years now, I want it over with. If I weren't innocent perhaps. . . . but I am. I'm ready to prove it. I'm ready for the trial."

In November 1997 the Assassinations Records Review Board (set up by Congress as a result of public pressure after the release of the movie 'JFK' and designed to expedite the release of all Government files relating to the assassination) released Clay Shaw's secret diary. In it he wrote of being wrongly persecuted:

"I am still dismayed to find myself charged with the most heinous crime of the century but I am completely innocent and the feeling of being a stunned animal seems to have gone now."

In another section of Shaw's diary he wrote about his feelings of being accused of having associated with Lee Harvey Oswald and David Ferrie:

"Aside from any questions of guilt or innocence, anyone who knows me knows that I would have better sense than to plot with two nuts like that."

Garrison, after surviving trials of his own on charges of income tax evasion and bribery, was driven from office. It was clear to many that Garrison had been seriously lacking in judgement and had not brought the case of Clay Shaw to trial to solve the assassination of President Kennedy but to further his own ambitions. Had Oliver Stone read works like 'American Grotesque' by James Kirkwood the movie would have been one based on truth, not lies. Instead Stone took Garrison's own version of his investigation, along with a number of other 'Conspiracy' works, and made a movie that will stand for all time as an aberration of justice and a grave slur on the reputations and standing of many people who were connected, directly or indirectly, with the assassination.

Garrison, the District Attorney who was discredited in the 1960's, became, after the release of 'JFK', the brave hero battling the dark conspiratorial forces of government. His book 'On The Trail of The Assassins' sold well and Conspiracy authors began to give him credence in the 1990's. The outrageous circumstances of the bogus Shaw trial had been forgotten.

CHAPTER 9

THE CONSPIRACY THEORISTS

"A truth that's told with bad intent
Beats all the lies you can invent."

Charles Blake.

"It is unfortunate, considering that enthusiasm moves the world, that so few enthusiasts can be trusted to speak the truth."

Arthur James Balfour.

"populus vult decipi" (the public is very ready to be deceived)

When Elvis Presley died, 21 years ago, it had a traumatic effect on many people. They could not just accept his death. The effects for many, especially his fans, were nothing short of traumatic.

The fact that a crazed psychotic could have changed the world in a single moment can be more unsettling than the prospect of an organised action, however corrupt. The idea of a conspiracy with a valid aim suggests control; the psychotic actions of a lone individual suggests chaos. And people are always looking for simple and straightforward answers or conspiratorial answers to questions. It gives them something to hate . It is also very difficult for any government to rebut allegations of conspiracy as the targets are often too numerous to understand- bureaucrats, a secret cabal of military officials and industrialists who 'control' the government, political leaders on both the right and the left who conspire together to maintain the status quo of the military-industrial complex, and many more.

Conspiracies, imagined or otherwise, abound in the culture of the United States. Far reaching and complex conspiracy stories seem to be the staple diet of Hollywood encompassing movies like 'The Manchurian Candidate', 'Three Days of the Condor', 'Seven Days in May, 'The Parralx View', 'The President's Analyst', 'Total Recall', 'The Conspiracy Theory' and many more suggesting the sinister and anti-Libertarian movies of various government organisations. Even television and the Internet have seemingly joined forces in propagating these myths. In 1998 the 'X-Files' and 'Dark Skies' became very popular with the viewing public. The Internet also cater for this need to see conspiracy everywhere. 'Majestic 12' a popular website is named after a supposed top secret division of the United States government set up to deal with Aliens. This site maintains that JFK was killed because he was about to reveal the sordid secret to the world. Another website 'The Illuminati Outline of History' reveals so called 'secrets' of the Illuminati an organisation that has been around since the 1700's who are lying in wait to take over the world. The 'Government Control' website maintains that the U.S. Government may have hidden away a cure for cancer, in case it damaged the economy. It also has interesting information about the secret 'Black Helicopters' believed by many to be piloted by the many 'MIBS' or 'Men in Black'. According to this website these helicopters have buzzed people for no apparent reason. Other websites promise to reveal that :

The F.B.I. murdered John Lennon

The American Government is promoting world government through the auspices of the United Nations which will take away all rights and freedoms of the American people.

The TWA airplane disaster over Long Island, New York was the work of the US Navy.

The C.I.A. became involved in drug distribution throughout American cities in order to decimate the African - American population.

The governments of the world are in league with Aliens.

Charles Paul Freund of the Washington Post captured the thinking of conspiracy theorists when he wrote:

"Let's say that everything you know is not only wrong, it is a carefully wrought lie. Let's say that your mind is filled with falsehoods - about yourself, about history, about the world around you - planted there by powerful forces so as to lull you into complacency. Your freedom is thus an illusion. You are in fact a pawn in a plot, and your role is that of compliant dupe - if you're lucky. If and when it serves the interests of others, your role will change: your life will be disrupted, you could go penniless and hungry; you might have to die.

"Nor is there anything you can do about this. Oh, if you happen to get a whiff of the truth you can try to warn people, to undermine the plotters by exposing them. But in fact you're up against too much. They're too powerful, too far-flung, too invisible, too clever. Like others before you, you will fail."

Understanding what has been going on over the past 35 years requires an understanding of American Politics and also the way in which Conspiracy

Theorists approach the study of President Kennedy's assassination. In many ways the two are linked. The study of the assassination and 'political conspiracy theory' reflect major shifts in American life.

Conspiracy Theorists come from both the American Left and American Right of the political spectrum. During the 1950's and 1960's Conspiracy Theorists were generally right-wingers like Senator Joseph McCarthy who saw America being subverted by the 'communists'. In the 1970's and 1980's the idealists of the left have tended to see America being subverted by right - wing conspiracies. It is interesting to note that the major Kennedy Conspiracy view since the late 1960's has been to see the President's death as a result of right-wing groups or agencies like the C.I.A., Anti-Castro Cubans or Right-wing Texas oilmen as the principle villains. Vietnam and Lyndon Johnson's lack of credibility in speaking to the American people on the progress of the war, Nixon's mis-use of Federal Agencies and the Watergate cover-up, Iran-Contra, fed the Conspiracy Theorists as they proclaimed 'see, we told you so'. America became paranoid and devised a sense of the secret manipulation of history- "The government is lying to us." While the Soviet Union and Castro's Cuba were busy subverting Democracies in Latin America and around the world Conspiracy Theorists looked inward to the subversion of Democratic institutions in America by faceless and powerful groups dedicated to the advancement of American corporations and Military Agencies.

There was certainly some form of cover-up in the assassination of President Kennedy but not a cover-up in the conventional sense. It was a cover-up involving bureaucracies, who, for their own warped understanding of the way government works, acted unconstitutionally in protecting what they considered to be 'National Security'. In this sense they conspired independently to protect their own 'turf' and incompetent/unconstitutional actions which occurred prior to the assassination. And bureaucracies are, of course, notoriously secretive, unwilling to adhere to the people's concept of 'Open Democracy'. Files sealed for a generation; files lost; official records kept from investigating agencies of the Congress in the name of protecting sources or disclosing methods; a general world view that 'we' know better than the American people and therefore can protect America if we were only allowed to get on with the job without political interference. Since Dallas Americans see conspiracy everywhere. Certainly the American people had faith in government before Kennedy was killed. That faith was deeply damaged, not only by the handling of the investigation and the agencies of government, but by later revelations concerning JFK's own Administration.

The Warren Commission tried to do a thorough job in investigating the assassination but as the years went by it became obvious that the Commission did not walk the last mile in settling anomalies and discrepancies in the evidence and it failed to chase up leads which would have put the conspiracy rumours to rest once and for all.

The Warren Commission should have cleared up the discrepancies arising from the initial reports of the Dallas doctors and the reports of the Bethesda doctors. The Commission should have followed up and reported on Jack Ruby's mob links. It should have received presidential approval in forcing the F.B.I. and C.I.A. to give them access to all the files pertinent to the circumstances surrounding the assassination. EVERY witness in Dealey Plaza should have been called to testify and Oswald's links to Russia and Cuba should have been explored deeper. The investigations of Oswald 'doubles', in Clinton, Louisiana, in Dallas, at the home of Sylvia Odio, and at the Cuban and Russian embassies in Mexico City were inadequate. The ballistics evidence, although relying on expert testimony, had too many loopholes on which Conspiracy Theorists could pounce.

But for all their faults the Commission members sought the truth. And genuine assassination researchers rightly pointed out the glaring errors and discrepancies in the report and their efforts should be commended. But they were quickly followed by Conspiracy Theorists who took these inaccuracies and mistakes to ludicrous extremes claiming all kinds of wild hypotheses and their rantings have continued unabated ever since. When confronted by the logical reasoning that claims of a cover-up had to involve hundreds if not thousands of people many fell back on a fail safe theory which would be practically impossible to discredit-a very powerful group of people killed the president, a group powerful enough to engage vast legions of workers to cover up the conspiracy-The C.I.A., F.B.I., Pentagon, White House, major arms manufacturers, oil industry and so on.

Having decided that the military-industrial complex's grip was a given fact many Conspiracy Theorists proceeded to approach the Kennedy assassination with a certain mind-set—if the facts did not fit they were discarded; Oswald's own history, character and inter-relationships which gave clues to his character were ignored; when a perceived pattern was firmly established, alternative explanations were ignored or rejected; they became predisposed to a certain point of view.

The first major conspiracy book, Mark Lane's "Rush to Judgement", published in 1966, started this trend.

In what judicious frame of mind Lane approached his task of examining the Warren Report can be deduced from an understanding of how he manipulated the evidence contained in the 26 volumes of the Warren Commission Hearings. His book, plausible only to those who do not know their way around the vast mass of material contained in these volumes, is virtually worthless.

Lane's technique is to assemble a wealth of 'evidence' and then by careful selection and arrangement and no less careful omission of the huge mass of evidence on the other side make the result look sinister. Lane's technique has been copied by many Conspiracy Theorists-taking perfectly reasonable mistakes and making them appear 'conspiratorial'. Take, for example, the autopsy notes written by Commander Humes at Bethesda Naval Hospital in Washington D.C. Conspiracy Theorists aver that the notes were destroyed because they indicated the wounds to President Kennedy were inconsistent with a single shooter theory. During the House Assassinations Committee hearings Humes was asked if the original autopsy notes were still in existence:

HUMES: "The original notes, which were stained with the blood of our late president, I felt, were inappropriate to retain to turn in to anyone in that condition. I felt that people with some particular ideas about the value of that type of material, they might fall into their hands. I sat down and word for word copied what I had on fresh paper."

(Investigator) Cornwall: "And then you destroyed them?"

HUMES: " Destroyed the ones that were stained with the President's blood."

The trouble, of course, is that to deal with Lane et al would require books at least as long as theirs. However for the sake of brevity I cite 3 examples from Lane's book. Mark Lane claims that Helen Markham, who witnessed Police Officer Tippit's murder, described the killer to him in a telephone conversation as "a short man, somewhat on the heavy side, with slightly bushy hair." But if we look at the actual transcript of that conversation in the actual volume of the Warren Commission we find not only that Lane put that entire description into her mouth in the conversation but she was only with difficulty persuaded to accept any of it from him, and one point (Lane's "somewhat on the heavy side") she in fact denied. ("And was he a little bit on the heavy side?")

"Uh, not too heavy."

"Not too heavy, but slightly heavy?"

"Uh, well, he was, no he wasn't, didn't look too heavy, uh-huh"

Lane uses Jack Ruby's Warren Commission testimony out of context: ".... There was no malice in me", (Ruby said). The reader is thus led to believe Ruby cold-bloodedly shot Oswald as a 'hit'. The true context of Ruby's statement is:

"I never called the man (Oswald) by an obscene name, because, as I stated earlier, there was no malice in me. He was insignificant, to my feelings for my love for Mrs. Kennedy and our beloved president."

Likewise Lane quotes Ruby as saying: "Take me back to Washington tonight to give me a chance to prove to the president I am not guilty." The reader is thus led to deduce that Ruby is not the truly guilty party but unknown 'conspirators'. Lane omits to say that Ruby was pleading that he was not guilty of the president's death and that "some persons are accusing me falsely of being part of the plot."

In another excerpt from his book witness Julia Ann Mercer's testimony is used by Lane to get a gunman on the Grassy Knoll before the shooting begins. Mercer said that she observed a green pickup truck blocking a lane on Elm Street near the Grassy Knoll and Triple Underpass. She recalled seeing a man "wearing a grey jacket, brown pants and plaid shirt, best as I can remember, get what appeared to be a gun case out of the back of the truck and walk up the Grassy Knoll."

In his book Lane imbues this incident with sinister connotations as there were 3 policemen standing nearby no doubt part of the conspiracy. What Lane fails to inform his readers is that Mercer originally described the objects in the rear of the truck as "what appeared to be tool boxes".

In building their case for foreknowledge of the assassination many Conspiracy Theorists like Anthony Summers and Jim Marrs mention the name of Joseph Milteer in their books. On November 9th. 1963, 2 weeks before the assassination, a Miami police informant William Somersett, met with Milteer, a right-wing extremist and recorded Milteer as saying "(During Kennedy's impending trip to Miami) You can bet your bottom dollar he is going to have a lot to say about the Cubans, there are so many of them here... The more bodyguards he has, the easier it is to get him... From an office building with a high powered rifle... he knows he's a marked man."

By selective use of the transcript of this tape Marrs and Summers ignore vital and telling parts of this story:

* Milteer talks about 15 Kennedy look-alikes who travel with the President.
* Milteer named the man who was going to kill the president as 'Jack Brown'.
* Summers and Marrs quote Milteer as saying a disassembled rifle would be taken up into a tall building but it was in the context of shooting Kennedy on the veranda of the White House.

Matthew Smith in his book 'JFK - The Second Plot' similarly mixed fact with speculation. Smith casts Oswald as an American intelligence agent who was sent to Russia as a bogus defector. On returning to America, he continued his secret agent work, taking orders from the C.I.A. Among other things, Oswald was supposedly innocent of the General Walker shooting. On November 22nd, according to Smith, Oswald was embarking on his latest assignment and was eating lunch when the assassination occurred: "Oswald left the Book Depository about five minutes later, and quickly realised he had a problem he had not bargained for." Having explained Oswald's whereabouts at the critical moment, Smith faced another hurdle-Oswald was arrested with the Tippet murder weapon in his hand. How does he explain this? As Smith tells it, Oswald was carrying the gun because he was on a 'mission' for the C.I.A. but it was someone else who shot Tippit who had been concealed in the bushes near Tippit's patrol car.

Smith, then, postulates that Oswald was on a 'mission' and only after his arrest did he realise that he had been set up. Oswald, on the morning of November 22nd was completing his latest assignment for the C.I.A. He was to report for work as normal and then later rendezvous with another agent who would take him to an airport to be flown to Cuba. However, another 'agent' killed Tippit and the plan went awry:

"The conspirators were devastated that their well laid plans had been fouled up. Lee Harvey Oswald had been selected very carefully as the patsy who would be blamed for shooting President Kennedy. That had been the intention from the beginning. The second plot had been interlocked with the shooting of the president so that the hapless Oswald would fly out to Cuba believing he was starting a new mission when, in fact, before he got into the air he would be being sought for questioning. Had he been picked up by Tippit he would have been at Red Bird Airfield, where his plane was being revved up and was waiting to take off, in 15 minutes. If Lee Harvey Oswald had reached Cuba there would not have been any doubt in any mind that he had killed the President and that Fidel Castro had sent him to do it."

And what evidence does Smith present for this speculative scenario?- Discrepancies in Tippit witness statements, anomalies in the Tippit murder ballistics evidence, uncorroborated witness statements etc., etc. Smith's conclusions about what happened that November day are pure speculation and are constructed cleverly from his biased interpretation of the evidence, yet the Sunday Times called his book, "JFK-The Second Plot", 'by far the best conspiracy book to date.' (1992)

The incredible implausibilities in 'JFK-The Second Plot', are implicit in most conspiracy books. They point to one suspicious looking anomaly after another and the authors devise scenarios to explain them without any credible evidence. They avoid incontrovertible facts which cause difficulties with their scenarios; for example why an INNOCENT Oswald went to Irving to collect 'curtain rods', left his wedding ring behind, fled the scene of the crime, appeared in full view of the Tippit murder witnesses, and so on. Conspiracy Theorists have, for 35 years, deployed a 'smokescreen' by making everything surrounding the assassination of President Kennedy obscure thus allowing Lee Harvey Oswald to escape blame.

When facts are presented that explain inconsistencies and investigatory mistakes Conspiracy Theorists fall back on another tactic. If the evidence proving a lone assassin involves a member of the public they say that person is wrong. If it involves the media they accuse the media outlet of covering up the "consortium / establishment / government" conspiracy. If it involves an agency of the U.S. government they are instantly dismissed as "tools". One can see that these tactics make it virtually futile in challenging their ideas. We are left, again with proving a negative- an impossibility.

For example, many Conspiracy Theorists pepper their narratives with phrases like "as we have found out" (we haven't), "it has been established" (it hasn't), "it is likely" (it isn't), 'it is to be expected' (is it?). Most Conspiracy Theorists are carried away by enthusiasm more than by fact. Their chains of reasoning lead to conclusions that are ill-founded and unprovable. Their hypotheses stand alongside claims made on Internet websites which say that Henry Kissinger and Queen Elizabeth were the supreme drug barons of Europe. Conspiracy Theorist's books are wildly speculative and indiscriminate. They treat all facts, all questions, all doubts, not merely as equally relevant but as equally decisive. They rightly belong on the shelves of fiction.

Matthew Smith, for example, describes the killers of Kennedy as the "Consortium" - a secret cabal of secret agents, politicians and businessmen - who conspired together because they wished to replace Kennedy. No credible evidence is presented, only imaginary hypotheses. Smith goes further than any Conspiracy Theorist in that he blames Edward Kennedy's tragic accident at Chappaquidick on the "Consortium".

Yet, in some ways, it should not be surprising that conspiracy theories like Smith's are accepted by the majority of Americans. In a country where, according to recent opinion polls 93% believe in the existence of angels and 45% are convinced that UFO's have visited Earth it was always to be expected.

It was in this climate that the defence lawyers in the O.J. Simpson criminal trial played their 'ace card'. Faced with overwhelming evidence showing that O.J. Simpson was guilty they chose to persuade the jurors that Simpson was set up by the Los Angeles Police Department, a 'patsy'. Simpson's lawyers knew the prevailing cynicism about police departments and government agencies. As if taking their cues from Conspiracy Theorists the jurors were thus 'persuaded' and found Simpson 'Not Guilty'.

In Smith's book "JFK, The Second Plot" the now famous "Sunday Times", "mysterious deaths" are mentioned:

"At one point, not very long after the assassination, a Sunday Times actuary took the number of material witnesses who had died by that time, and calculated the odds against the group dying from any cause. His oft-quoted result was 100,000 trillion to 1 against." Smith cleverly introduces scepticism about these figures but eventually decides they do indeed require a sinister interpretation:

"But in spite of any arguments that nature may have intervened to deprive us of the potential testimony of some important witnesses, when it comes to a coincidence factor we would do well to consider the dimensions of the coincidence involved."

What Smith fails to say is that the Sunday Times admitted their statistics were wrong and retracted the story. In a statement to the House Assassinations Committee they said:

"Our piece about the odds against the deaths of the Kennedy assassination was ... based on a careless journalistic mistake and should not have been published ... there was no question of our actuary having got his answer wrong. It was simply that we asked him the wrong question. He was asked what were the odds against 15 named people out of the population of the United States dying within a short period of time, to which he replied-correctly -that they were very high. However, if one asks what are the odds against 15 of those included in the Warren Commission index dying within a given period, the answer is, of course, that they are much lower. Our mistake was to treat the reply to the former question as if it dealt with the latter - hence the fundamental error."

The "mysterious" deaths can, of course, be explained by a more rational and logical method. Thousands of people were directly or indirectly involved in this momentous event, from the friends and relatives of Oswald to the witnesses, reporters and government agencies involved in the investigation. Simple laws of probability would indicate that some "witnesses" would have to die in some kind of criminal act. One example of a 'mysterious' death that most Conspiracy Theorists mention is the case of William Whaley, the taxi driver who took Oswald to his rooming house after the assassination. Whaley was killed in a car crash involving an 80 odd year old woman who was also killed in the crash. What are we to make of this 'suspicious' death? Whaley was killed by a 'geriatric kamikaze pilot' ? It begs the question, if conspirators were trying to eliminate all those witnesses who have given evidence indicating a conspiracy why have so many survived- like Jean Hill and Beverly Oliver who supposedly saw "shooters" behind the Grassy Knoll?

The movie JFK is a typical example in the use of these subtle techniques with which to circumvent logic and the true facts of the case. 'JFK' is a typical example of how Conspiracy Theorists mislead the American public. Stone cleverly builds his theories by omitting critical evidence, taking out of context statements made by key witnesses, relying on erroneous conclusions by alleged experts like Robert Groden, and at the same time making false accusations that respected and honourable investigators like Arlen Specter and David Belin instituted some kind of cover-up.

Stone's thesis, based upon books by Jim Marrs and Jim Garrison, states that the C.I.A., military-industrial complex, anti-Castro Cubans and elements of the Mafia conspired together to murder President Kennedy.

Both Stone and other Conspiracy Theorists, for example, contend that Jack Ruby played an important role in the conspiracy. They claim that Ruby's murder of Oswald was so precise that it had to be 'arranged'. In order to reach this conclusion, Stone et al have first to overcome the testimony of Postal Inspector Holmes which disproves their theory as we have seen in Chapter 5. Stone and many Conspiracy Theorists fail to disclose the existence of Postal Inspector Holmes and the circumstances of the extended interrogation and subsequent and aborted jail transfer. (Stone's movie is analysed in Appendix 2, scene by scene, showing how he has manipulated and misrepresented the evidence in the case.)

Conspiracy Theorists use discrepancies in witness testimony to build their cases. How could witnesses recall things that were different from the official reports on the assassination? Why were there so many people, named by the Conspiracy Theorists, who had different perspectives from the witnesses who made up ' the preponderance of evidence'? It is quite evident that some witnesses testified for monetary gain. Others changed their stories when interviewed by television documentary teams, or conspiracy authors, many years after the assassination. Not a few were simply publicity seekers. Yet others were simply mistaken in their judgements. In conspiracy theories people don't make mistakes.

Psychologists know that even well meaning and expert observers are often mistaken when they 'remember' a particular event. Each time the event is recalled it is 'coloured' by a different perception. Over time memory does not fade ;it grows. But with every reconstruction of a memory a little bit is added and contributions are made to the memory by others who experienced the same events.

Psychologists also recognise that people are susceptible to 'cognitive dissonance', that is the ability to view 'reality' through a particular world view and personal prejudices which act as a framework for incoming information. When a perceived pattern of events are firmly established alternative explanations are rejected. For example, Oswald was 'fingered' during his arrest at the Texas Theatre. Johnny Brewer, the man who 'fingered' Oswald, did not, initially, identify himself leading to rumours of a 'mystery plotter'. Conspiracy Theorists, looking for conspiratorial intrigue, opined that the 'mystery man' was an 'agent', ignoring alternative and rational reasons as to who this 'mystery' man might be.

Conspiracy Theorists also generally ignore Oswald's attempted assassination of right-winger General Edwin A Walker in April 1963. The evidence for Oswald's attempted killing of Walker is overwhelming. So why do Conspiracy Theorists tend to ignore this event ? It is quite obvious - why would conspirators use someone who could endanger their plot to kill the President? It is also unlikely conspirators would put their plot at risk by carrying out a "dummy run".

When Lee Harvey Oswald's body was exhumed in 1981, re-examined by pathologists and re-buried, a conspiracy theory put forward by Michael Eddowes was shown for what it was-a conspiracy theory built upon inconsistencies and bureaucratic mistakes. Eddowes theory began with Oswald's Marine record which showed his height to be 5feet 11 inches. Yet after Oswald was arrested in Dallas, his height was recorded as 5 feet 9½ inches and the autopsy report later recorded his height as 5 feet 9 inches. In conspiracy theories people do not make mistakes but it has been seen that in many famous criminal cases mistakes and anomalies often occur.

Take for example four major criminal cases of the last 30 years-The Manson murders, the trial of Jeffrey MacDonald, the O.J. Simpson case and the Jon Benet Ramsey case. In the O.J. Simpson investigation an on-scene detective, Mark Fuhrman, left himself open to allegations that he planted the bloody glove worn by the murderer of Nicole Simpson and Ronald Goldman. His simple mistake was in not securing the witnessing of the gloves retrieval by his detective colleague.

The Boulder, Colorado, police committed their share of blunders in the Jon Benet Ramsey murder case. In the first 48 hours they made crucial mistakes including not conducting a thorough search of the Ramsey house; not separating Mr. and Mrs. Ramsey for initial questioning and not taking everyone involved down to the police station for questioning. And, crucially, the police failed to seal the crime scene. Boulder police detective Linda Arndt, without permission from the police department, gave Ramsey lawyer Patrick Burke a copy of the 'ransom note'.

Vincent Bugliosi, in his excellent book 'Helter Skelter' vividly demonstrates how the police investigation of the Tate-LaBianca murders included many errors and inconsistencies: Various police officers who arrived at the scene of the Tate murders recorded different times of arrival. One of the officers at the scene of the crime obliterated a bloody fingerprint. Evidence at the scene of the crime was unaccountably moved. The forensic team failed to collect all the samples of blood at the crime scene and the victims wounds were not properly measured. Furthermore Dr. Noguchi, the Los Angeles Coroner who performed the autopsies, made numerous mistakes.

Author Joe McGinniss in his best-selling book 'Fatal Vision' demonstrated how numerous investigative errors were made in the Dr. Jeffrey MacDonald case. A bloody footprint was destroyed. Fingerprints of the victims were not taken and other fingerprints were poorly documented. Objects at the scene of the crime were handled before examination by experts and the garbage at the scene of the crime was not investigated. And so on and so forth.

Conspiracy theorists often cite the phrase "reasonable doubt" as to Oswald's guilt. Ipso Facto, if reasonable doubt exists then we must assume Oswald's innocence. The real question to be asked should be - 'Is the doubt reasonable outside one's own subjective feelings on the matter?'. If the doubt is unreasonable-that is, it is not linked with other important areas of the investigation, then we cannot assume this doubt can be a matter of rational discourse. People can wrongly believe their doubts are 'reasonable'. This suggests that the inquirer, for example Kennedy assassination investigators or conspiracy buffs, have a responsibility to investigate whether any doubt is, as a matter of objective fact, reasonable. In the context of the Kennedy case, the only alternative to Oswald's guilt is an implausible conspiracy, and therefore a reasonable doubt about Oswald's guilt must imply that it is reasonable to entertain the possibility of an implausible conspiracy.

Reasonable doubt is not, then, "Doubt with a reason" as many lawyers define it. The true meaning of the term is not simply "possible doubt" because everything relating to human affairs is open to some possible or imaginary doubt. Reasonable doubt cannot be used to examine an isolated anomaly in the evidence. If the preponderance of evidence points to the guilt of the accused it is not reasonable to say a particular anomalous piece of evidence shows innocence. Even when more than one anomaly arises it is still not 'reasonable' to assume innocence if the preponderance of evidence shows guilt.

This misunderstanding about reasonable doubt was compounded by the amount of evidence in the case. The problem with this crime is, rather than too little evidence there was too much. In trying to explain the events of the Kennedy assassination investigations became bogged down in details about bullet trajectories, police files, witness statements, autopsy reports. Because of the magnitude of the crime it was inevitable this would happen.

If only a fraction of the evidence had been accumulated there would still have been no room for 'reasonable doubt'. Yet because we have many times as much evidence it seems that some people have many times as much doubt.

We have so much evidence it was inevitable that mistakes, inaccuracies, misstatements and human error would occur. Take any crime and investigate it to the nth degree and the same anomalies, mysteries and mistakes will surface sooner or later.

Given this propensity, it is welcome to Conspiracy Theorists, faced with a preponderance of evidence pointing to Oswald acting alone, to complicate matters by raising doubts about small details. There is always the chance that the reader will be confused and not understand the complex issues involved. But even if they understand the issues, the confusion and doubts about some of the evidence may influence their assessment of the totality of the evidence.

Conspiracy Theorists use yet another tactic in order to propagate their theories. They repeat discredited testimony time after time. For example, Ray and Mary La Fontaine, in one of the most recent conspiracy books published in 1996, use Delphine Roberts' testimony that she had seen Oswald and Guy Banister together at Banister's New Orleans office at 544 Camp Street. They have ignored Posner's interview with Robert's in which she began to dissemble, rambling on about her mystical experiences. It is quite evident from Posner's research that Delphine Roberts was mentally unbalanced. The LaFontaines write:

"In her account to Anthony Summers (and to the HSCA) Banister's secretary and mistress, Delphine Roberts, reported that her ex-F.B.I. boss employed some strange characters. They included David Ferrie ... and a young ex-marine whom she believed had use of an office on the second floor. His name was Lee Harvey Oswald." The LaFontaines thus fail to use Posner's interview with Roberts which invalidates her testimony.

The Fontaines made the same mistake when they used Jack Ruby's statement in which he talks about the need to be taken to Washington so he can tell the truth about the 'conspiracy'. The Fontaines write:

"... Ruby pleaded repeatedly with his visitors to take him with them back to Washington where he would feel more free to talk. Warren, whose Commission Report three months later would absolve Ruby of any connection with organised crime or the assassination of President Kennedy, denied the request."

The use of witness testimony by Conspiracy Theorists is troubling because they generally believe that all witnesses have equal authority. This is not true. For example, take a hypothetical murder scene and spots of blood are found. If the witness is a professional, say a detective, his testimony about the blood drops would be superior to the testimony which might be given by a lay person who has had no experience in the field of forensic science.

The detective is thus given 'professional authority'.

Furthermore, a witness whose testimony is corroborated by a wealth of evidence which supports his statement is superior to a witnesses whose testimony has no supporting evidence. For example, take the testimony of Warren Commission witness Howard Brennan, who saw Oswald in the 6th floor window, and the testimony of S.M. (Skinny) Holland who saw puffs of smoke behind the Grassy Knoll. Why is Brennan's testimony superior to Holland's? Precisely because Brennan's statement is supported by the preponderance of evidence which shows that Kennedy was fired at from behind and not from in front; evidence about the rifle; Book Depository employees etc. It should also be self-evident that witnesses who gave their testimony at the time of the assassination are more credible than 'Grassy Knoll shooter' witnesses like Jean Hill who changed her story frequently or other 'witnesses' like Ed Hoffman, who did not speak out until the late sixties or seventies.

Conspiracy Theorists continually lend support to the specious claims that the acoustics testimony before the House Assassinations Committee proves there was a fourth shot. This testimony was discredited by the Ramsey Panel of Experts in 1982 yet David Scheim in his 1988 book "Contract on America" goes into detail about the acoustics testimony and relies heavily on the conclusion that "'with a probability of 95% or better', the third shot was fired from the Grassy Knoll." Mention is made of the panel of scientists who discredited the House Assassinations Committee acoustics evidence but Scheim relies on 'dissenting' members of the scientific community to rebut the findings. Similarly the dissenting member of the Committees pathologists panel, Dr Cyril Wecht, is the person most quoted to shore up the theory that Kennedy was shot from in front.

Fakery has had an important place in the world of conspiracy theories. Various document forgeries have muddied the waters of Kennedy assassination research., the latest a batch of 'original' documents from the personal papers of purported Kennedy Attorney Lawrence X. Cusack. They were discovered by the late lawyer's son "Lex" Cusack and marketed by document dealer Thomas G. Cloud.

The documents purport to show a relationship between JFK and the Mafia and that the president had been blackmailed by Marilyn Monroe. The documents were examined by Pulitzer prize winning investigative journalist Seymour Hersh and were authenticated by 5 'experts'. Hersh became convinced they were genuine and were documentary proof that JFK was killed by Chicago crime boss Sam Giancana. "I just solved the Kennedy assassination", Hersh told assassination researcher Michael Ewing, "It was Sam Giancana."

However, Hersh had to eventually retreat from his position when the documents were finally, in July 1997, proven to be bogus. Microscopic analysis of the typewriting on the Monroe document showed evidence of fakery. Some of the characters had been lifted off and replaced- a process involving a 'ball-style' IBM Selectric typewriter which was not invented until 1973. The use of typewriter ribbons, which were not around when the documents were supposedly written, also proved they were fake. Other proofs were the sizes of the commas and full-stops which were subtly different from those used at the time and the spacing between individual letters were different in the late 50's and early 60's.

Hersh continued with his book 'The Dark Side Of Camelot' but naturally he did not use the documents to prove JFK was killed by the Mafia.

The media must also take some responsibility for the growing acceptance of Conspiracy Theories by the American public. In the 1970's and 1980's there was something almost frightening in the intensity of the public doubts about the role played by government agencies in the assassination. The media, in it's new found virility after the Watergate scandal, reported any theory that popped up, including the most ludicrous implicating President Johnson, without any sense of incredulity. It felt engulfing and all-encompassing as if there was no room for an anti-conspiracy view. This atmosphere was created, I believe, by the media's scepticism about politicians or those government servants who worked for the security agencies. It was also created by the media's hesitation in putting forward the government's side of the issues.

In joining the conspiracy bandwagon the media propagated the belief that the public was susceptible to conspiracy theories and thus helped to silence the opposition. At the same time those who made the decisions about how to present new evidence arising from newly published conspiracy books and the release of government files, appealed to the current national obsession that the body politic was corrupt and did not serve the interests of American Democracy. Cover- ups existed everywhere. There MUST have been a government cover-up in the Kennedy Assassination. The Conspiracy Theorists were the good guys rooting out abuses of power. Supporters of the lone-assassin theory were the bad guys protecting a sinister and corrupt government.

True, the media were reporting what they perceived to be the public consciousness. But the conspiracy issue appealed to their own way of looking at government. Post-Watergate reporting methods were in vogue - 'And we were right about Watergate weren't we?'

For example, Jean Davison's excellent examination of Oswald's life and the way in which Conspiracy Theorists had misused the Warren Commission's Volumes of Hearings was not well publicised by the media. Although she left many questions unanswered (which I attempt to address in my work) her methodology and interpretation of the facts of the case were far superior to that employed by Conspiracy Theorists. Yet their books have been continually acclaimed throughout the United States. Thus the media were not only reporting events but framing it by their choices. Davison's lone-assassin book did not meet the demands of drama and excitement unlike Summers' conspiracy book. Thus the media entered the debate and helped to mould it. In doing so they made Conspiracy Theorists more bolder and the lone-assassin theorists more timid. For a long time it was the act of a 'philistine' in disagreeing with conspiracy theories. Publicity was also a problem as lone assassin theories do not meet the demands of 'prime-time' drama.

In not presenting the full and complex facts surrounding the assassination the media did not just report the story they were part of it-shaping it and creating it by the choices they made over the years while they themselves were also responding to the intense public reaction (especially after the release of the movie JFK) and their need to meet it. It is such a process of giving the public what they want that creates a distorted picture of events.

Conspiracy Theorists do not believe in coincidences but it is a simple fact of life that they do occur and more often than we like to think.

Some writers try to imbue strange coincidences between the assassinations of Kennedy and Lincoln giving them almost mystical traits. But they are what they are-coincidences. For example, there are the same number of letters in the names of the assassins. Lincoln's assassin ran from a theatre to a warehouse. Kennedy's assassin ran from a warehouse to a theatre (cinema). Lincoln's assistant was named Kennedy. Kennedy's assistant was named Lincoln. Both presidents were killed on a Friday. They both were seen as presidents who fought for civil rights for African- Americans. Both presidents were shot in the head from behind.

Coincidence, then, is not as unique a phenomenon as we think it is. For example, if we plotted the movements of, say, 7 people on a computer over a given period of time would we not discover some intriguing crossed paths? Would we not discover an intriguing web of associations? This case is no different from other tragedies in many respects—What if we did this or what if we did that-would the outcome have been different? Airline crash investigators, for example, constantly quote cases where chains of events all seemingly unconnected and independent on one another, interact together to cause an aeroplane crash.

Sometimes, then, these chains of occurrences take on bizarre traits. For example, some Conspiracy Theorists write that because the protective covering on the presidential limousine was removed on the morning of the assassination sinister moves were afoot. Others point to the change of the motorcade route which forced the limousine to slow down as it passed the Texas Book Depository; the change was necessary as it was the correct route to the Trade Mart where Kennedy was to give his speech. The original route was blocked by a concrete road divider. The Texas Employment Commission was about to offer Oswald a job outside the vicinity of Dealey Plaza when Ruth Paine found him a job at the Book Depository. Fellow employees moved from the 6th to the 5th floor just before the arrival of the motorcade. If all or one or two of these events had not happened the tragic turn of circumstances may not have been put into effect.

Conspiracy Theorists frequently eschew coincidences but use them if they suit their purposes. For example, Ray and Mary LaFontaine maintain that a man named Harry Elrod, along with others in the vicinity of the railroad tracks near the depository building, was picked up by Dallas police and placed in the same cellblock as Oswald. Just coincidentally, Elrod's cellmate had seen Oswald before the day of the assassination 'conspiring' with Jack Ruby and others and receiving a share of some money. Apart from the obvious problems with this story- why would 'conspirators' meet in full view of a stranger- Elrod's 'proof' is hearsay and unverifiable. The only verifiable part of the story are the Dallas Police records which prove that Elrod was indeed arrested in Dealey Plaza that day as one of many 'suspects' in the assassination.

Coincidence is linked to human error and negligence. What would have happened if the F.B.I. had done their job properly and kept tabs on Oswald? Were the reactions of the Secret Service slow, when the first shots rang out, because many of them had been drinking at a Fort Worth night Club the previous evening? There are plenty of 'what ifs' in this case.

Like many who suffer fools gladly Americans suffer Conspiracy Theorists reverently. Similarly, Conspiracy Theorists are predisposed to accept any witness whatever their 'credentials'. Some of these 'witnesses' have claimed to have seen Oswald in places where he shouldn't have been. One of the most famous of the 'multiple' Oswald sightings involved a gundealer who produced a tag with Oswald's signature. This caused problems with the investigation as Oswald was supposed to be elsewhere during the time period given by the dealer. The gunshop tag was later found to be faked but by this time many people were persuaded that an Oswald impersonator proved conspiracy. Indeed, many other JFK Assassination documents have eventually proven to be bogus- for example a letter supposedly written by Oswald implicating oil- billionaire H.L. Hunt in the assassination. These Oswald 'sightings' have caused problems for investigators as they often coincided with Oswald's placement elsewhere and many can not be verified. Many can be explained as mis-identification or a desire for publicity. Others can simply be neither proven nor disproven.

Conspiracy Theorists are very trusting of these so-called 'witnesses' who frequently turn up in their books claiming that they observed, or were part of, all kinds of intrigue in the Kennedy assassination. If all the events had actually occurred that 'witnesses' claimed the events in Dealey Plaza would have been nothing less a phenomenon than a landing by a UFO on the White House lawn.

Some witnesses, like Matthew Smith's 'Hank Gordon', use pseudonyms, thus making their claims unverifiable. Conspiracy Theorists jump at the chance to secure the exclusive stories of these witnesses but fail to check out their veracity. Many statements are not checked until years later. For example Henry Hurt writes:

"One of the most convincing of these Grassy Knoll witnesses is Gordon Arnold who for 15 years was believed by assassination experts to be a lump on the ground- perhaps a pile of earth. That is how he appeared to many of those who made intense studies of the photographs of the scene. That was precisely Arnold's desire as he felt the powerful reverberations of a bullet zing just past his left ear that afternoon."

Arnold appeared in the documentary "The Men Who Killed Kennedy" in 1988, and repeated his story. To me, his story lacks verisimilitude and is led by the documentary makers in accepting the claims of 'photographic experts' that he is the man supposedly dressed in army uniform who is throwing himself to the ground. Gerald Posner has named another person who was the soldier and the colourised and enhanced photograph showing the Grassy Knoll shooters (one of whom is named 'badgeman' by Conspiracy Theorists) has been shown to be nothing but light and shadows. Arnold, according to Posner's very persuasive investigation, was not even in Dealey Plaza at the time of the assassination.

Did Arnold give his statement to the Dallas Police or the F.B.I. at the time of the assassination. Apparently not. But this does not prevent Conspiracy Theorists from accepting his claims. After all, he was frightened of the conspirators wasn't he?

Another witness Ed Hoffman, investigated by Bill Sloan in his work "JFK-Breaking The Silence" and interviewed for the Channel 4 documentary "The Men Who Killed Kennedy", claims he saw the man who shot the President from where he was situated on the Grassy Knoll and railway overpass area and it was not Oswald. He was not able to communicate it to the authorities because he was deaf and mute. Posner checked out Hoffman's story and found out he must have been lying as he changed his story a number of times and his line of sight to where the 'shooter' was hidden was impossible because of the layout of trees and billboards. Hoffman, like Jean Hill, spends a lot of his time signing autographs in Dealey Plaza; an almost mystical place now which still attracts huge crowds coming to see the place where the 'conspirators' killed Kennedy. How long will it be until these uncorroborated witnesses finally dissemble?

In my research I have not been able to find any substantial consideration by Conspiracy Theorists about how Oswald, a supposed hired assassin, managed to work for the 'conspirators' whilst living in what amounted to penury. This may account for why many Conspiracy Theorists insisting

Oswald was a 'patsy'. There is no evidence whatsoever that Oswald was paid for his troubles which begs the question —Would not the conspirators have assisted Oswald financially?

The Warren Commission investigated Oswald's finances and their conclusions have been supported by Marina Oswald:

"During the 17-month preceding his death, Oswald's pattern of living was consistent with his limited income. He lived with his family in furnished apartments whose cost, including utilities, ranged from about 60 to 75 dollars per month. Witnesses testified to his wife's disappointment and complaints and to their own shock and misgivings about several of the apartments in which the Oswald's lived with relatives and acquaintances at no cost. Oswald and his family lived with his brother Robert and then with Marguerite Oswald from June until sometime in August 1962. As discussed previously, Marina Oswald lived with Elena Hall and spent a few nights at the Taylor's house during October of 1962; in November of that same year, Marina Oswald lived with two families. When living away from his family Oswald rented rooms for 7 and 8 dollars per week or stayed at the YMCA in Dallas where he paid 2 dollars 25 cents per day. During late April and early May 1963, Oswald lived with relatives in New Orleans, while his wife lived with Ruth Paine in Irving, Tex. From September 24, 1963, until November 22, Marina stayed with Ruth Paine, while Oswald lived in roominghouses in Dallas. During the period Marina Oswald resided with others, neither she nor her husband made any contribution to her support.

The Oswald's owned no major household appliances, had no automobile, and resorted to dental and hospital clinics for medical care. Acquaintances purchased baby furniture for them, and paid dental bills in one instance. After his return to the United States, Oswald did not smoke or drink, and he discouraged his wife from doing so. Oswald spent much of his time reading books which he obtained from the public library, and periodicals to which he subscribed. He resided near his place of employment and used buses to travel to and from work. When he visited his wife and the children on weekends in October and November 1963, he rode in a neighbour's car, making no contribution for gasoline or other expenses. Oswald's personal wardrobe was also very modest. He customarily wore T-shirts, cheap slacks, well-worn sweaters, and well-used zipper jackets. Oswald owned one suit, of Russian make and purchase, poor fitting and of heavy fabric which, despite its unsuitability to the climates of Texas and Louisiana and his obvious discomfort, he wore on the few occasions that required dress.

Food for his family was extremely meagre. Paul Gregory testified that during the 6 weeks that Marina Oswald tutored him he took the Oswald's shopping for food and groceries on a number of occasions and that he was "amazed at how little they bought". Their friends in the Dallas-Fort Worth area frequently brought them food and groceries. Marina testified that her husband ate "very little". He "never had breakfast. He just drank coffee and that is all. Not because he was trying to economise. Simply he never liked to eat." She estimated that when he was living by himself in a roominghouse, he would spend "about a dollar, 1 dollar 30 cents" for dinner and have a sandwich and soft drink for lunch."

For each and every circumstance surrounding the assassination Conspiracy Theorists will offer a dramatically different, but I believe inherently illogical, interpretation of it. This is especially true when Conspiracy Theorists misinterpret Oswald's stay in New Orleans in the summer of 1963. Nearly every conspiracy writer suggests that Oswald was acting as some kind of agent provocateur manipulated by plotters. Oswald's actions should be seen for what they were-the delusions of a fantasist.

Conspiracy Theorists put forward good points and bad alike, mingle discredited testimony with valid evidence and make up for weak links in their hypotheses by making false accusations and unlimited calumny against innocent people. They offer no connected account of what they think occurred and content themselves with issuing a barrage of rhetorical questions and innuendo.

But how does the public fall for the demonologists world view? In the majority of cases conspiracy theories are too often like the Hydra-cut off one of it's heads and a score of others take it's place.

Gary Wills and Ovid Demaris wrote their excellent biography of Jack Ruby in 1968 and it stands as probably the best examination of the people who were caught up in the tragic events of that November weekend. Like James Kirkwood, who was to write his book about the New Orleans fiasco in 1970, they understood more than any Conspiracy Theorist that the assassination story was about tragic lives not sinister plots. As Wills and Demaris wrote:

"All our private hells-surviving our beliefs - arose out of the national catastrophe, invaded us in our privacies we did not know we had. A shrewd instinct of self-preservation made us drive the threat back out, make it public, reduce it to a 'plot'. . . . This explains the widespread audience the theorists enjoy, the willingness vaguely to believe it is 'all politics', that in some such terms it all makes sense. Human ambition, venality, greed, crime-all these we live with and can handle; no matter how criminal, such acts are at least conventional in their sequence of cause and effect; things done by man, and so within man's power. There is this much, at least, of reason and light in the darkness of the darkest plot. Better that than the vision of total night, of superhuman or subhuman forces revealing themselves, at last, as anti-human, erasing all man's pretensions, all reason, order, law."

CHAPTER 10

QUESTIONS ANSWERED- WHY LEE HARVEY OSWALD KILLED PRESIDENT KENNEDY.

"Fanatics have their dreams
wherewith they weave,
A paradise for a sect."

John Keats.

"The resenters, those men with cancer of the psyche, make the great assassins."

Richard Condon-"The Manchurian Candidate".

The explanation of Oswald's motive for killing President Kennedy was buried with him. But I believe the mystery can be solved by penetrating Oswald's personal life, his ideological beliefs and his increasingly disturbed behaviour in the months leading up to the assassination. Whilst such a study is not subject to absolute verification and, I confess, is in the manner of Conspiracy Theorists, relying on speculation, it does in this instance reveal much to the discerning mind. In this chapter we are dealing with imponderables which are not subject to conclusive proof, but it is not, I believe, an impenetrable darkness. My understanding of Oswald's personality and character is in direct contradiction to that of Conspiracy Theorists. And my approach is a psychological one deriving from my research. I hope to paint a picture of Oswald, as I see him, who is the same person that his family, colleagues, friends and acquaintances have recognised as true. This is a man whose psychological make-up can be understood and thus reveal that his act was not just explicable but inevitable-given the chance that provided the opportunity; that had he not killed Kennedy it would have been some other prominent figure.

The Warren Commission, in 1964, and the House Assassinations Committee, in 1977, rigorously investigated Oswald's tortured life but fell short in explaining his motives:

"While Oswald appeared to most of those who knew him as a meek and harmless person," said the Warren Commission, "he sometimes imagined himself as the 'Commander' and, apparently seriously, as a political propheta man who said that after 20 years he would be prime minister. His wife testified that he compared himself with great leaders of history. Such ideas of grandeur were apparently accompanied by notions of oppression. He had a great hostility toward his environment, whatever it happened to be, which he expressed in striking and sometimes violent acts long before the assassination."

In this chapter I hope to show that all of Oswald's actions, however seemingly irrational, are part of the same believable figure. After researching Oswald's life for so long his act of killing Kennedy appears to me as a 'natural' one. He was not the conspiring genius or patsy he is portrayed by Conspiracy Theorists. Oswald was a man who had experienced a deprived if not depraved childhood. His craving for attention which was not fulfilled as a child passed on into adulthood. Witness after witness have testified to his malevolence and maladjustment in his formative years; as an adolescent and as a young man. His period in the Marine Corps was marked by disillusion and antagonism to authority. His relationship with his wife contributed to the spark of violence which led, in the final year of his life, to a violent eruption. His burning desire to be recognised as a revolutionary is perhaps the cornerstone in understanding how his need to enter history testifies to his perverted ambitions. It is clear to me that this man could never have been a KGB agent; that, though he was a secretive liar, he could never have lived a lie; that he shot Kennedy because Kennedy was there to be shot; and that, in his mind he could be a truly revolutionary figure who would be a hero in the coming world communist system. Lee Harvey Oswald was an accident about to happen.

Born October 18th 1939, two months after his father died, Oswald was raised under the influence of a domineering mother. The relationship had an obvious traumatic effect on the boy. Young Oswald once told a probation officer, "Well, I've got to live with her. I guess I love her."

Lee was the third boy born to Mrs. Marguerite Claverie Oswald. After the death of Oswald's father Mrs. Oswald went to work as a saleswoman about two years after the birth of her new son, holding a series of different jobs. His mother was at home with Lee during his first two years, and later, when she went to work, her sister Lillian or whoever else she could get to baby-sit cared for him. When Lee was three he was placed in a boarding school which accepted children either orphaned or with one parent. His brother Robert and half-brother John had been lodged at the boarding school a year earlier. Mrs. Oswald took the children home on weekends but protested that she couldn't look after them and work too.

In 1944 Mrs. Oswald met Edwin A. Eckdahl, an industrial engineer from Boston who was working in the Southern United States. They were married-she for the third time-in May 1945, and took off on a car holiday so she could meet his family in Massachusetts. Instead of returning to New Orleans, the family settled in a small house in Fort Worth, not far from Dallas. The two older boys were sent to a military school in Port Gibson, Mississippi; Lee lived at home with his mother and stepfather.

Records show that Lee did not enter primary school until January 1947, when he was 7. The family home at that time was on the south side of Fort Worth and Lee entered the first grade at Lily B. Clayton school. His marks were average. Lee did not make any close friends.

In March 1948 Lee transferred from Clayton school to the George Clark Elementary school in the same area on Fort Worth's South side. In that year Edwin Eckdahl sued for divorce. In his suit Eckdahl complained that his wife nagged him all the time and argued about money. He testified that she once threw a bottle at his head and another time scratched and struck him. A jury upheld Eckdahl and gave him a divorce. Marguerite returned to her former name of Oswald and moved into a one-story frame house in the Ridglea district of Fort Worth. She and Lee-and occasionally the two other boys-lived there for the next four years. Neighbours remember Lee as quick-tempered and anti-social.

Lee's teacher Mrs. Clyde Livingstone, remembered Lee as a boy who was lonely, quiet and shy, who did not easily form friendships with other boys. His abilities at school gradually declined.

Lee finished the 6th grade at Ridglea West in June 1952. He was approaching his 13th birthday-fairly tall for his age, well-built and athletic. But he appeared lonely and became noticeably resentful and antagonistic to authority. At this time his mother decided to move to New York to be near her first son John Pic who was stationed with the Coast Guard.

They arrived in New York in September, moved into an apartment in the Bronx and Lee entered Trinity Lutheran school. He soon began to play truant and he was judged to be unsatisfactory in co-operation, dependability and self-control.

His truancy resulted in his first brush with legal authority-in this case the New York children's court. It was at this time that Oswald was interviewed by a psychiatrist Dr. Renatus Hartogs, a Ph.D. in clinical psychology and an M.D. Hartogs considered Lee dangerous, a fact often overlooked by Conspiracy Theorists who give only lip service to Dr. Hartogs testimony. Dr. Hartogs said that Lee had a potential for explosive behaviour and an aggressive, assaultive acting out which he said was rather unusual to find in a child who was sent to the Youth House on such a mild charge of truancy from school. He thought Lee was 'self-centred' and showed a 'cold, detached outer attitude'.

The Warren Report stated: "Dr. Hartogs did find Oswald to be a tense, withdrawn, and evasive boy who intensely disliked talking about himself and his feelings. He noted that Lee liked to give the impression that he did not care for other people but preferred to keep to himself, so that he was not bothered and did not have to make the effort of communicating. Oswald's withdrawn tendencies and solitary habits were thought to be the result of "intense anxiety, shyness, feelings of awkwardness and insecurity ... (Dr. Hartogs said in his report that) ... "Lee has to be seen as an emotionally, quite disturbed youngster who suffers under the impact of really existing emotional isolation and deprivation, lack of affection, absence of family life and rejection by a self involved and conflicted mother."

Lee's withdrawal was noted by a social worker, Evelyn Siegal who gave testimony to the Warren Commission. Siegal found Oswald to be a "seriously detached, withdrawn youngster ... emotionally starved, affectionless." She thought he had detached himself from the world because "no one in it ever met any of his needs for love." Siegal concluded that Lee "just felt that his mother never gave a damn for him. He always felt like a burden that she simply just had to tolerate." Lee admitted to Seigal his fantasies about being powerful and sometimes hurting and killing people. Seigal concluded that Lee had suffered serious personality damage. She believed that Lee's mother Marguerite, "Didn't seem to see him (Lee) as a person at all, but as an extension of herself." Seigal described Marguerite as a "smartly dressed, gray haired woman, very self-possessed and alert and superficially affable, "but essentially, "a defensive, rigid, self-involved person who had real difficulty in accepting and relating to people" and who had "little under-standing" of Lee's behaviour and of the "protective shell he has drawn around himself." Dr. Hartogs reported that Marguerite did not understand that Lee's withdrawal was a form of "violent but silent protest against his neglect by her and represents his reaction to a complete absence of family life."

Lee's truant officer, Dr. John Carro stated:

"When you get a thirteen year old kid who withdraws into his own world, whose only company is fantasy, who wants no friends, who has no father figure, whose mother doesn't seem to relate either - then you've got trouble." The boy's mother, Carro added, "was detached and non-involved. She kept saying that Lee wasn't any problem, and she didn't understand what the fuss was all about."

Her son John Pic saw his mother's obsession as money and her placing of money where other values should have been. He said no decision had ever been made on the basis of the children's well being, but only on the basis of what was cheapest and best for Marguerite. Robert, too, believed his mother's character had a profound influence on the family. Priscilla Johnson McMillan has related how, after Lee's arrest for the murder of President Kennedy, Robert was approached by his mother in the Dallas police jail: "I would like to speak to you alone, " she told Robert, "This room is bugged. Be careful of what you say." Robert thought, "All my life I've been hearing her tell me about conspiracies, hidden motives and malicious people." Robert believed Lee was a lot like his mother. Both of them craved attention.

John Pic has testified to the change in his brother on seeing him after his arrival in New York. John recalled that the day they arrived, Lee was waiting for him at the subway exit about ten blocks from the apartment and seemed glad to see him. He took a few days leave to show Lee around the city and noticed that Lee had definitely become the 'Boss'. If he decided to do something he did it. Pic thought he had no respect for his mother at all.

As time went by, tension developed at the Pic's apartment when Marguerite made no effort to help with the food or lodging. When Pic's wife was interviewed by the F.B.I. after the assassination she remembered how Lee kept damaging their bookcase by putting beverage glasses down on it. She also remembered that one day she asked Lee not to turn on the T.V. set Marguerite had brought with them and Lee pulled out a small pocket-knife with a blade opened. He moved toward her, she said, and she backed off. When Pic got home that night, she told him about it and this was the end of Pic's relationship with his brother. All of Lee's life John had expected "some great tragedy to strike" his younger brother.

In 1954 Lee and his mother were back in New Orleans, and Lee entered Beauregard Junior High School. Shortly before he graduated from Beauregard in 1956 Lee's emotional problems were increasing. He was having more trouble with his classmates and was friendless.

Immediately after his 16th birthday Lee tried to enlist in the Marines but was rejected because of his age. He managed to get several jobs-one as a messenger on the Mississippi River docks, another as a runner for a dental laboratory in New Orleans. In between jobs he read and according to his mother he brought home books on Marxism and socialism.

In August of 1956, Lee and his mother moved to Fort Worth and he entered Arlington Heights High school. The pattern of disaffection and separation from the other students, which had it's beginning in New York, continued.

On October 18th 1956 Lee was old enough to enter the Marines and got his mother to sign a false affidavit that he was 17. On October 24th he enlisted in the Marines in Dallas. Lee went to training camp at San Diego, California. At first he was quite serious with his training but then he became troublesome and difficult towards authority. His Marine commanding officer, Captain John E. Donavan, told the Washington Evening star, shortly after the assassination:

"(Oswald was) a wise guy... His revolt was against any kind of authority. He wasn't expelled from society. He expelled himself from it. (He) used to read most of the time- history books, magazines and a Russian newspaper he used to get. He also spent a lot of time studying the Russian language. There were no pocket books or comics for him. One of his tricks was to lay a trap for some officer, particularly a field-grade officer if he could catch one. He'd study up on some particular world situation and then go up to the officer and say 'Sir, could you please explain the Venezuelan or Cambodian situation, sir?' He always put a sir before and after speaking to an officer, but said it in such a supercilious, pointedly obsequious way that it became an insult rather than a courtesy. The poor officer would make a valiant attempt to answer the question, probably not knowing a whole lot about the specifics of whatever Oswald brought up. Then Oswald would turn to me and say 'Sir, what do you think of that, sir?' I knew what he was up to. He was just trying to show off his superior knowledge. He was smart enough. You have to have a GCT score of 110 to get into radar.

That's the same score for getting a commission. But you could tell he was a self-educated man because there were rough edges to his knowledge."

Oswald was court- martialled twice in 1958. On April 11th, he was convicted of violating Article 92 by failing to register a personal weapon, a pistol. As a result some of his privileges were taken away. His second court-martial came two months later. He had talked to an NCO when both were off duty and had tried to pick a fight with him. The NCO reported him. Because it was his second offence, Oswald was demoted from private first class to private.

In October 1958 Lee celebrated his 19th birthday and was shipped back to the United States, his tour of duty overseas completed. He was reassigned to the 3rd Marine Air Wing at El Toro Marine base near Santa Ana, California.

Oswald's plans were set by this time. He began to study Russian by himself and he tried to enter a military language school by taking a test in Russian, but he failed the qualifying test. He continued to study on his own.

In the summer of 1959 Oswald applied for a hardship release from the Marine Corps. His mother, working in a Fort Worth Department store was injured when a box of glass jars fell and struck her on the head. She was forced to remain in bed for 6 months and the medical bills rapidly exhausted her savings.

Shortly before his release Oswald applied for admission to Albert Schweitzer College in Switzerland, a private college with a curriculum in world problems, philosophy, religion, sociology and languages. He was accepted for the spring term of 1960, but he never appeared. Lee spent only 3 nights at his mother's house. He had saved 1,600 dollars from his Marine Corps pay and it is likely he had other plans in mind.

Oswald's mother realised what he had had in mind when a newspaper reporter called in late October 1959 and said that her son had defected to Russia. Lee was only a few days past his 20th birthday.

Oswald told officials that he was in Russia as a tourist. After two and a half weeks in Moscow, on October 31st. he appeared at the U.S. Embassy, slapped his passport on the counter and declared his intention to defect. He said he had applied for Soviet citizenship. The next day he was interviewed by Aline Mosby, United Press International reporter. The interview gave him the opportunity for the first time in his life to feel important. He struck Mosby as naive and emotionally unbalanced.

Oswald was also interviewed by Priscilla Johnson another reporter who was in Moscow at the time and she also considered him to be unstable.

On November 14th, a month after he first turned up in Moscow, Soviet officials told Oswald he would not be granted citizenship. After an unsuccessful suicide bid Soviet officials considered him to be unstable, but because they did not want an international embarrassment, allowed him to stay as a resident alien and sent him to Minsk where he was given work in a factory. A high ranking member of the Politburo found out about Oswald's rejection so she used her influence with Kruschev to allow Oswald to stay.

The Warren Commission explained why Oswald was allowed to stay in Russia:

"When compared to five other defector cases, this procedure seems unexceptional. Two defectors from US Army intelligence units in West Germany appear to have been given citizenship immediately, but both had prior KGB connections and fled as a result of Army security checks. Of the other three cases, one was accepted after not more than 5 weeks and given a stateless passport (like Oswald) apparently at about the same time. The second was immediately given permission to stay for a while, and his subsequent request for citizenship was granted three months later. The third was allowed to stay after he made his citizenship request, but almost two months had passed before he was told that he had been accepted. Although the Soviet Ministry of Foreign Affairs soon after told the US Embassy that he was a Soviet citizen, he did not receive his document until five or six months after initial application. We know of only one case in which an American asked for Soviet citizenship but did not take up residence in the USSR. In that instance, the American changed his mind and voluntarily returned to the United States less than three weeks after he had requested Soviet citizenship."

The KGB have always claimed they had never interrogated Oswald but now after the end of the Cold War KGB agents have spoken the truth about those events. According to the head of the KGB at the time, Vladimir Semichastny, the KGB moved Oswald from the hospital where he had been treated for the injuries sustained in the suicide attempt, to a hotel while they considered his fate. They did indeed question Oswald about his military service. Semichastny said in an interview with BBC 'Timewatch' researchers, in 1993:

"Counter intelligence and Intelligence both looked him over to see what he was capable of but unfortunately neither could find any ability at all. ..... We were not convinced this would be his last act of blackmail (Oswald's suicide attempt). We expected he would try again which would be difficult to deal with in Moscow so we decided to send him to Minsk."

Two and a half years of KGB surveillance had revealed nothing which would suggest Oswald had been planted by American Intelligence. Semichastny said:

"We concluded that he was not working for U.S. intelligence. His intellectual training and capabilities were such that it would not show the F.B.I. and the C.I.A. in a good light if they used people like him."

Oleg M. Nechiporenko, a KGB agent who read the Soviet Secret Service's file on Oswald confirms this observation. The KGB wondered if Oswald was a spy and kept tabs on him throughout his stay in Russia. Nechiporenko maintains that when Oswald defected in 1959 an agent, cover-named 'Andrei Nikolayevich', interviewed Oswald and was unimpressed. According to Nechiporenko, Oswald was a resentful person whose vainglory and pent-up capacity for violence made him unsuitable by almost any group that would have wanted JFK dead. He was simply too undependable to have been a likely cog in a conspiracy. His psychological portrait of Oswald suggests this.

Oswald became embittered with his new communist paradise and his entries to his 'Historic Diary' as he called it, is perhaps the best description of Oswald's state of mind at this time:

"As my Russian improves I become increasingly conscious of just what sort of sociaty (sic) I live in. Mass gymnastics, compulsory afterwork meeting, usually political information meeting. Compulsory attendance at lectures and the sending of the entire shop collective (except me) to pick potatoes on a Sunday, at a state collective farm: A 'patroict (sic) duty' to bring in the harvest. The opions (sic) of the workers (unvoiced) are that it's a great pain in the neck: they don't seem to be esspicialy (sic) enthusiastic about any of the 'collective' duties a natural feeling. I am increasingly aware of the presence, in all thing, of Lebizen, shop party secretary, fat fortyish, and jovial on the outside. He is a no-nonsense party regular ... I am stating (sic) to reconsider my desire about staying the work is drab the money I get has nowhere to be spent. No night clubs or bowling allys (sic) no places of recreation acept (sic) the trade union dances I have had enough."

Ironically it was because of Embassy consul Richard Snyder's persuading Oswald not to renounce his citizenship when Oswald arrived in Russia, that Oswald was allowed to return to the U.S. Had Snyder allowed Oswald to act impulsively in giving up his American citizenship he would have been trapped in the Soviet Union.

An exit visa was finally obtained and Oswald's two and a half year Russian sojourn was finally at an end. On June 22nd he and his Russian wife Marina left for America. They disembarked in New York and flew on to Dallas.

Conspiracy Theorists are astounded that Oswald was not debriefed by the F.B.I. or C.I.A. on his return to the United States. To investigate the possibility that he was debriefed and that the C.I.A. was covering up the House Assassinations Committee "reviewed the files of 22 other defectors to the Soviet Union (from the original list of 380 who were born in America and appeared to have returned from the United States between 1958 and 1963). Of these 22 individuals, only 4 were interviewed at any time by the C.I.A. ... Based on this file review, it appeared to the Committee that, in fact, the C.I.A. did not contact returning defectors in 1962 as a matter of standard operating procedure."

On Oswald's return to the States there was a family reunion at his brother Robert's house in Fort Worth. Robert thought that Lee was disappointed because there were no reporters to greet him when he disembarked in New York. Lee and his family stayed only briefly, however, then moved in with his mother, who had an apartment in Fort Worth. Further evidence that Oswald had not been working for American Intelligence during his period in Russia is the fact that he was unable to find work or to hold down a job on his return; an unlikely reward for a government agent.

In early July, with help from the Texas Employment Commission, Oswald got a job at a welding shop in the industrial section of Fort Worth. He was a sheet metal helper, a job similar to that he held in Minsk. He was paid 50 dollars per week barely enough to sustain a family of three.

After his return from the Soviet Union Oswald's behaviour was becoming increasingly violent and erratic. He forbade his wife to smoke and the Russian exile community in Dallas, who had befriended the Oswald's, noticed how bad Oswald was treating his wife. He frequently beat her and forbade her to speak English fearing he would lose his proficiency in Russian if she did. Oswald was sullen, arrogant and bullying towards his wife, members of the Dallas Russian community have testified.

"I'd have thought it was a conspiracy, " one of the Russians said, "if only I hadn't known Lee."

Another has said, "Lee couldn't have been bought-not for love, not for money and not for the sake of a political plot." They all agree that Lee acted on impulse and only decided 2 or 3 days before to shoot Kennedy.

In early October, 1962, Oswald having quit his Fort Worth job decided to look for work in Dallas. He moved to the Dallas Y.M.C.A., rented a Post Office box and began looking for work. After about 3 weeks he found employment with a photographic printing firm, Jagger, Chiles and Stovall in downtown Dallas. He rented a small apartment nearby and his family joined him.

Oswald celebrated his 23rd birthday that month. He had tried military life and failed; he was now failing in civilian life. He had tried communism and did not like it. He was not any happier living in a democracy. He had one year and one month left to live.

In November, Marina arranged to have their daughter June baptised in an eastern orthodox church in Dallas and the ceremony had to be performed in secret because Oswald was an atheist and would have vehemently objected.

During this period Lee and Marina met Mrs. Ruth Paine, the 31 year old estranged wife of a Bell Helicopter engineer. Ruth was studying Russian because of her interest in the national Quaker young people's group which sponsored cultural exchanges of young Russians and Americans. Ruth was estranged from her husband Michael, but he often visited the Paine household to see his children. Michael befriended Lee and they talked about politics often. Michael has described Lee's activities in Dallas as 'spying' on right-wing groups like the John Birch Society:

"There is no doubt in my mind", Michael told the BBC 'Timewatch' team, "that (Oswald) believed violence was the only effective tool. He didn't want to mess around with trying to change the system."

Marina became pregnant again. The baby was due in October 1963. Then Lee lost his job. He lied about the reason saying it was because there was not sufficient work. He was sacked, however, because of his incompetence.

On April 10th 1963, Oswald committed an attempted murder, the evidence of which cannot be explained away by Conspiracy Theorists. It is the overriding explanation for Oswald's propensity for violent 'revolutionary' action. That evening he left the apartment after dinner. At about 11 o' clock Marina found a note in their bedroom from Lee. In Russian, it told her what to do if he left or was arrested:

"1. This is the key to the mailbox which is located in the main post office in the city on Ervay Street. This is the same street where the drugstore, in which you always waited is located. You will find the mailbox in the post office which is located 4 blocks from the drugstore on that street. I paid for the box so don't worry about it ...

2. Send the information as to what has happened to me to the Embassy and include newspaper clippings (should there be anything about me in the newspapers). I believe that the Embassy will come quickly to your assistance on learning everything.

3. I paid the house rent on the 2nd so don't worry about it.

4. Recently I also paid for water and gas.

5. The money from work will possibly be coming. The money will be sent to our post office box. Go to the bank and cash the check.

6. You can either throw out or give my clothing, etc., away. Do not keep these. However, I prefer that you hold on to my personal papers (military, civil, etc.).

7. Certain of my documents are in the small blue valise.

8. The address book can be found on my table in the study should need same.

9. We have friends here. The Red Cross also will help you (Red Cross in English). (sic)

10. I left you as much money as I could, 60 dollars on the second of the month. You and the baby (apparently) can live for another 2 months using 10 dollars per week.

11. If I am alive and taken prisoner, the city jail is located at the end of the bridge through which we always passed on going to the city (right in the beginning of the city after crossing the bridge)."

When he returned home, he told her that he had fired a rifle shot at former Major General Edwin A. Walker, a leader of ultra-conservative groups. The bullet, fired through a window, barely missed Walker as he sat at his desk.

Conspiracy Theorists argue that the bullet did not come from Oswald's rifle. However, as the Warren Commission found:

"Although the Commission recognises that neither expert was able to state that the bullet which missed General Walker was fired from Oswald's rifle to the exclusion of all others, this testimony was considered probative when combined with the other testimony linking Oswald to the shooting ... The admission made to Marina Oswald by her husband are an important element in the evidence that Lee Harvey Oswald fired the shot at General Walker. ... the note and the photographs of Walker's house and of the nearby railroad tracks provide important corroboration for her account of the incident. Other details described by Marina Oswald coincide with facts developed independently of her statements. She testified that her husband had postponed his attempt to kill Walker until that Wednesday because he had heard that there was to be a gathering at the church next door to Walker's house on that evening. He indicated that he wanted more people in the vicinity at the time of the attempt so that his arrival and departure would not attract great attention."

Marina asked Lee why he had fired a shot at General Walker. He said that Walker was an extremist who deserved to die. She secreted the note in a cook book and warned him that she would show it to the police if he ever did anything similar. The next day newspaper reports indicated that the shooter had escaped by car. Lee was contemptuous of the police. As Marina related the story to Priscilla Johnson McMillan:

"Americans are so spoiled," Lee told Marina, "It never occurs to them that you might use your own two legs. They always think you have a car. They chased a car. And here I am sitting here!" Lee also laughed at the police for their ballistics mistakes. "They got the bullet-found it in the chimney," he said, "They say I had a .30 calibre bullet when I didn't at all. They've got the bullet and the rifle all wrong. Can't even figure that out. What fools!"

This was not the only unbalanced act committed by Oswald in this period. Two other incidents are generally overlooked by Conspiracy Theorists and one has to conclude that Marina was part of the 'conspiracy' to disbelieve them. The first involved a plan to assassinate Former Vice-president Richard Nixon even though Nixon was not in Dallas at the time. Oswald had probably confused Lyndon Johnson with Nixon as the title Vice-president was still used in reference to Nixon. Marina testified that Oswald had been reading the Dallas Morning News which had a banner headline "Nixon calls for Decision to Force Reds Out of Cuba". The lead story, accompanied by a front page photograph of Nixon, reported Nixons comments in a speech he made in Washington, accusing President Kennedy of being too soft on Castro and demanding a 'command decision' to force the Russians out of Cuba. The speech has been interpreted as a call for a new invasion of Cuba. According to Marina's statement to Priscilla Johnson McMillan:

"(Oswald) got dressed and put on a new suit. I saw that he took a pistol. I asked him where he was going, and why he was getting dressed. He answered 'Nixon is coming. I want to go and have a look'. I said 'I know how you look'."

She did not know who Nixon was but she knew his life was in danger and that was enough. She locked Lee in the bathroom saying she could lose the baby. Lee relented.

The second incident occurred during the third week in August when he was in New Orleans looking for work. He was desperately seeking to go to Cuba and live out his fantasies of working for the Cuban revolution. He came up with the idea of hi-jacking a plane to Cuba and he tried to enlist Marina's help. She refused.

Priscilla Johnson McMillan described Marina as a woman who eventually came to believe that Lee "had no sense of right and wrong; no moral sense at all; only egotism, anger at others because of his failed life and he was unable to understand his mistakes."

About April 24th Ruth Paine visited the Oswald's in Dallas and saw that Lee's bags were packed. Marina had suggested that Lee go to New Orleans to look for work. Lee had agreed but was insisting that Marina go back to Russia where he would join her, presumably after his sojourn in Cuba. Ruth felt sorry for Marina and invited her to stay with her in Dallas while Lee sorted himself out in New Orleans. They agreed on this.

Conspiracy theorists have indicated that Oswald's time in New Orleans was spent becoming enmired in conspiracy and intrigue with anti-Castro Cubans, the C.I.A., F.B.I., and the Mafia. The evidence seems to suggest otherwise although no-one can disprove a negative and Oswald's time alone in the Louisiana city must be speculative whilst relying on known facts. The dates, in particular are the time from July 19th onwards, when he was unemployed, and the two days between Marina's departure for Texas on September 23rd and Lee's own departure for Mexico City on September 25th Clandestine meetings and conspiratorial relationships have been attributed to Oswald during this period but the evidence suggests that both were unlikely if not impossible. Taking Marina's evidence of Lee's activities, the testimony of neighbours, his visits to the library, visits to the Louisiana Employment Exchange, job-hunting, his picketing of a radio station, handing out 'Fair Play for Cuba' leaflets, his trips with his daughters Marina and June to relatives, trips to Lake Ponchartrain, trips to the zoo and botanical gardens - all of these well documented and investigated times leaves little or no time for Oswald's supposed planning, with the help of others, the 'crime of the century'.

During his time in New Orleans Oswald was serious and committed to his 'agent provocateur' and political activities. He wrote to the Fair Play for Cuba Committee in New York and he was anxious to become more active, deciding to stir things up with the Anti-Castro groups in New Orleans by approaching an exile group leader, Carlos Bringieur, introducing himself as an ex-marine and saying he had the experience to fight Castro. This was evidently a ploy. Oswald desperately wanted publicity to shore up his credentials as a 'revolutionary'. A few days later Bringuier and some friends spotted Oswald distributing Pro-Castro leaflets and a scuffle ensued resulting in Oswald's arrest. It is likely Oswald was 'proving' that he had the qualifications to serve as a 'revolutionary soldier' . He would now have more documentary evidence with which to present to the Cubans at their embassy in Mexico City.

On September 26th Lee Oswald was on his way to Mexico. In Mexico City Oswald booked into a cheap Hotel not far from the bus station. He brought a file of his political activities in New Orleans and in it he detailed the distribution of pro-Castro leaflets, publicity about his arrest and appearances on radio and T.V. He also described himself as a Marxist, political organiser and street agitator who had infiltrated Carlos Bringuier's anti-Castro group. That same day Oswald went to the Cuban Consulate where he was met by Sylvia Duran who told him that he could only enter Cuba on a temporary visa and only if he was in transit to Russia. So Oswald walked the short distance to the Soviet Diplomatic compound.

At the Soviet Embassy Oswald was met by 3 consular officials who were, in fact, 3 KGB officers acting under diplomatic cover. They recalled, in 1993 for the BBC 'Timewatch' researchers, after the end of the Cold War, that Oswald's hands were shaking and he was in a nervous condition, at one time taking out a pistol and placing it on the table in front of him saying he was afraid of the F.B.I., who he claimed had been harassing him because of his previous defection.

KGB Colonel Oleg Nechiporenko told BBC researchers: "We all thought the man had an unstable nervous system. He was extremely agitated." One of the other agents, Valery Kostikov, said that Oswald kept feeling in his pockets and taking out all sorts of papers during their discussion: "Then he took out a gun and put it in front of him. I took the gun away and put it on Pavel's desk. Pavel (Yatskov) asked him, 'Why did you come here with a gun? What do you need a gun for?' He said 'I'm afraid of the F.B.I.. I'm being persecuted. I need a gun to protect myself, for my personal safety.' That's what he said. Pavel Yatskov said, "His behaviour certainly served to confirm this. Valery (Kostikov) saw that when he left the Embassy he wrapped himself tighter like somebody who was hiding from someone."

It was going to take months to get a visa and without one entry to Cuba was barred. When Sylvia Duran explained this Oswald became upset. After a short time the consulate was called and Oswald was ejected. In 1993, speaking to the 'Timewatch' team, Duran repeated her version of the events in the Cuban Embassy:

"I explained and he couldn't believe what I was saying. He said 'That's impossible because I have to go to Cuba right now because I only have ... 3 or 4 days in Mexico City so I have to go.'... I thought he would cry because he was red and excited. His eyes were shining like he was in tears. He didn't want to understand. So I called the consulate." (Oswald called the consul a petty bureaucrat after losing his temper) ... Then the consul says 'Listen, get out, get out'. Then he went to the door and said, 'If I see you again I'll kick you out.'"

There have been many suggestions that it was not Oswald who actually made the visits to the Soviet and Cuban embassies and that it was a double of Oswald who was seen entering and leaving the embassies. The problem of Oswald "doubles" first arose immediately after the assassination and for the last 35 years they have grown incrementally. Literally dozens supposedly turned up in places across the United States in the months before the assassination. They are too numerous to list and nearly all are unverifiable, depending, as they are, on one person's sighting. One photo of a second "Oswald", however, became famous and has been mentioned by most Conspiracy Theorists.

After the assassination the C.I.A. searched its files on the surveillance activities of C.I.A. agents who were watching the Soviet Embassies in Mexico City in the period of Oswald's visit. The staff went through its photographs of persons seen entering and leaving the Embassy and found one of a heavy set blond man who it guessed might have been Oswald. This tentative identification caused the C.I.A. considerable embarrassment later on. The man in the photograph was never identified, but he evidently had no connection with Oswald. He may even have been a Russian diplomat. The circumstance led to theories that he had impersonated Oswald. The confusion was based simply on the fact that the C.I.A. did not have any pictures of Oswald in its files and the teletype it sent to Washington was replete with errors.

Oswald returned to Dallas. He did not mention his trip to Mexico when he was re-united with Marina. Lee hitchhiked to Irving, a Dallas suburb (yet another example of cheap conspiracies?) where Marina was staying with Ruth Paine and spent the weekend with his family before going to Dallas to look for work. Ruth had given him a map of the city and on Monday October 14th Lee presented himself to Mrs, A. C. Johnson, who ran a rooming house in the Oak Cliff section of Dallas. Secretive as ever, he signed his name O.H. Lee.

Lee Oswald got his last job on a tip from Ruth Paine, who had heard from a neighbour there were vacancies at the Texas School Book Depository in Dealey Plaza, Dallas. The Depository received books from publishers and delivered them to schools and other customers. Lee promptly applied to Roy S. Truly, the manager of the warehouse. Truly hired Oswald and guaranteed him a 40 hour week. His job description was to collect order sheets and roam throughout the building collecting books. Truly said Oswald made no friends on the job and there was a chance that he may have been required to work at a warehouse 2 blocks away. It was chance that Oswald was picked to work in the main building and another worker who was hired at the same time was sent to the other warehouse. The weekend he was hired, Marina gave birth to the Oswald's second child Audrey Marina Rachel Oswald. On Wednesday, October 23rd, Oswald attended a large right-wing rally in Dallas and heard General Edwin A. Walker speak.

The first two weekends in November, Oswald rode out to Irving with Buell Wesley Frazier who lived near Ruth Paine. He spoke hopefully of renting an apartment in 1964 and re-uniting the family. But events in the Paine household were to take a turn for the worse. Arguments erupted between Marina and Lee and she constantly berated him for his failure in his marriage and in his life.

On Thursday November 21st. Oswald asked Frazier to give him a lift back to Irving. He showed up about 5.15 and Marina and Ruth were surprised to see him as he had not been invited by Ruth and he usually only returned to Irving on weekends.

Oswald had dinner with Marina, Ruth and the children and went to bed early. He had tried to make up with Marina but his advances were spurned. The subject of the President's visit the next day was not discussed. In the morning Oswald rose, told Marina to buy something nice for herself and the children and she wondered why he was being so kind all of a sudden. He then made himself some coffee. Before leaving the house he placed his wedding ring in a favourite cup belonging to Marina and he left nearly all the money he had -170 dollars- in a wallet they kept in a drawer. Conspiracy Theorists rarely mention this telling act.

In the garage Oswald picked up his rifle he had secretly wrapped in brown paper the night before. Then he rode to work with Frazier. Frazier had noticed the package in the back of the car and asked Oswald what it was. Oswald replied that it was curtain rods for his rooming house in Dallas. The two men were silent on the way to Dallas and when they arrived, shortly before 8am Oswald got out of the car with the package under his arm and walked into the Book Depository ahead of Frazier.

Apparently Oswald put in a routine morning on the job. Roy Truly saw him filling orders and remembered greeting him. A few minutes before noon an employee, Charles Givens saw Oswald on the 6th floor and said "Let's go down and watch the President". Oswald declined the invitation but asked Givens to send the lift back up. The culmination of Oswald's fantasies and hopes were about to be fulfilled. In his own mind he was probably seeing himself as a great man, fighting for the Cuban Revolutionary cause; a man who would one day go down in history as a revolutionary martyr.

When Lee Harvey Oswald left the Paine's house that morning, after telling his wife to buy something nice and leaving his wedding ring in a small cup, it is likely assassination was his supreme goal. But how could he be assured of success? He couldn't. The only thing he could be sure of was appearing at the Book Depository with rifle in hand, or perhaps eventually pointing his rifle at the motorcade.

There was no way he could have known the activities of the Secret Service. Would they have stationed men opposite the Book Depository? Would they have stationed men inside the Book Depository? Would they spot him and take appropriate action? Might one of the depository employees have found the rifle? There are endless possibilities of what might have happened that Friday morning which may have prevented Oswald from fulfilling his evil ends.

Oswald did know, however, that he could, at least, attract attention even if he merely attempted to kill the president. Attracting attention and propagating his political ideals were the central aims of his life, especially in the year leading up to the assassination. It is likely, given these facts about Oswald's character, he would have been satisfied at having been arrested with a rifle on the motorcade route.

But chance provided the opportunity for a greater role and it is likely he realised this only at the moment he pulled the trigger. We will never know for sure.

What, then, ignited Oswald's passions in taking his rifle to the Book Depository that fateful Friday morning? I believe the answer lies in those tell-tale pieces of Oswald's life which are overlooked by most Conspiracy Theorists, precisely because they do not fit in with 'a well-organised and sophisticated conspiracy to assassinate the President'. In most conspiracy scenarios authors describe Oswald as either an innocent 'patsy', a heroic ex-marine, or a naive and gullible co-conspirator who is not responsible for the fatal shot. Those Conspiracy authors who say Oswald was part of a conspiracy, ipso facto, deny his personal background has any relevance in understanding the plotter's motives.

The question of why Oswald killed Kennedy was not satisfactorily answered by the Warren Commission The House Assassinations Committee, in it's erroneous conclusion that there was a plot, made the issue of Oswald's motives a moot point.

As I have attempted to demonstrate, it is highly unlikely a conspiracy took place therefore Oswald's motives are the sine quo non of the assassination.

The first point to consider in understanding Oswald's motives is the question of his sanity. Most Conspiracy Theorists argue that Oswald was not insane therefore his state of mind has little bearing on the investigation. Robert Sam Anson is typical in ridiculing the Warren Commissions considerations as to Oswald's sanity:

"Whatever their eloquence the Commission and it's defenders could only surmise that Oswald was crazy, and then only in disregard of the facts. For the facts, troublesome as they were, showed Oswald not only to be sane, but sober, bright, and confident of his eventual vindication. The only emotion he displayed out of the ordinary was anger and amazement that he had been arrested at all."

An article, published in "The American Journal of Psychiatry" (July 1960) is, I believe, particularly instructive in understanding Oswald's state of mind. Written by Dr. Joseph Satten, in collaboration with three colleagues, Karl Menninger, Irwin Rosen, and Martin Mayman, the article is chilling in it's delineation of a criminally intentioned mind.

"In attempting to asses the criminal responsibility of murderers, the law tries to divide them (as it does all offenders) into two groups, the 'sane' and the 'insane'. The 'sane' murderer is thought of as acting upon rational motives that can be understood, though condemned, and the 'insane' one as being driven by irrational senseless motives. When rational motives are conspicuous (for example, when a man kills for personal gain) or when the irrational motives are accompanied by delusions or hallucinations (for example, a paranoid patient who kills his fantasised persecutor), the situation presents little problem to the psychiatrist. But murderers who seem rational, coherent, and controlled and yet whose homicidal acts have a bizarre apparently senseless quality, pose a difficult problem, if courtroom disagreements and contradictory reports about the same offender are an index. It is our thesis that the psychopathology of such murderers forms at least one specific syndrome which we shall describe. In general, these individuals are pre-disposed to severe lapses in ego-control which makes possible the open expression of primitive violence born out of previous, and now unconscious, traumatic experiences."

The authors had examined four men convicted of seemingly unmotivated murders. All had been found 'sane'. The authors examined areas of similarity:

"The most uniform and perhaps the most significant, historical finding was a long standing, sometimes lifelong, history of erratic control over aggressive impulses ... during moments of actual violence, they often felt separated or isolated from themselves, as if they were watching someone else."

(RUTH PAINE: (At the Dallas jail) " he seemed utterly 'apart' from the situation he was in.")

"... In all these cases, there was evidence of severe emotional deprivation in early life ...

(ROBERT OSWALD: "The idea even crossed (my) mind that (my) mother might want to put (me) and John up for adoption; anything to be rid of the burden.")

" ... This deprivation may have involved prolonged or recurrent absence of one or both parents, a chaotic family life in which the parents were unknown, or an outright rejection of the child by one or both parents with the child being raised by others ..."

(ROBERT OSWALD: "We learned very early that we were a burden ... she wanted to be free of responsibility.")

" ... Most typically the men displayed a tendency not to experience anger or rage in association with violent aggressive action. None reported feelings of rage in connection with the murders, nor did they experience anger in any strong or pronounced way, although each of them was capable of enormous and brutal aggression ... "

(LEE OSWALD: "Americans are so spoiled ... They chased a car. And here I am sitting here ... What fools ...")

(DETECTIVE JAMES LEAVELLE: "He was a cool character.")

(CARLOS BRINGUIER: "He was really cold-blooded ... he was not nervous ...)

" ... Their relationships with others were of a shallow, cold nature, lending a quality of loneliness and isolation to these men. . ."

(WILLIAM WULF: "We were 16 ... he seemed to me a boy that was looking for something to belong to. I don't think anybody was looking for him to belong to them.")

" ... People were scarcely real to them, in the sense of being warmly or positively ... or even angrily ... felt about ..."

(MICHAEL PAINE: "People were like cardboard (to Lee) ...")

" ... The 3 men under sentence of death had shallow emotions regarding their own fate and that of their victims ..."

(LEE OSWALD: "Poor dumb cop.")

"Guilt, depression, and remorse were strikingly absent ..."
(MARINA: "Lee had no moral sense at all ... only egotism, anger at others on account of his failures.")

" ... The murderous potential can become activated, especially if some disequilibrium is already present, when the victim-to-be is unconsciously perceived as a key figure in some past traumatic configuration. The behaviour, or even the mere presence of this figure adds a stress to the unstable balance of forces that results in a sudden extreme discharge of violence ..."
(Lee learned of a past boyfriend of Marina's - he bore a startling resemblance to JFK).

Lee Oswald described himself as "the son of an Insurance salesman whose early death left a fair mean streak of independence brought on by neglect". Oswald therefore felt he was the person he was because his father had died before he was born, ignoring the fact that it was his mother's life choices and her neglect of him on the one hand and indulgence of him on the other, which were the primary factors in the development of his personality. When Lee was 6 his mother married Edwin Ekdahl, who became the father that Lee had never known. This could have turned the tide in the one-parent environment yet Marguerite, it seemed, was destined to think only of herself and constantly berated her husband for his inadequacies. She eventually used her devious and vindictive personality in getting her son Robert to conspire in the marriage break-up. Divorce ensued. Thereafter Marguerite spoiled her youngest son allowing him to 'rule the roost' and excusing his misbehaviour. Often his mother could not handle Lee, especially as he grew into adolescence. Her future relationships with men were thereafter shallow and irregular.

Oswald's mother, then, was a widow and twice-divorced. Lee Oswald was, for most of his youth, separated from his brothers who attended military academies and boarding schools. They were thus immunised against their neurotic mother and as they grew older there was little in the way of affection for her. Although a domineering woman, Marguerite was unable to control her youngest son who became a truant and displayed such neurotic tendencies he was eventually remanded by a New York court for psychiatric observation. He fantasised about hurting and killing people. This fantasy of fame through murder grew in his mind as he matured into adulthood. He struck his mother, threatened his sister-in-law with a knife and was disruptive in school. Later he beat his wife repeatedly. Inadequate parenting had produced inner corruption which removed any sense of decency or conscience. Nearly all of the people who knew Oswald spoke of him as a person whose personality lacked any warmth or compassion for his fellow human beings. Writers have often written about Oswald's dedication to humanitarian ideals yet they miss the point - Oswald's ideals only existed in an abstract, impersonal, way.

Just as some lives are destined for accomplishment Oswald's was damned to preparation for external and internal destruction. I believe this preparation had it's roots in his childhood.

Stated in its simplest terms the assassination of President Kennedy and the murder of Police Officer J.D. Tippit occurred because two factors came together - a psychopathic individual dedicated to his political ideals and wanting to grasp fame through a violent acting out of those ideals and a society which abrogated it's responsibilities in propagating moral outrage about the decline in family values and sexual morality. American society, after the second world war, became non-judgemental and embraced moral relativism. A society that does not have any sense of moral outrage, or the individuals within it a sense of shame, is one which is destined to self-destruct.

Writers have continually refused to examine the effect that a fatherless upbringing had on the young Oswald. In an age of 'political correctness' that unwillingness is even more pronounced. Furthermore, an America which treats divorce and unmarried mothers as the 'norm' can hardly be expected to criticise it's own moral foundations when it comes to family life and the nurture of it's children. As recently as the early 90's Vice-President Dan Quayle was castigated by the U.S. establishment media for criticising the story line of a popular soap comedy, 'Murphy Brown', in which the star character decided to have a baby out of wedlock. The lead character in the story felt that a lasting and firm relationship with the father was unnecessary.

I believe fatherlessness had a crucial effect on young Oswald moulding and forming a personality which hid some of his darkest impulses having their origins in childhood and the lack of a meaningful male role model.

The young Oswald, whose real father died in a car accident when he was a baby, had only weak relationships with his mother's many boyfriends whose personalities were often weaker than the domineering and unstable Marguerite's. He was unable to connect with a 'father' to learn his emotionality and the unique way of how to compete and to channel aggression effectively. Oswald was denied a nurturing system which was male-driven, in which discipline, morality teaching and emotional sustenance were provided by males for males.

Recent events in the United States and over the past generation confirm the lack of control many divorced parents have over their offspring. I am speaking here, of course, of those divorced fathers who maintain no links at all with their children. Similar research on the subject of fatherless youths has been carried out in the United Kingdom, notably by Professor Norman Dennis of Newcastle University and George Erdos. In their well-researched books, "Families without Fatherhood" and "Rising Crime and the Dismembered Family" they clearly reveal the disturbed nature of many young men, born to unwed mothers whose partners had only sporadic and irregular connections with their children, and the links between their home life and involvement in criminal activity.

In the introduction to the book "Families Without Fatherhood" this proposition is supported by Professor A.H. Halsey when he writes:

"No one can deny that divorce, separation, birth outside marriage and one-parent families as well as cohabitation ... have increased rapidly. Many applaud these freedoms. But what should be universally acknowledged is that children of parents who do not follow the traditional norm (i.e. taking on personal, active and long term responsibility for the social upbringing of the children they generate) are thereby disadvantaged in many major aspects of their chances of living a successful life. On the evidence available such children tend to die earlier, to have more illness, to do less well at school, to exist at a lower level of nutrition, comfort and conviviality, to suffer more unemployment, to be more prone to deviance and crime, and finally to repeat the cycle of unstable parenting from which they themselves have suffered ... Dennis and Erdos draw particular attention to an overlooked consequence of family breakdown -- the emergence of a new type of young male, namely one who is both weakly socialized and weakly socially controlled so far as the responsibilities of spousehood and fatherhood are concerned."

Michael Gurian, author of 5 books and the recently published (1998) "A Fine Young Man" puts the problem of fatherlessness in a contemporary context. He believes the solution for raising healthy adolescent boys involves increasing the presence of men and decreasing the presence of women. American culture, he maintains, puts adolescent boys in peril and the solution is to get fathers and the masculine nurturing system to work better. He has linked the school shooting in Springfield and Jonesboro to this problem.

Lee Harvey Oswald believed he was an important man and his wife often ridiculed him for this 'unfounded' belief:

"At least his imagination, his fantasy, which was quite unfounded, as to the fact that he was an outstanding man. (I) always tried to point out to him that he was a man like any others who were around us. But he simply could not understand that. . . .".

Aline Mosby, a reporter, interviewed Oswald in Moscow after his defection and this interview gives a 'clue' to the way Oswald acted out his political dramas. Oswald told her he became interested in communist ideology when "an old lady handed me a pamphlet about saving the Rosenburgs..."

After a controversial trial in 1951, Julius and Ethel Rosenburg were convicted of conspiracy to commit wartime espionage and sentenced to death. They had been accused of transmitting atomic bomb secrets to the Russians. After several legal appeals President Eisenhower refused to commute the death sentence and they were executed in New York's Sing Sing prison on June 19th 1953. During their final months campaigns were mounted to save the Rosenburgs and pamphlets were distributed around New York City when Oswald was living there with his mother.

The pamphlet led Oswald to change the direction of his life for it was from this period he became enamoured with left-wing politics. The memory of the Rosenburg case, I believe, lasted until his incarceration in the Dallas police jail. Oswald had made repeated requests the weekend of the assassination, for John Abt to defend him. Abt was a left-wing New York lawyer who had defended communists and a newspaper story about Abt had appeared on the same page as the President's visit to Dallas. In attempting to contact Abt Oswald was revealing something about himself - I believe his action suggests he was already preparing for his appearance on the political stage, emulating the Rosenburgs by becoming a 'cause celebre'.

Oswald, therefore, had a desperate desire to act in a political way to further the cause of his commitment to communism and to the Cuban Revolution and in so doing elevate himself as an important 'revolutionary'. He needed a cause to belong to; to inflate his self-image and sustain it. Oswald said that nothing kept him in the United States and he would lose nothing by returning to the Soviet Union. His real destination, of course, was Cuba. Cuba was a country which embodied the political principles to which he had been committed since he was an adolescent. As Marina testified to the Warren Commission:

"I only know that his basic desire was to get to Cuba by any means and all the rest of it was window dressing for that purpose."

Marina has testified to Oswald's view of Castro as a 'hero' and said Lee had wanted to call their second child 'Fidel' if it had been a boy.

Michael Paine told BBC 'Timewatch' researchers that Lee "wanted to be an active guerrilla in the effort to bring about the new world order."

Nelson Delgado, Oswald's friend in the Marine Corps said that Oswald's hero was William Morgan, a former sergeant in the U.S. Army who became a major in Castro's army. In August 1959 Morgan received considerable press coverage when he lured some anti-Castro rebels into a trap by pretending to be a counter-revolutionary. This may explain Oswald's 'counter-revolutionary' activities in New Orleans when he visited anti-castroite Carlos Bringuier. Oswald wanted to emulate Morgan.

To Oswald Cuba was the last gambit- his last chance to fulfil his political fantasies.

Trying to portray Oswald, as some Conspiracy Theorists do, as a right wing anti-Castro conspirator flies in the face of the mountains of evidence which indicates that Oswald's commitment to his political ideals from the age of 16 was genuine. An incident from Oswald's time in the Marine Corps testifies to this genuine commitment. Marine associate, Kerry Thornley testified to the Warren Commission about an incident " which grew out of a combination of Oswald's known Marxist sympathies and George Orwell's book '1984'" After Thornley finished reading the book Thornley and Oswald both took part in a parade they were assigned to. While waiting for the parade to start they talked briefly about '1984' even though Oswald "seemed to be lost in his own thoughts." Oswald remarked on the stupidity of the parade and on how angry it made him, to which Thornley replied: 'Well, comes the revolution you will change all that." Thornley testified:

"At which time he looked at me like a betrayed Caesar and screamed, screamed definitely, 'Not you, too, Thornley'. And I remember his voice cracked as he said this. He was definitely disturbed at what I had said and I didn't really think I had said that much. ... I never said anything to him again and he never said anything to me again."

I believe those political ideals remained with him up to the moment of his death and there is convincing, but still speculative, evidence to support this.

It was inevitable that someone as politically motivated as Oswald would eventually reveal his political self that weekend. Someone like Oswald needed a stage to show the world he was a true revolutionary. But he did not do this by confessing. Instead he showed his commitment to his ideals by a clenched fist salute, a symbol of left-wing radicalism - as he was paraded around the Dallas police station. Most Conspiracy Theorists have assumed that Oswald was merely showing the photographers his manacled hands. But there is a definite clenched-fist salute portrayed. He repeated this gesture as he lay dying in the ambulance. According to Dallas policeman Billy Combest, he made a " definite clenched fist".

Conspiracy Theorists have dismissed this vital evidence claiming that a clenched-fist salute did not come into vogue until the late 1960's. Communists and left-wing militant groups had however, used the salute since the 1930's - in the political elections in Germany in 1930 and in Spain during that decade.

Oswald was influenced in his beliefs and his desire to act them out by a number of people and events during the last year of his life. Firstly, there is evidence that the periodicals that Oswald subscribed to may have influenced his actions. As the Warren Report pointed out:

"The October 7th, 1963, issue of the 'Militant' reported Castro as saying Cuba could not accept a situation where at the same time the United States was trying to ease world tensions it also 'was increasing its efforts to 'tighten the noose' around Cuba'. Castro's opposition to President Kennedy's attempt to reduce world tensions was also reported in the October 1, 1963, issue of the 'Worker', to which Oswald also subscribed. In this connection it should be noted that in speaking of the 'Worker', Oswald told Michael Paine, apparently in all seriousness, that "you could tell what they wanted you to do ... by reading between the lines, reading the thing and doing a little reading between the lines."

In the month before the assassination Oswald may have entered into his revolutionary fantasies whilst watching television. According to a Secret Service interview with Marina, and which was first recognised by Jean Davison as a telling indication of Oswald's state of mind, on Friday, October 18th Oswald had watched two movies on T.V. and, according to Marina, he had been 'greatly excited'. The first movie was 'Suddenly', in which Frank Sinatra played an ex-soldier who planned to shoot an American president. Sinatra's character was to shoot the president with a high powered rifle from the window of a house overlooking a railway station. The second movie was 'We Were Strangers' and was based on the overthrow of Cuba's Machado regime in 1933. John Garfield had played an American who had gone to Cuba to help a group of rebels assassinate the Cuban leader. Oswald's reactions to these movies made a strong impression on his wife according to the Secret Service report. I believe that, given Oswald's orientation to violence as evidenced by his willingness to take General Walker's life, his treatment of his wife and his belief in revolutionary violence these movies are a vital piece of evidence in understanding Oswald's motives.

As the movie plots suggested, Oswald could see a way in which he could strike out against a government he detested and support a government he admired. It is feasible that Oswald could have known about C.I.A. plots to assassinate Castro. On September 9th the New Orleans 'Times Picayune' published a story about Castro's warning about assassination plots against him. Castro declared that United States leaders would be in danger if they aided anti-Castro terrorist plans to assassinate Cuban leaders. It is possible that Oswald's 'revolutionary heroic actions' in killing Kennedy were a response to these plots. Although the American people as a whole did not learn of C.I.A. plots to murder Castro until the 1970's it would have been easy for newspaper readers in New Orleans to 'read between the lines' because it was common knowledge in New Orleans in the summer of 1963 that anti-Castro murder plots were ongoing.

Oswald's first reply to a police officer when he was arrested inside the Texas Theatre was, "I haven't anything to be ashamed of." He did not say, "I didn't shoot anyone" at this time. He was obviously giving himself time to think of an answer to the inevitable questions he would be asked when interrogated. His answer "I haven't anything to be ashamed of" is a natural one for a true believer in the Castro revolution. He may have committed murder but to Oswald it was an act of war putting himself outside moral culpability. If Oswald was innocent why didn't he say "I didn't shoot the police officer."?

Some commentators on the assassination have expressed the belief that after the flight from the scene of the assassination Oswald was intending to catch a bus which would have taken him to the Mexican border. Could it be possible that Oswald, with his own warped sense of revolutionary action, have believed that the Cuban Embassy in Mexico City would have squirreled him away to Cuba as a hero of the revolution?

Lee Oswald, in his revolutionary fervour, needed only a catalyst to spur him on. And it came in the form of an aristocratic member of the Dallas emigre community. George De Mohrenschildt had an important influence on Oswald in the months leading up to the assassination. De Mohrenschildt and his wife befriended the Oswald's, and became Lee's mentor. Unlike the other members of the community De Mohrenschildt had a soft spot for Oswald and sympathised with his left-wing views. In reality DeMohrenschildt thought Oswald was a pathetic individual who saw himself as a self-important intellectual and revolutionary.

At the time of the Kennedy assassination, De Morenschildt was an oil geologist employed by the U.S. State Department in Haiti. He had known Oswald for a year and he told the Warren Commission in 1964 that he knew nothing of Oswald's role in the Kennedy killing. But during a series of meetings with Willem Oltmans, a Dutch T.V. reporter, beginning in 1966, De Mohrenschildt began to remember things differently. By 1975, during an interview with Oltmans on Dutch television, he insisted that Oswald was led by others.

However, by this time De Mohrenschildt was suffering from depression and had twice attempted suicide. He began to have bizarre hallucinations and distortions. De Mohrenschildt would vacillate between claiming his conspiracy tale was a hoax and asserting it was true. In addition to De Mohrenschildt's instability doubts are thrown on to his tale by an examination of Warren Commission testimony that shows De Mohrenschildt last saw Oswald 6 months before the assassination. Furthermore, in a letter to a friend shortly before he committed suicide he confessed that what he had written about the assassination were "stupidities" and he was gripped by remorse at having possibly influenced Oswald to shoot the president.

Even so, De Mohrenschildt could be morally culpable for the assassination in another sense. Marina has testified as to De Mohrenschildt's influence on Lee and how Lee looked up to the older man as a 'father figure'. Most of the emigre community were rabid anti-communists, except for George, who sympathised with Lee's world views. George had always been a rebellious figure who had expressed unconventional views. Telling evidence of De Mohrenschildt's influence on Oswald was provided in Marina's conversations with Priscilla Johnson McMillan:

"Then they began to speak in English, a sign that George and Lee were talking politics. Marina could not follow what they were saying but she has always felt that this evening was a turning point in Lee's life. She believes that Lee pounced on some remark that affected his later actions. She suspects that George said something that inadvertently, in her words, 'influenced Lee's sick fantasy', and that Lee, having seized the idea, squirreled it away out of sight so that neither she nor George would guess where it came from."

It is possible that George's statements to Lee had something to do with assassination. George referred to General Walker as the 'Hitler of tomorrow' and Lee, according to Marina, often repeated unoriginal things which she believed may have come from George. One of Lee's often repeated sayings was that if Hitler had been assassinated it would have benefited the world. It is therefore possible that the anti-fascist George contributed to Lee's attempt on the life of General Walker (and concomitantly on President Kennedy) and that Lee was acting to impress his 'surrogate father'. According to Samuel Ballen who was De Mohrenschildt's close friend during the time he knew Oswald: "(In De Mohrenschildt's conversations with Lee) his unconventional, shocking, humorous and irreverent ideas would have been coming out of George all the time." Ballen stated that he thought De Mohrenschildt could have influenced Oswald to kill General Walker.

And there is evidence that De Mohrenschildt was a malevolent influence on others. Tito Harper, for example, who was De Mohrenschildt's roommate in the 1940's later committed suicide. Harper's parents blamed George for his atheistic and anti-social influence and their son's disintegration.

Oswald's potential for violence is often unnoticed by most Conspiracy Theorists. Yet the evidence is clear that Oswald, like O.J. Simpson, had a history of wife battering. Henry Hurt for example writes:

"The Commission's account of Tippit's and Oswald's movements leading up to the policeman's murder is as speculative as anything the Commission produced. All of it is squarely aimed at one conclusion: that the brutal deed was done by Lee Harvey Oswald. Before that day, there is no corroborated evidence that this mild-mannered young man had ever committed an act of serious violence- much less murder. The evidence suggesting his capacity for violence is as tenuous today as it was 2 decades ago."

Oswald's treatment of his wife is in direct contradiction to this statement. As the Warren Report stated:

" The instability of their relations was probably a function of the personalities of both people. Oswald was overbearing in relations with his wife. He apparently attempted to be 'the commander' by dictating many of the details of their married life. While Marina Oswald said that her husband wanted her to learn English he made no attempt to help her and their are other indications that he did not want her to learn that language. Oswald apparently wished to continue practising his own Russian with her. Lieutenant Martello of the New Orleans police testified that Oswald stated that he did not speak English in his family because he did not want them to become Americanised. Marina Oswald's inability to speak English also made it more difficult for her to have an independent existence in this country. Oswald struck his wife on occasion, did not want her to drink, smoke or wear cosmetics and generally treated her with a lack of respect in the presence of others". According to Ruth Paine, Marina was worried about Lee's "mental state".

Domestic violence did not have the high profile in the 60's as it does today. In the 1995 criminal trial and the 1997 civil trial evidence of O.J. Simpson's wife - battering was indeed relevant in supporting the prosecution's case for Simpson's guilt. Similarly, Oswald's treatment of his wife is pertinent to an understanding of his propensity for violence. And the evidence is corroborated by the Russian emigre community in Dallas. At one stage Oswald tried to strangle his wife. There were incidents when Oswald hit Marina and she ended up with bruises on her body. At one stage in their relationship some members of the emigre community 'rescued' Marina but she returned to her husband after a 2 week separation.

Mahlon Tobias, who managed one of the buildings in which the Oswald's lived, said on one occasion, when a neighbour complained to him about the violent arguments, "I think he's really hurt her this time ... I think that man over there is going to kill that girl."

Michael Paine was shocked that Lee treated his wife like a vassal and he believed Marina was a person who acted as though she were in 'bondage and servitude'.

These kinds of abusive behaviours are all about control of the victim. A variety of seemingly unconnected events are part of that strategy to maintain that control - methods like telling her who she can be friends with, how much she can spend, what kind of clothes she can wear, belittling her, demeaning her. All of these things accomplish the end objective - control. The ultimate act of control is violence - the classic pattern to which Lee Harvey Oswald fitted. Why did Marina return to her husband? It is evident she was suffering from the battered woman's syndrome, a form of traumatic stress disorder. This helped explain why it was difficult for her to leave. And of course she was a Russian, speaking no English. How could she escape? Oswald, indeed, fitted a batterers profile.

The relationship took a turn for the worse especially in the few months leading up to the assassination and particularly the evening of November 21st when Oswald arrived at Ruth Paine's home unexpectedly. Clues as to Oswald's state of mind and the volatile love/hate relationship between Oswald and his wife can be gleaned from her Warren Commission testimony:

Q. Did your husband give any reason for coming home on Thursday?

A. He said that he was lonely because he hadn't come home the preceding weekend, and he wanted to make peace with me.

Q. Did you say anything to him then?

A. He tried to talk to me but I would not answer him, and he was very upset.

Q. Were you upset with him?

A. I was angry, of course. He was not angry - he was upset. I was angry. He tried very hard to please me. He spent quite a bit of time putting away the diapers and played with the children on the street.

Q. How did you indicate to him that you were angry with him?

A. By not talking to him.

Q. And how did he show that he was upset?

A. He was upset over the fact that I would not answer him. He tried to start a conversation with me several times, but I would not answer. And he said that he didn't want me to be angry at him because this upsets him. . . On that day, he suggested that we rent an apartment in Dallas. He said that he was tired of living alone and perhaps the reason for me being so angry was the fact that we were not living together. That if I want to he would rent an apartment in Dallas tomorrow-that he didn't want me to remain with Ruth any longer, but wanted me to live with him in Dallas. . . He repeated this not once but several times but I refused. And he said that once again I was preferring my friends to him, and that I didn't need him.

Q. What did you say to that?

A. I said I would be better if I remained with Ruth until the holidays, he would come, and we would all meet together. That this was better because while he was living alone and I stayed with Ruth, we were spending less money. And I told him to buy me a washing machine, because with two children it became too difficult to wash by hand.

Q. What did he say to that?

A. He said he would buy me a washing machine.

Q. What did you say to that?

A. Thank you. That it would be better if he bought something for himself-that I would manage.

Q. I understood that when you didn't make up he was quite disturbed and you were still angry, is that right?

A. I wasn't really very angry. I, of course, wanted to make up with him. But I gave the appearance of being very angry. I was smiling inside, but I had a serious expression on my face.

Q. And as a result of that, did he seem to be more disturbed than usual?

A. As always, as usual. Perhaps a little more. At least when he went to bed he was very upset.

It is, of course pure speculation as to what would have happened had Marina and Lee made up but I believe the speculation is indeed relevant in understanding Oswald's frame of mind on that fateful day.

Conspiracy Theorists omit further evidence which shows Oswald's propensity for violence. They overlook the fact that as far back as the 1950's Oswald had spoken about shooting an American President. Palmer McBride has testified that, in 1956, he befriended Oswald and they often discussed politics. McBride said that one central theme in their discussions was the 'exploitation of the working class' and on one occasion, after they began discussing President Eisenhower, Oswald made a statement to the effect that he would like to kill the president because he was exploiting the working class. McBride said that the statement was not made in jest.

Finally I want to try and connect a somewhat 'mysterious' piece of evidence about Oswald's actions that tragic Friday, which may give some insight into Oswald's state of mind. Why did Lee Harvey Oswald fire 3 shots at President Kennedy? Most commentators have assumed that it was because of the time span available as the Presidential limousine drove down Elm Street heading for the turnpike. But I believe there is a telling, if only speculative, clue in the conversations Marina had with Priscilla Johnson McMillan in the months after the assassination. During one conversation Marina told McMillan about Lee's fascination with the number 3 and how he was obsessed by it.

"Marina knew that her husband attributed an altogether magical significance and was obsessed by it. She remembered that one year earlier, on November 11th 1962, when the DeMohrenschildts took her away from Lee because of his violence toward her, then, too, had begged her 3 times not to leave him, but after the 3rd time gave up. And on the bottom right-hand corner of the Fair Play For Cuba Committee card on which he had asked her to forge the name 'A. J. Hiddell' the previous summer, he had written the number '33' to signify he was the 33rd member of his fictitious chapter-still another sign of the power he attached to the number three."

EPILOGUE - A Disabled Life.

" ... the human fish swim about at the bottom of the great ocean of atmosphere and they develop psychic injuries as they collide with one another. Most mortal to these are the wounds gotten from the parent fish."

Andrew Salter (Pavlovian Psychologist).

Most crime does not happen in a vacuum. They do not happen by blind chance - something causes them. Sometimes the reasons are social, sometimes psychological, most often both.

This case has disturbed America deeply over the past 35 years. The general disturbance lies in the widening distrust that Americans now have for their government. But I believe their concerns should be about how boys like Lee Harvey Oswald grow up as misfits having no real control or moral guidance with which to exist in, and poorly equipped to meet, the demands of society. As long as today's society can rear vicious minded youths like Oswald it can be no source of smug content. Something was wrong in the rearing of Oswald, something was left out of his make-up and his up-bringing.

The attempted murder of General Walker and the murders of Police Officer Tippit and President Kennedy have their origins in the early years of Lee Oswald. The early phases of personality growth involve the child and the mother. There must be a nurturing and a provision of security from the mother. It was not present in this case.

Lee Harvey Oswald existed with a mask of sanity. His mask was convincing to many except those who knew him well. What lay beneath the surface was Oswald's fatally crippled personality, a dark side, a defensive and surly character that no-one could penetrate not even his wife Marina. He tried to exercise control over others by his manipulating, lying and fantasising. He even maintained this control during his interrogation at Dallas Police headquarters when he "toyed" with his interrogators.

Now and then, in the final year of his life, Oswald would gravitate toward normalcy, seeking work and interacting with others. But the rare occasion gathering with friends was tempered by the realisation that when the social hour was over he would eventually return to his life of despair and unfulfilled political fantasies.

Oswald's friends in the Dallas Russian community recognised in Oswald traits which have been ignored and overlooked by Conspiracy Theorists. There is little doubt in their minds that this was a man whose personality featured some distinctly and probably dangerous, paranoid characteristics.

Lee Oswald's lifelong isolation left him without the resources for the kind of role-modelling and parental guidance most of us take for granted. People who are close to others turn to them in moments of stress and doubt to interpret the meaning of an event or an interaction. As an adult, Lee Oswald did not do this with the only person who was truly close to him - his wife Marina. He was too domineering and insistent she follow his "commands". He could not ask her if his thoughts and actions were consistent with the world around him, seeking out reassurances, communicating ideas. To Lee, Marina had to follow and admire.

Without this kind of relationship with another, we are wholly dependent, as Lee Oswald was, on our own internal understandings of people and events. Without it, we all can get lost in the quagmire of our own thoughts and feelings, of distorted perceptions that have little relationship to reality, of fears that are projections of our own insecurities.

Oswald, as seen by Conspiracy Theorists, was a one- dimensional character who participated willingly or unwillingly in the assassination. Gathering evidence which did not fit into a lone assassin theory, they assembled and constructed elaborate plots fitting in "evidence" to prove their theories. But the whole is more than the sum of the parts; the parts that look suspicious should be taken with the incontrovertible evidence linking Oswald's tragic life with the circumstances surrounding the assassination. To say, as Conspiracy Theorists do, that Oswald was a patriotic American, flies in the face of the total knowledge of Oswald's past, his personality, character and ideological beliefs.

Psychologically, Oswald had always been an outsider. He had always lived in a situation that had intrigue, mystery and drama. He had been subjected to years of bad parenting. In adolescence he embraced a controversial and subversive ideology - communism. He yearned to follow in the footsteps of his brothers in taking up a life in the military. In moving to the Soviet Union he was choosing drama yet again. And it was the attacks on his psyche in childhood - his father dying, living in a household headed by unstable stepfathers and an angry, unstable and domineering mother - that helped turn Lee's psyche in adulthood into an embittered and angry one. Psychologists know that a child who lives an isolated life, as Oswald did, often sees the world as an adversary. Without moral grounding the child is unable to recognise moral prerequisites for living in an adult world. Without the attention only a mother can give, the child is denied the necessary 'socialisation'. The angry and embittered Marguerite Oswald was unable to provide that background. This was recognised by Lee's brother Robert when he said that mother and son's world views were alike in many ways. They both saw themselves as victims, isolated and surrounded by people and government agencies who failed to understand their special place in the scheme of things. As Norman Mailer wrote:

" ... it seems certain at the least that every malformation, or just about, of Lee Harvey Oswald's character had it's roots in her."

Psychologists know that the kind of contempt Lee Harvey Oswald showed for authority, for those who disagreed with his vision of the world, the absolutist sentiments he harboured in the face of complex issues he spoke of, generally are expressions of self-aggrandisement. Until 1963 this side had been kept in check by his place in the world. When he began to see himself as "the commander", the learned revolutionary who was given only menial jobs, the gifted politician who headed an imaginary chapter of the Fair Play For Cuba Committee, "the hunter of the right wing fascists" - the grandiose side was coming out of hiding. If Lee Oswald had not assassinated President Kennedy he would have committed another tragic act of an embittered and angry misfit - shooting at innocent people from a clock tower in Austin, Texas as Charles Whitman was to do in 1966, for example. Or bombing a government building like the radical right- wing 'Oklahoma Bomber' Timothy McVeigh was to do.

Lee Harvey Oswald was not unusual or anomalous to American society, or indeed, any so-called contemporary 'civilised' society. We are surrounded by them. Power mad bombers, terrorists who believe they can circumvent the political process acting out their violent fantasies in order to bring about their ideal world order where they will be recognised as the geniuses they truly believe they are.

In many ways Oswald's actions in killing Kennedy were a protest - undoubtedly a product of his feelings toward the authoritarian approach to life. He had built up a need to protest. So much of what he did was egocentric, ego-satisfying. What he did, especially in his political world, wasn't done in order to help others but to draw attention to himself; to satisfy his narcissistic tendencies.

He not only saw himself as an unappreciated revolutionary but a person who was superior and more learned than any of his contemporaries who he conversed with. This is born out by the many people who crossed Oswald's path, especially in the years after his return from the Soviet Union. Although psychologists have long believed that low self-esteem causes aggression and other pathologies the concept of high self-esteem had not really been considered until lately. High self-esteem that is unjustified and unstable, as in Oswald's case, has led in many instances to violence. Like Oswald many narcissists are supersensitive to criticism or slights, because deep down they suspect their feelings of superiority are bogus. Because his grandiosity was challenged (Marina laughed at his notion that he would eventually become a statesmanlike leader) he reacted violently. Oswald's inflated self-esteem had a powerful effect on his aggression. When the real world failed to recognise his 'superior gifts' he exploded.

Oswald desperately wanted to become famous. His brothers and his wife have testified to the many occasions when they sensed a bitter disappointment in Oswald when he failed to gain due recognition.

Oswald turned to radical politics for the purpose of ego-building. Marina believed that learning Russian gave Lee a reputation for being intelligent, making up for the fact that he had a reading disability which gave him feelings of inadequacy. He got from his politics something he couldn't get from individuals. It shows the poverty of Oswald's emotional relationship with people - a psychopathic tendency. He also subordinated his personality, what little personality he had, to a messianic, charismatic leader, Fidel Castro.

Oswald was a bitter and angry young man. As a youth his mother had little or no control over him and, indeed, conspired with him in his rebellion. He was ruthless in his determination to get what he wanted. Prison files are full of case histories like his. He learned very early in life to hate the world, learned early that he had to take what he wanted for himself on his own. Lessons learned in childhood are carried into adulthood. Marina has testified he was given to fits of unreasonable domineering rage. His history is full of examples that he was secretive, aggressive and arrogant - to a degree almost paranoid. His brother Robert said Lee liked to create drama and mystery around him. He was suspicious of everyone and withdrew from all who loved him - his mother, his brothers. And he was rent by deep inner conflict.

At the time he killed President Kennedy he was in an extremely critical stage in his life. In June 1963 he suffered the same kind of anxiety attacks and nosebleeds which occurred just before he shot at General Walker, shaking from head to foot without waking up. The evening prior to the assassination he tried to make-up to his wife after a series of bitter disagreements about their lives together. She rejected his advances. It must have been a terrible blow to his ego.

Oswald's struggle was to get what he wanted-to be recognised as an important political figure. He achieved a modicum of recognition when he appeared on television and radio in New Orleans in the summer of 1963, when his 'Fair Play for Cuba' activities were noticed. However, his esteem was damaged when Bill Stuckey, the television presenter, ambushed Oswald with statements about his defection to Russia which took away Oswald's status as an objective spokesman for Castro's communist regime.

Oswald's ego and esteem must have been affected when he was rejected by the only country left in the world that could fulfil his warped idealism and his plans to journey to Cuba had to be abandoned. He returned to Dallas more embittered than ever. He was now desperate. He hated the American way of life. Years earlier he had come to detest his beloved Russia. And now his entry to his brave new world was barred. Failure seemed to follow him everywhere. He had nowhere to turn except inwards to his embittered and disillusioned self.

In a sense President Kennedy died at the hands of a boy who was the product of a new phenomenon in western society - the one parent family. His lack of a paternal role-model left Oswald psychologically disabled, leaving only his egocentric and bitter mother to nurture him. The pattern of fatherless criminals has been repeated over and over again since the assassination - the Charles Mansons, the Richard Specks. The degeneration of family morals reflected modern attitudes towards the developing consumer society - if the marriage did not work a woman could find a new husband, a man could find a new wife. The consumer society was transferred by a process of osmosis to the family thus weakening child care across the nation.

It is true that not all American fatherless boys become Presidential assassins - many have the internal strengths to overcome their disability as

Lee's brother Robert testifies to. But it is also true that prisons in America and Europe are full of young men who did not have the gift of a stable parental background. One has only to look at contemporary society to recognise this stark fact.

I acknowledge this theory is controversial and will inevitably be met by an incredulous response from the liberal elements within our society. Nevertheless, as I stated at the beginning, crimes do not occur in a vacuum. There has to be a reason. I believe Lee Harvey Oswald acted alone in carrying out the murders of President Kennedy and Police Officer Tippet therefore his motives should be open to examination. I have tried to explain these motives and in doing so I have necessarily sought to explain Oswald's character and psyche. I believe Oswald's upbringing bears directly on his actions as a young man. Poor parenting from a single unstable mother affected Oswald greatly, warping his sense of right and wrong and creating an individual who was continually frustrated in his relationships with others. His failure as a man, a husband, a worker, a son, a soldier began shortly after his birth.

The child is the father of the man.

AFTERWORD

My years of research were validated and my conclusions confirmed, by the release of the final report of the Assassination Records Review Board in October 1998. The ARRB had been set up by Congress in 1992 as a response to the growing public concern, stimulated by Oliver Stone's 'JFK', that the U.S. Government had kept many government agencies' files secret in order to cover up the 'real' truth of the assassination.

The ARRB dug deep into the mountain of secrecy and decided there was no 'smoking gun', no concealed evidence and no reasons for secrecy apart from the normal bureaucratic onces of concealing sources and methods of operations. More than 60,000 secret documents were released on the assassination in an unprecedented opening of the records of the C.I.A., F.B.I. and other agencies which were involved in the investigation of the assassination or had prior knowledge of the president's assassin.

The released documents, which run to more than 4 million pages, included previously unknown original notes of Oswald's interrogation after the assassination, and statements from doctors who performed the post-mortem on the president. The documents confirmed that Secret Service agents destroyed intelligence files covering threats to Kennedy in the Dallas area, his travels in the weeks before the assassination and activities of the Fair Play for Cuba Committee, the pro-Castro organisation to which Oswald was drawn. It also uncovered some records showing that the F.B.I. tried to keep track of Oswald in the Soviet Union and monitored the money sent to him by his mother.

The 5 Board members, Judge John Tunheim, Kermit Hall, professor of history and law at Ohio State University, William Joyce, archivist at Princeton University and historians Henry Graff and Anna Nelson, did not confirm or deny the existence of a conspiracy; they wanted the public to draw their own conclusions; but the report's implications are clear -- there is no evidence of a conspiracy and Oswald had acted alone. There was also no evidence of a conspiracy involving Jack Ruby and Lee Harvey Oswald. The Board, which was given unprecedented power to review and release records locked in government vaults, said in it's 208 page report that it confronted a cold war culture of secrecy that had not significantly changed:

"The Federal government needlessly and wastefully classified, and then withheld from public access, countless important records that did not require such treatment.... Change is long overdue. It is a matter of trust. Making historical documents public is essential to maintaining our freedom... (Such secrecy) led the American public to believe that the government had something to hide."

Commenting on the work of the Warren Commission it said that it was set up to dispel public fears surrounding the assassination, but sealed it's records and misstated some evidence and was denied some facts from important government agencies; (read C.I.A.).

According to one of President Clinton's top aides there were two mysteries that the newly - elected president wanted to clear up after he came to power. One was whether there was any credible evidence in government files which would confirm the existence of UFO's. The second was whether or not his boyhood hero, President Kennedy, had been assassinated as a result of a conspiracy. As far as the first mystery is concerned the jury is still out. With regard to the second, President Clinton must now acknowledge that the truth about the assassination has now been established to the satisfaction of history.

Mel Ayton.
October 1998.

APPENDIX 1

QUESTIONS CONSPIRACY THEORISTS MUST ANSWER:

* How could 'conspirators' have been sure that the protective 'bubble top' on the presidential limousine would have been taken down on the morning of the assassination?

Had the rainy weather continued it would have remained on the limousine making the possibility that bullets would be deflected.

* How could 'conspirators' have been sure that Bonnie Ray Williams, a Book Depository employee, would leave the 6th floor of the Book Depository and join friends on the 5th floor moments before the assassination?

* How could 'conspirators' have been sure that the protective security forces would be negligent in not securing the windows of high buildings along the presidential route as they normally did? The only answer is that these security personnel were part of the 'conspiracy', a preposterous notion.

* How could 'conspirators' have been sure that the presidential route would be changed at the last minute to facilitate easier access to Stemmons freeway? The new route, as we have seen took the limousine past the Texas School Book Depository where the limousine would have to slow down to turn into Elm Street. If the original route was adhered to the 'conspirators' would have had an extremely difficult, if not impossible, moving target. One can see how some Conspiracy Theorists dismiss Mafia involvement in the assassination. The Mafia would not have had the power to facilitate all of these security changes therefore more powerful forces had to be involved-i.e. the government.

* If a shooter was firing from the 'Grassy Knoll' why didn't any 'credible' witness come forward? As stated earlier in this chapter many 'witnesses' who supposedly 'saw' a Grassy Knoll shooter or smoke came forward many years after the assassination making their claims very suspect.

* Many Conspiracy Theorists claim that there was a second shooter but the bullet missed the president. If so why wasn't anyone standing across

the street from the Grassy Knoll shot or saw/heard the impact of the bullet? Police searched the area and found nothing.

* If Oswald had no connection to the rifle why were his fingerprints and palmprint found on the rifle? Are we to believe the claims of Oliver Stone et al, that 'Government Agents' lifted Oswald's prints after his murder and applied them to the rifle? And if they did why haven't any of them come forward or 'leaked' this information these past 35 years?

* The identification of the rifle initially as a German Mauser was an honest mistake. If it was not a mistake and there was indeed a second rifle why haven't any of the dozens of Dallas policeman who investigated the 6th floor of the Book Depository come forward to testify to this? In an age when government employees have been leaking everything from secret documents to incriminating information about presidents are we to believe these policemen are still afraid of the 'conspirators'?

* If Oswald was innocent, a 'patsy', why did he:

Lie about having lunch with 'Junior' Jarman, a Book Depository employee?

Leave the building after the assassination?

Collect his pistol from his rooming house?

Shoot Officer Tippit?

Try to shoot his arresting officers?

Leave his wedding ring in a cup before leaving for work?

Lie about the 'rifle photographs'?

Say "It's all over now." when he was arrested?

* Isn't it curious that someone who was extremely interested in politics, who subscribed to political periodicals and conversed frequently about political issues, did not take time out, along with the other Book Depository employees, to see the most important political figure in the country?

* If Oswald had made arrangements to spy for the C.I.A. or military intelligence why did he attempt suicide in Moscow?

* If Oswald had returned to the United States as a KGB agent why would he have brought with him a Russian wife whose very presence would be likely to attract the attention of local and federal officials?

* Why didn't the 'conspirators' silence Ruby as swiftly as they took care of Oswald?

*If Oswald was involved in the conspiracy why was he financially insecure?

Oswald owed his New Orleans landlord 15 or 16 days rent shortly before he left on his Mexico trip. If Oswald was conspiring to kill Kennedy at this time, as some Conspiracy Theorists claim, why would he risk arrest by the police?

* Oswald arrived at the Book Depository on the morning of November 22nd 1963 wearing a blue jacket. It was later found in the 'Domino room' of the Book Depository late in November. If Oswald was correct in saying he left the building because he guessed there would be no further work that day why didn't he take his jacket with him?

When considering Ruby's part in that tragic weekend there are a number of questions that Conspiracy Theorists have never satisfactorily answered.

* Because of Postal Inspector Holmes' unintentional movements which delayed the transfer of Oswald does this mean that Holmes was conspiratorially involved?

* If Ruby had wanted to silence Oswald, why didn't he kill Oswald on Friday evening, when he had a perfect opportunity? There is nothing to show that Ruby knew on Friday evening that he would be back downtown at the police station on Sunday morning, just as there is nothing to show that he knew that the transfer of Oswald from the police station to the county jail would be delayed by the Postal Inspector's arrival. Given these facts, if Ruby were conspiratorially involved and wanted to kill Oswald, would he not have done this on November 22nd?

* If Ruby were conspiratorially involved, why did he volunteer to take a lie detector test against the wishes of his lawyers?

* If Ruby were conspiratorially involved isn't it logical to assume that Rabbi Silverman would have found some evidence of conspiracy in his many conversations with Ruby?

* Conspiracy Theorists must take into account Ruby's emotional state that tragic weekend. There is no reason whatsoever to disbelieve Ruby's sister Eva in her descriptions of her brother and his distraught state. If Ruby was a Mafia hitman why did he put on such a great 'act' that weekend? Was it all a charade? Eva described Ruby as follows:

"He was sitting on this chair and crying. . . he was sick to his stomach. . . and went into the bathroom. . . he looked terrible. . . one of the things he loved about this president he didn't care what you were, you were a human being and Jack felt this was one time in history that Jews are getting the break. He (Kennedy) put in great Jewish men in office. . . that lousy commie. Don't worry, the commie we will get him. . . . He looked pretty bad. . . I can't explain it to you. He looked too broken, a broken man already. He did make this remark, he said, 'I never felt so bad in my life, even when Ma and Pa died. . . . someone tore my heart out.'

*. Why do Conspiracy Theorists still refer to Ruby's shooting of Oswald as a 'typical mob hit'? In the annals of Mafia activities in the United States there is no evidence that Mafia hit men have carried out their 'hit' in an area surrounded by police officers so that the gunman can be immediately captured and put in jail and subject himself to life imprisonment or execution; or alternatively 'turn state's evidence' and name the co-conspirators.

* Why did Ruby leave his dog Sheba in the car when he walked to the Dallas police department from the Western Union Office? Friends of Ruby have said he would never have done that if he had planned the shooting in advance and known he would be taken into custody. Furthermore Ruby was so attached to his dogs, he referred to Sheba as his 'wife' and the other dogs as his children.

APPENDIX 2

OLIVER STONE'S " JFK " - LIES AND DISTORTIONS.

"The paranoid message will give more and more, and then it will give even more. The entertainment resources of the paranoid message are unrivalled. It offers puzzles, drama, passion, heroes, villains and struggle. If the story line can be tied to an historical event, especially one that involves romantic characters and unexpected death, then fiction, history, and popular delusion can be joined in the pursuit of profit. The story, moreover, need never end. If evidence appears that refutes the conspiracy, the suppliers of the discrediting material will themselves be accused of being part of the conspiracy. The paranoid explanatory system is a closed one. Only confirmatory evidence is accepted. Contradictions are dismissed as being naïve or, more likely, part of the conspiracy itself."

"Political Paranoia as Cinematic Motif Stone's 'JFK'" - presented at the 1997 Annual Meeting of The American Political Science Association by political scientist Robert S. Robins and psychiatrist Jerrold M. Post.

Scene: Before President Kennedy's visit to Dallas Rose Cheramie is hurled from a moving car and is taken to a hospital where she reveals a plot to kill the president.

FACT: Rose Cheramie (real name Melba Christine Marcades) was a prostitute and drug addict. From the hospital medical records the House Assassinations Committee discovered that she had been in heroine withdrawal and physical shock when she was checked into the hospital by police officer Francis Fruge. Fruge testified to the HSCA that Cheramie had told him, on the 20th November, that she was going to Dallas to 'kill Kennedy'. When Fruge returned to the hospital on the Monday, one day after Ruby killed Oswald, she embellished her story saying she worked for Ruby, was involved in a drugs run and her two companions said they were going to kill Kennedy. Dr. Victor Weiss, who attended to Cheramie could not recall that her comments about the murder of Kennedy occurred before or after the assassination. Cheramie had been confined to mental hospitals in the past and had a history of providing the F.B.I. and U.S. Customs with elaborate and false stories about drug deals. There is, however, a puzzle in the whole affair which needs further investigation- Fruge said that Cheramie named one of her travelling companions as Sergio Arcacha Smith, a notable Cuban exile with ties to Marcello, Ferrie and Bannister.

Scene: An eye-witness to the assassination is interviewed and states the shots came from the fence on the knoll. Later in the movie Garrison asserts that 51 witnesses heard shots from the 'Grassy Knoll'.

FACT: See Chapter 3 for an account of contradictory eyewitness testimony.

The number of witnesses who claimed to hear shots from the 'Grassy Knoll' was far fewer. Conspiracy Theorist Josiah Thompson only claims 33 and the House Assassinations Committee only classified 20 as 'Grassy Knoll' witnesses.

Scene: Guy Bannister pistol whips Jack Martin after he discovers that Martin may have rifled his files. In a later scene Martin states that Oswald, Ferrie, Shaw and Bannister knew each other.

FACT: The source for this statement is Jack Martin, an alcoholic who was investigated by the F.B.I. and found to be without credibility. See Chapter 8 for an examination of Martin's F.B.I. report.

Scene: Garrison is informed by one of his assistants that David Ferrie was a known acquaintance of Oswald.

FACT: The source was anonymous. For 35 years Conspiracy Theorists have tried to link Oswald with Ferrie with little success. A photograph of Air Cadet Oswald and Ferrie has, however, surfaced since the publication of Gerald Posner's 'Case Closed'. Ferrie, in combat dress, is seen in the foreground speaking with a group of young cadets. Oswald is in the background. The photograph was taken in 1955 and belongs to John Ciravolo. To claim this is evidence that Oswald and Ferrie 'knew' each other is a little like saying a scout would 'know' every member of his Scout Troop.

Scene: Garrison asks Ferrie his whereabouts on November 22nd. Ferrie replies that he went 'Duck-Hunting' in Texas. The implication is clear. The journey taken by Ferrie at the time of the assassination was for sinister purposes. Garrison would later claim that Ferrie went to Texas as the 'getaway' pilot for the conspirators. .

FACT: See Chapter 8 for an explanation of this innocuous trip.

Scene: A United States Senator discusses the assassination with Jim Garrison. He states that Oswald was a poor shot.

FACT: See chapter 3. Oswald was far from being a 'poor shot'. The Senator was speaking from a position of ignorance as to the mechanics of the rifle, the scene of the assassination and the evidence which was presented to the Warren Commission as to Oswald's capabilities with a rifle.

Scene: Lee Bowens is giving evidence before the Warren Commission saying he saw suspicious activity in the railyard shortly before the arrival of the motorcade; "a flash of light" and "smoke". He was later found dead. The implication is clear. Bowers was killed by plotters who were apparently concerned that he had seen them at the scene of the crime.

FACT: Bowers did not mention either a "flash of light" or "smoke" to the Warren Commission. He later told Conspiracy Theorist Mark Lane that he saw "a flash of light or smoke or something which caused me to feel like something out of the ordinary had occurred". The circumstances surrounding Bowers' death in a car accident were investigated by researcher David Perry who conclusively proved that Bowers' death was an accident and he was not forced off the road.

Scene: Garrison is surprised that Oswald was given a Russian test whilst in the Marines.

FACT: There was nothing unusual in Oswald's learning the Russian language whilst a Marine. Jim Garrison claimed Oswald was learning Russian because he was an intelligence agent. If this were true why would his operatives allow him to be bullied by his fellow Marines? From all accounts of his time spent as a Marine Oswald was constantly picked on by his colleagues and he did not improve matters by his unwillingness to engage the other members of his unit in any meaningful relationships. Oswald's superiors did not see any sinister reasons in Oswald studying the Russian language or in subscribing to a Russian language newspaper. Lieutenant Donavan has testified that he thought Oswald subscribed to a Russian newspaper to learn another language and to get another view of international affairs. Indeed, another officer had questioned Oswald about the 'Left-wing' literature and Oswald, disingenuously stated that he was indoctrinating himself in Russian theory in conformance with the Marine Corps policy of 'getting to know the enemy'.

Scene: Garrison notices that Guy Bannister worked at the same building as the address Oswald stamped on his 'Fair Play For Cuba' leaflets - 544 Camp Street.

FACT: The 'witnesses' who supposedly saw Oswald enter 544 Camp Street were found by investigating bodies to be without credibility. The issue is discussed in Chapter 8 with an explanation as to why Oswald used this address on his 'Fair Play For Cuba' leaflets. Furthermore, the Camp Street and LaFayette Street entrances went to different offices. Guy Bannister's office could not be reached from 544 Camp Street.

Scene: Lawyer Dean Andrews is asked by Clay Bertrand (Clay Shaw) to defend Oswald after the assassination.

FACT: Andrews has admitted that he made many statements which he knew were lies. See Chapter 8 for an examination of Andrews' testimony.

Scene: Convict 'Willie O'Keefe'(a composite character of witnesses Perry Russo, David Logan, Raymond Broshears and William Morris) speaks to Garrison about Clay Bertrand (Shaw) and David Ferrie. He states that he saw Oswald meeting with Shaw and Ferrie.

FACT: All 4 witnesses had severe credibility problems. Other witnesses, however, have testified to seeing Shaw and Oswald together and their claims are dealt with in Chapter 8. Conspiracy Theorist Robert J. Groden has produced a photograph of Oswald handing out leaflets on the streets of New Orleans and a figure resembling Shaw can be seen in the background. A person resembling Shaw does appear in the background of a WDSU-TV newsfilm. Garrison maintained this was Shaw but this proves nothing as the International Trade Mart, where Shaw worked, is nearby.

Scene: 3 tramps are arrested in Dealey Plaza by the police and released. The Dallas Police Department finally released their files on the assassination in the early 1990's and the tramps were identified as Harold Doyle, Gus Abrams and John Forrester Gedney. Assassination researchers have confirmed they were not conspiratorially involved in the assassination.

Scene: One of Garrison's investigators states that the government will not release the C.I.A., F.B.I. and other government documents on the grounds of national security.

FACT: A natural occurrence given the circumstances of the time. US Government bureaucracies were notoriously secretive fearing their methods of operation and information gathering would be compromised. They were also fearful that these files could lead to embarrassing disclosures they had failed to protect the President.

Scene: Garrison's investigator states that Marina's father was with Soviet intelligence.

FACT: The man referred to was Marina's uncle who can more truthfully be described, in a western sense, as a "policeman". He had risen to become a high-ranking member of the Communist party and he was also a Lieutenant-colonel and head of the Timber Administration of the Belorussian Republic's Ministry of Internal Affairs (MVD). It is possible he supervised the use of convict labour in the timber industry in the area in which he worked. He was not a 'KGB' officer.

Scene: Conspirators fake the photo of Oswald holding the rifle and pistol.

FACT: See Chapter 3 for a full account of the history of the 'Backyard Photographs'.

Scene: Garrison implies that Marina Oswald was rehearsed by the government in giving fake and incriminating evidence.

FACT: Marina was indeed intimidated by the numerous government investigators and police officers who invaded her life in the days weeks and months after the assassination. However, notwithstanding the fact that she now claims that Lee was working with others or was a 'patsy', she has not retracted the testimony she gave to the Warren Commission or to the House Assassinations Committee. Her fuller story was told in a more relaxed atmosphere when she spent many months with author Priscilla Johnson McMillan, after she gave evidence to the Warren Commission. Marina's story, as told to McMillan, is more incriminating of her husband.

Scene: Oswald's palm print was lifted from his corpse and planted on the rifle.

FACT: There is no evidence whatsoever that this occurred. The actual movie scene looks 'real' but this is another of Stone's techniques with which he fools the audience into believing that he has used genuine 'news footage'.

Scene: Jean Hill states she was standing with her friend Mary Moorman in Dealey Plaza and saw a flash of light in the bushes (on the Grassy Knoll) and saw the last shot when Kennedy's head was impacted by the bullet. She was arrested by 'Secret Service' agents and taken to a building and her camera confiscated.

FACT: A reporter named Featherstone of the Dallas Times Herald escorted Hill to the Sheriff's office . Within half an hour of the assassination she was interviewed by a local Dallas television crew and stated she saw nothing untoward. In later years she has embellished her preposterous story.

Scene: Julia Ann Mercer saw Jack Ruby get out of a truck on the morning of the assassination and deliver a rifle to Dealey Plaza.

FACT: Investigations have revealed that the truck, which was stalled, belonged to a local construction company. The truck held three men who took tools from the rear of the truck to fix it. They were under constant surveillance by 3 Dallas policemen.

Scene: Beverly Oliver tells Garrison that Oswald and Ferrie met with Jack Ruby in Ruby's Carousel Club.

FACT: Oliver's testimony has never been corroborated. She claims Jack Ruby introduced Oswald to her as 'Lee Oswald of the C.I.A.' and to have told this story to one of Jack Ruby's strippers, Jada. Jada told her son that nothing of the kind occurred. Oliver was never known to Jim Garrison, or anyone else until years later. Her story is extremely implausible. Jada (Janet Conforto) never linked Ruby and Oswald and she did not 'disappear'. She died in a motorcycle accident in 1971.

Scene: Jack Ruby tells chief Justice Earl Warren that he must go to Washington in order to tell the truth.

FACT: See Chapter 5 for a full explanation.

Scene: Garrison and his investigator try firing the Mannlicher Carcano rifle from the 6th floor window of the Book Depository and say it is impossible.

FACT: See Chapter 3 for experts' opinions as to the difficulty of the shots and the performance of the Mannlicher-Carcano rifle. The feat was entirely possible and 3 shots fired in 8 or 9 seconds is entirely consistent with the Zapruder film.

Same scene: The best shot would be when the Kennedy limousine approached the Book Depository from Main and Houston Street.

FACT: This would have put Oswald in full view of Kennedy's protectors, the car full of Secret Service Agents.

Scene: Oswald test drives a car and insults the salesman. He shoots at another mans target on a rifle range, both incidents are designed to show that Oswald impersonators were used by the conspirators in order to set up Oswald as a 'patsy'.

FACT: Albert Bogard said Lee Oswald visited him on November 9th

1963, two weeks before the assassination and drove one of his cars. His manager, who Bogard was supposed to have introduced Oswald to, nor his co-workers could remember the meeting.

Floyd Davis, owner of the Sportsdrome Gun Range near Grand Prairie, Texas, was quoted in an AP news story, as saying that 3 people had told him that they had seen Oswald at the range, though he conceded he never saw Oswald himself. The F.B.I. sent two men to collect expended cartridges to be sent to the F.B.I. laboratory in Washington where they were examined and found to have no similar conformities with Oswald's rifle. Among the eyewitnesses were Malcolm H. Price, Jnr., Garland G. Slack, Sterling G Wood and Dr. Homer Wood who said the man they saw was definitely Oswald. The Warren Commission investigated the incident and found that other witnesses present at the rifle range remembered the same individual but, though noting a similarity to Oswald, did not believe that the man was Oswald. Furthermore, when interviewed, Slack recalled that the individual who he saw had 'blond' hair and Price stated that on several occasions when he saw 'Oswald' he was wearing a 'Bulldogger Texas style' hat, which is not characteristic of Oswald or consistent with other so-called witness statements.

Scene: The Sylvia Odio incident. Oswald, together with 2 other men are supposed to have visited Sylvia Odio's apartment in Dallas where Oswald remarked that Kennedy should be killed.

FACT: See Chapter 6 for the most logical explanation of this event.

Scene: The photo the C.I.A. takes outside the Cuban Embassy in Mexico of a man called "Lee Harvey Oswald" is not Oswald.

FACT: See Chapter 6 for an explanation of the C.I.A.'s activities in surveilling Oswald in Mexico City and the bureaucratic mistakes which led to claims of C.I.A. involvement in the assassination

Scene: David Ferrie is supposedly murdered.

FACT: The Coroner, Dr. Nicholas Chetta reported that death resulted from a berry aneurysm, a weak spot in a blood vessel that suddenly blows out, causing a cerebral haemorrhage and the death was due to natural causes. If the death was caused by an external blow there would have been tissue damage and none was found. The autopsy also revealed no evidence of drugs which might have been used to induce such a condition. Ferrie had a history of high blood pressure. Furthermore if conspirators had the means to induce such a condition why did they go to the trouble of doing away with Ferrie by such means which would only attract suspicion if the autopsy had revealed it? Well -heeled conspirators had the swampy marshes of Louisiana at their disposal where a body could never have been found. Ferrie went to his death denying he knew Lee Harvey Oswald.

Scene: "Mr. X" meets Garrison in Washington DC and says he is close to the intelligence community and the assassination was the work of the military-industrial complex and the intelligence community.

FACT: This scene is based on a meeting Garrison had with Richard Case Nagell but 'Mr. X' voices the views of Colonel Fletcher Prouty a Conspiracy Theorist who did not meet Garrison until many years later and whose comments on the assassination have been found to be without credence. The foundation for Prouty's claims is an edition of a New Zealand newspaper which published details of Oswald's life supposedly before Oswald was charged with murder. The implication is that the C.I.A./military were ready to implicate Oswald. His claims are spurious and there is no reason why the newspapers should not have had the information if the international time differences are taken into consideration.

Scene: "Mr. X" tells Garrison that the "establishment" is trying to destroy his credibility.

FACT: There was no need for the 'establishment' to destroy Garrison's credibility. He did that all by himself. See chapter 8.

Scene: Clay Shaw, on being indicted for conspiracy to assassinate President Kennedy is fingerprinted and logged at the police Dept. where he tells a police officer his alias is "Clay Bertrand".

FACT: See Chapter 8. The preponderance of evidence shows that Habighorst was mistaken.

Scene: Clinton witnesses.

FACT: See Chapter 8 for an examination of the credibility of the Clinton witnesses.

Scene: Oswald visits the F.B.I. office. The movie implies that the note was describing the assassination plot.

FACT: See chapter 6 and F.B.I. Agent Hosty's testimony. The scene contradicts all witness testimony.

Scene: Garrison shows the Zapruder film to the court. Says that JFK's head snaps back indicating a shot from the front.

FACT: What appears to be Kennedy's head snapping backwards is consistent with evidence presented to the House Assassinations Committee which concluded, on the basis of evidence presented by their panel of pathologists, that the head shot came from the rear.

Scene: Garrison tries to destroy Arlen Specter's "Single- Bullet Theory".

FACT: See Chapter 3 for a description of events connected to the 'Magic Bullet'.

Scene: Garrison states in court that 51 witnesses heard shots coming from the Grassy Knoll area.

FACT: As explained in Chapter 3 the acoustics of Dealey Plaza were consistent with witness confusion as to the direction of the shots.

Scene: Garrison states in court that the Dallas doctors considered JFK's throat wound as a "wound of entry".

FACT: As the Dallas doctors testified they were trying to save the President's life and were not too concerned, at this time, whether the wounds were ones of entry or exit.

Scene: Conspirators at the Grassy Knoll and picket fence produce Secret Service credentials to Dallas Police Officer Joe Smith.

FACT: Chris Mills has given the most logical explanation to these curious events as discussed in Chapter 3 .

Scene: Garrison tells the court about the discrepancies in eyewitness testimony in the Tippet Shooting.

FACT: See Chapter 4. The majority of witnesses identified Lee Harvey Oswald as the shooter and discrepancies in eyewitness testimony for any crime occur frequently.

Scene: Jim Garrison in a lengthy speech does the summing up for the prosecution.

FACT: Jim Garrison spent very little time in the courthouse during the Shaw trial which is not surprising given the fact that his case was so weak.

Scene: Jim Garrison tells of the C.I.A./F.B.I. files which are sealed until the year 2038.

FACT: Where issues of national security are concerned Government agencies frequently seal files.

BIBLIOGRAPHY

The following selective bibliography includes all the main sources consulted for this work.

Unless otherwise stated in the narrative all quotations, testimony and evidence is taken from the following government documents:

Report of the President's Commission on the Assassination of President John F. Kennedy, and 26 accompanying volumes of Hearings and Exhibits published by the US Government Printing Office in 1964. Also 'The Warren Report', without supporting volumes, published by Doubleday with forward by Louis Nizer and afterward by Bruce Catton. (1964).

Alleged Assassination Plots Involving Foreign Leaders, conducted by the Select Committee to Study Governmental Operations with respect to Intelligence Activities, United States Senate, published by the US Government Printing Office in 1975.

The Investigation of the Assassination of President John F. Kennedy, conducted by the Senate Select Committee to study Governmental Operations, Published by the US Government Printing Office in 1976.

Investigation of the Assassination of President John F. Kennedy, conducted by the Select Committee on Assassinations of the US House of Representatives, published by the US Government Printing Office in 1979.

I owe a debt of gratitude to the following authors. A nearly silent minority, these authors did not jump on the 'Conspiracy Bandwagon'. Their books are courageous, intelligent and well-researched- Gerald Posner, Jean Davison, Ovid Demaris, Gary Wills, James Kirkwood, Priscilla Johnson McMillan.

BOOKS:

The Day Kennedy Was Shot by Bishop, James A. (HarperPerennial) 1992.
Blumenthal, Sid, and Yazijian, Harvey, eds. Government by Gunplay: Assassination Conspiracies from Dallas to Today. New York: New American Library, 1976.
Demaris, Ovid, and Willis, Gary B. Jack Ruby. (DaCapo Press N.Y.) 1994.
Eddowes, Michael. November 22: How They Killed Kennedy. London: Spearman, 1976

Inquest: The Warren Commission and the Establishment of Truth by Epstein, Edwad J. New York: Viking, 1966.

Legend: The Secret World of Lee Harvey Oswald by Epstein, Edward J. (Hutchinson) 1978.

Oswald: Assassin or Fall Guy? by Joesten, Joachim. (Merlin Books)1964.

American Grotesque: An Account of the Clay Shaw-Jim Garrison Affair in the City of New Orleans Kirkwood, James. (HarperPerennial) 1992.

Rush to Judgment by Lane, Mark. New York: Holt, Rinehart, 1966.

The Scavengers and Critics of the Warren Report by Lewis, Richard Warren. New York: Delacorte, 1967.

Best Evidence: Disguise and Deception in the Assassination of John F. Kennedy by Lifton, David. (Carroll and Graf Publishers) 1988. .

Marina and Lee by McMillan, Priscilla Johnson. (Collins), 1978.

The Death of a President: November 20-November 25, 1963 by Manchester, William R. (Michael Joseph) 1967.

The C.I.A. and the Cult of Intelligence by Marchetti, Victor, and Marks, John D. (Jonathan Cape), 1974.

Conspiracy by Summers, Anthony. (Sphere Books), 1989.

JFK - The Second Plot by Matthew Smith (Mainstream Publishing) 1992.

Vendetta - The Kennedys by Matthew Smith (Mainstream Publishing) 1993

Oswald Talked - The New Evidence in the JFK Assassination by Ray and Mary LaFontaine (Pelican Publishing Co. Gretna) 1996.

The Hoffa Wars - The Rise and Fall of Jimmy Hoffa by Dan E. Moldea (SPI Books) 1994

First-hand Knowledge How I Participated in the C.I.A.-Mafia Murder of President Kennedy by Robert D. Morrow (SPI Books) 1994.

LBJ and the JFK Conspiracy by Hugh McDonald and Robin Moore (Condor) 1979.

The C.I.A. and American Democracy by Rhodri Jeffreys-Jones (Yale University Press) 1989.

The Web - Kennedy Assassination Cover-Up by James R. Duffy (Alan Sutton Publishing) 1988.

Case Closed - Lee Harvey Oswald and the Assassination of JFK. by Gerald Posner. (Warner Books) 1993.

Cause of Death by Cyril Wecht, M.D., J.D. with Mark Curriden and Benjamin Wecht (Dutton) 1993.

Crime of the Century - The Kennedy Assassination from an Historian's

Perspective by Michael L. Kurtz. (The University of Tennessee Press) 1993.

Crossfire - The Plot That Killed Kennedy by Jim Marrs (Carroll and Graf Publishers) 1992.

For The President's Eyes Only - Secret Intelligence and the American Presidency from Washington to Bush by Christopher Andrew (HarperCollins) 1995

The JFK Assassination - The Facts and the Theories by Carl Oglesby (Signet) 1992

On The Trail Of The Assassins by Jim Garrison (Penguin Books) 1992.

Case Open - The Omissions, Distortions and Falsifications of Case Closed by Harold Weisberg (Carroll and Graf) 1994.

The Agency - The Rise and Decline of the C.I.A. by John Ranelagh (Sceptre) 1988

Fidel Castro by Robert E. Quirk (WW Norton and Co.) 1993.

Never Again by Harold Weisberg (Carroll and Graf Publishers) 1995.

Mafia Princess by Antoinette Giancana with Thomas C. Renner (George Allen and Unwin) 1984.

Contract on America - The Mafia Murder of President John F. Kennedy by David E. Scheim (Shapolsky Publishers Inc.) 1988.

JFK - Breaking the Silence by Bill Sloan (Taylor Publishing Co.) 1993.

Oswald's Tale by Norman Mailer (Random House) 1995.

Mortal Error - The Shot That Killed JFK by Bonar Menninger (Sidgewick and Jackson) 1992.

J. Edgar Hoover - The Man and the Secrets by Curt Gentry (WW Norton and Co.) 1991

The Very Best Men by Evan Thomas (Simon and Schuster) 1995.

Gentleman Spy - The Life of Allen Dulles by Peter Grose (Andre Deutsch) 1995.

The Last Investigation by Gaeton Fonzi (Thunder's Mouth Press) 1994

JFK - The C.I.A., Vietnam and the Plot to Assassinate John F. Kennedy by L. Fletcher Prouty (Carol Publishing Group) 1992.

Plausible Denial - Was the C.I.A. Involved in the Assassination of JFK? by Mark Lane (Plexus, London) 1992.

Marita - From Castro To Kennedy: Love and Espionage in the C.I.A. by Marita Lorenz. (Warner) 1994

Lyndon - An Oral Biography by Merle Miller (Ballantine Books, N.Y.) 1987

Passport To Assassination: The Never-Before-Told Story of Lee Harvey

Oswald by The KGB Colonel Who Knew Him by Oleg M. Nechiporenko, Todd P. Bludeau (Translator) (Birch lane) 1993.

A Mother in History by Jean Stafford (Chatto and Windus) 1966

Deep Politics and the Death of JFK by Peter Dale Scott (University of California Press) 1993

Deadly Secrets - The C.I.A.-Mafia War Against Castro and the Assassination of JFK by Warren Hinckle and William Turner (Thunder's Mouth Press, N.Y.) 1992

In Search of History by Theodore H. White (Jonathan Cape) 1978

Oswald and the C.I.A. by John Newman (Carroll and Graf) 1995

Honourable Men - My Life in the C.I.A. by William Colby with Peter Forbath (Hutchinson of London) 1978

Cold Warrior - James Jesus Angleton by Tom Mangold (Simon and Schuster) 1991

Oswald's Game By Jean Davison (WW Norton) 1983.

Mafia Kingfish - Carlos Marcello and the Assassination of John F. Kennedy by John H. Davis (McGraw-Hill Publishing Company) 1989

Act of Treason - The Role of J. Edgar Hoover in the Assassination of President Kennedy by Mark North (Carroll and Graf Publishers inc.) 1992

Double Cross - The Story of the Man Who Controlled America by Sam and Chuck Giancana (MacDonald) 1992

President Kennedy by Richard Reeves (Simon and Schuster) 1993

Kennedy by Theodore Sorenson (Harper and Row) 1965

A 1000 Days - John F. Kennedy In The White House (Andre Deutsch) 1965

Crime Inc. by Martin Short (Thames Methuen) 1984

The Search For Lee Harvey Oswald by Robert J. Groden (Bloomsbury) 1995

The Killing of A President by Robert J. Groden (Bloomsbury) 1995

A Good Life - Newspapering and Other Adventures by Ben Bradlee (Simon and Schuster) 1995

Reasonable Doubt - An Investigation Into The Assassination of John F. Kennedy by Henry Hurt (Sidgewick and Jackson) 1986

The Kennedy Women - The Saga of An American Family by Laurence Leamer (Villard Books, N.Y.) 1994

Life in Camelot - The Kennedy Years Edited by Philip B. Kunhardt Jr. (Little Brown and Co.) 1988

Treachery In Dallas by Walt Brown (Carroll and Graf, Inc.) 1995

The Dallas Times Herald (original copies) November 22 - 24 1963

The New York Times (original copies) November 22 - 24 1963
Who was Jack Ruby? by Seth Kantor (New York-Everett House) 1978
Helter Skelter by Vincent Bugliosi (Dell Publishing) 1994
Fatal Vision by Joe McGinniss (Warner Books) 1993
'They've Killed The President' by Robert Sam Anson (Bantam Books) 1975.

ARTICLES

NEWSWEEK, 10.3.75 - "J. Edgar Hoover's Secret Files"
NEWSWEEK, 27.11.67 - "A New Assassination Theory"
"Executive Action"- 1973 - Facts behind the making of the film(Cinema Magazine)
NEWSWEEK, 2.10.78 - "A Tremendous Insanity"
NEW YORK TIMES, 18.11.88 - "Who Killed John Kennedy? After 25 Years, More Theories Than Certainty"
AMERICAN JOURNAL OF PSYCHIATRY July 1960. Article by Dr. Joseph Satten, Dr. Karl Menninger, Dr. Irwin Rosen and Dr. Martin Mayman.
TIME 23.6.75 - "Kennedy Assassination"
NEWSWEEK 2.6.75 - "Target Castro"
TIME 4.8.75 - "C.I.A. Tantalizing Bits of Evidence"
NEWSWEEK 29.9.75 - "Of Dark Guns and Poisons"
TIME 7.7.75 - "The C.I.A.-Tales of an Old Soldier"
TIME 2.6.75 - "The Kennedy Connection"
LIFE 1.9.67 - "The Mob".
LIFE 8.9.67 - "The Mob Part 2"
NEWSWEEK 20.1.75 - "A True-Blue-Ribbon Panel"
NEWSWEEK 20.1.75 - "Good and Bad Secrets"
TIME 23.6.75 - "Rocky's Probe: Bringing the C.I.A. to Heel"
TIME 19.12.77 - "The F.B.I. Story on J.F.K's Death"
TIME 28.11.88 - "Was Connally the Real Target"
TIME 28.11.88 - "A Shattering Afternoon in Dallas" by Hugh Sidey
NEWSWEEK 19.12.77 - "JFK: What the F.B.I. Found"
NEWSWEEK 25.9.78 - "Marina Oswald's Story"
TRUE DETECTIVE June 1964 - "The Jack Ruby I Knew, Why I Didn't Put Him On The Stand" by Melvin Belli.
EMPIRE MAGAZINE Oct 1993 - "Who Shot JFK?"

TIME 20.3.64 - "Death For Ruby"

ARENA MAGAZINE 1993 - "The Killing of a President"

THE INDEPENDENT 24.8.93 - "800, 000 more clues to the JFK Mystery".

NEWSWEEK. 5.12.66 "Eyewitness in Dallas"" JFK: The Death and the Doubts"

LOOK 26.8.69."The Persecution of Clay Shaw"

NEWSWEEK 14.11.66 "The Missing Link"

INTERNATIONAL HERALD TRIBUNE 3.11.66 "National Archives Get Kennedy Death Photos".

THE OBSERVER 25.9.66 "The Flaw in the Warren Report"

THE LONDON EVENING NEWS 22.9.66 "Kennedy: The Case for a Second Assassin"

THE SUNDAY TIMES 25.9.66 "Dallas: Pandora's Box is Opened"

TIME 14.2.64 "The Warren Commission: Probing Kennedy's Death"

THE SPECTATOR 23.9.66. "Warren in the Dock" by R.A. Cline.

THE MAIL ON SUNDAY 1.8.93 "Marina Oswald's First Visit To The Site Where her Husband Killed Kennedy"

UNDERCOVER No.5 July 1993. "The Secrets of 544 Camp Street".

DAILY MAIL 24.11.92 "Now I Know My Husband Didn't Kill Kennedy".

LIFE December 1991 "JFK: Why We Still Care".

TIME 2.12.74 "Hoover's Closet".

DAILY MAIL 30.12.78. "Did Two Men Shoot Kennedy?".

NEWSWEEK 3.10.77 "Recipe For Paranoia".

EVENING STANDARD 22.9.66 "Who Else Killed Kennedy?".

GUARDIAN WEEKLY 22.8.93 "The Ruin of a Counterspy"

EVENING CHRONICLE 19.11.93 "A World Wept".

UNDERCOVER April/May 1993 "Doppelganger: Oswald... Or Oswalds?".

TIME 6.12.63 "The Man Who Killed Kennedy".

NEWSWEEK 15.1.79. "Rush To Judgment"

TIME 29.11.68 "Assassinations: A Warning Five Years Later".

TIME 5.4.76 "The F.B.I.: Just How Incorruptible?".

NEWSWEEK 26.1.76 "Memoirs: Lady In Waiting".

TIME 9.6.75 "Mafia Spies In Cuba"

"The C.I.A.: Prying Into Mail, Plotting Murder".

THE ECONOMIST 6.8.66 "Was Oswald Alone?".

NEWSWEEK 16.8.66 "Again, The Assassination".

THE TIMES 22.11.93 "JFK Cult Proclaims Denial of President's Death".

NEWSWEEK 27.1.69 "Curtains For The D.A.".

TIME 25.9.78 "Facing The Bad: Marina Oswald On The Stand".

NEWSWEEK 3.2.69. "Trials: Round One".

NATIONAL ENQUIRER Vol.71 No.25 "O.J.'s Photo Expert is a Phony"

NEWSWEEK 24.2.75 "C.I.A.: The Constant Witness".

NEWSWEEK 18.9.78 "JFK: Settling Some Doubts".

TIME 16.6.75 "The Momo and Cain Connection".

TIME 16.6.75 "C.I.A.: Leaving Murky Murders To The Senate".

NEWSWEEK 12.12.77 "Opening The JFK File".

NEWSWEEK 12.12.63 "The Day Kennedy Died".

TIME 11.4.77 "Assassination: Now A Suicide Talks".

TIME 2.10.64 "The Warren Commission Report".

GUARDIAN WEEKLY Nov.93 "Murdered By The Mob?".

EVENING CHRONICLE 2.3.67 "Kennedy: Ex-War Hero Is Arrested".

DAILY MIRROR 20.2.67 "Kennedy: Clue of Convict X".

"Kennedy: New Doubts About His Death Shock America"

"Oswald: Did He Act Alone or Was He Hired?".

THE TIMES 24.2.67 "New Orleans 'Man In Fear' Disappears".

THE TIMES 14.6.66 "Jury Finds Jack Ruby Sane".

THE DAILY EXPRESS 14.6.66 "Ruby Sane, Rules Jury".

DAILY MIRROR 31.8.67 "This Gun For Sale...To Pay Jack Ruby's Taxes".

NEWSWEEK 12.10.64 "Reporting The Report".

NEWSWEEK 30.11.64 "And Then It Was November 22 Again".

NEWSWEEK 17.10.64 "Back To Dallas".

DAILY TELEGRAPH 4.1.67 "Ruby Dies Denying He Was In Plot".

GUARDIAN 4.1.67 "Ruby Is Dead: In JFK's Hospital".

DAILY SKETCH 4.1.67 "Ruby: The Most Public Killer In History. Strangely He Dies In His Bed. 17 Others With Knowledge of the Kennedy Assassination Have Met Violent or Bizarre Deaths".

THE TIMES 4.1.67 "Jack Ruby Dies In Dallas Hospital".

THE NEW YORK TIMES INTERNATIONAL EDITION 6.10.66 "Court Reverses Ruby Conviction In Oswald Case".

TIME 14.10.66 "Ruby Revisited".

DAILY EXPRESS 22.11.65 "That Day In Dallas".

EVENING CHRONICLE 2.11.66 "A Kennedy Mystery Is Solved".

THE TIMES 28.3.68 "New Controversy On Kennedy Killing"

NEWSWEEK 4.12.67 "The Assassination Scene of the Crime".

TIME 24.2.67 "Historical Notes: The Full Record".

ESQUIRE December 1993 "The Secret Life Of Lee Harvey Oswald" by Anthony Summers.

TIME 16.9.66 "Autopsy On The Warren Commission".

THE TIMES 21.6.67 "Investigator Garrison Investigated".

NEWSWEEK 17.2.69 "Mardi Gras Season".

THE TIMES 30.12.67 "Garrison Denies Mental Record"

THE TIMES 15.11.66 "Photograph Mystery of Dallas Rifleman".

NEWSWEEK 24.2.69 "Trials: What Conspiracy?".

DOCUMENTARY VIDEOS AND RECORDED NEWS PROGRAMMES.

NEWSLINE (ABC NEWS) Ted Koppel interviews David Belin, Anthony Summers and Louis Stokes.(1992)

BBC NOVEMBER 1993 "The Zapruder Footage-The World's Most Famous Home Movie".

CNN November 1993 "30 Years later: Reflections of the F.B.I." James Hosty, Vincent Drain and Cartha (Deke) DeLoach interviewed by Larry Woods.

CNN November 1993 "Larry King Live" Kal Korff and Gaeton Fonzi interviewed by Larry King.

CHANNEL 4 Documentary 1988 "The Trial Of Lee Harvey Oswald".

DISCOVERY CHANNEL 1992 "The JFK Conspiracy-Final Analysis" Hosted By James Earl Jones.

CHANNEL 4 November 1993 "As It Happened: The Killing Of Kennedy".

CNN 1992 "Larry King Live" Larry King Interviews Dr. Lundberg, Editor Of 'The Journal Of The American Medical Association.'(JAMA).

BBC 'TIMEWATCH' 1993 Documentary. "The Mysterious Career Of Lee Harvey Oswald".

CBS NEWS 'NOVA' Documentary 1988. "Who Shot President Kennedy?" Hosted By Walter Cronkite.

CS FILMS INC./Castle Communications 1988. (Video) "Reasonable Doubt-The Single-Bullet Theory and the Assassination of John F. Kennedy". Produced and Directed by Chip Selby.

EXPOSED FILMS LTD. 1988 "The Day The Dream Died". (Video).

BLUE RIDGE/FILM TRUST/BRAVEWORLD VIDEOS 1992 (Video) "The JFK Assassination: The Jim Garrison Tapes".

FABULOUS FILMS LTD. 1990 (Video) "Best Evidence: The Research Video".

CENTRAL INDEPENDENT TELEVISION 1989 (Video) "The Men Who Killed Kennedy-The Incredible True Facts". Produced and Directed By Nigel Turner.

BBC "The Nazis" (Broadcast September 1997)

LP RECORDS.

THE INFORMATION COUNCIL OF THE AMERICAS (INCA) 1965. "Oswald-self-Portrait In Red".

THE INFORMATION COUNCIL OF THE AMERICAS (INCA) 1967. "Lee Harvey Oswald Speaks".

AMERICAN SOCIETY OF RECORDED DRAMA, BEVERLY HILLS, CALIFORNIA. "The Assassination Of A President: The Four Black Days" Written and Narrated By Richard Levitan.

CAPITOL RECORDS/EMI RECORDS 1967 "The Controversy: The Death: The Warren Report". Produced By Lawrence Schiller.

INTERNET DOCUMENTS: "The Man Who Wasn't There" By Chris Mills.